Teach Yourself VISUALLY™

iPhone® 7

by Guy Hart-Davis

Visual
A Wiley Brand

Teach Yourself VISUALLY™ iPhone® 7

Published by
John Wiley & Sons, Inc.
10475 Crosspoint Boulevard
Indianapolis, IN 46256

www.wiley.com

Published simultaneously in Canada

Wiley publishes in a variety of print and electronic formats and by print-on-demand. Some material included with standard print versions of this book may not be included in e-books or in print-on-demand. If this book refers to media such as a CD or DVD that is not included in the version you purchased, you may download this material at http://booksupport.wiley.com. For more information about Wiley products, visit www.wiley.com.

Library of Congress Control Number: 2016950308

ISBN: 978-1-119-29415-3

Manufactured in the United States of America

10 9 8 7 6 5 4 3

Trademark Acknowledgments

Contact Us

For general information on our other products and services please contact our Customer Care Department within the U.S. at 877-762-2974, outside the U.S. at 317-572-3993 or fax 317-572-4002.

For technical support please visit www.wiley.com/go/techsupport.

Sales | Contact Wiley at (877) 762-2974 or fax (317) 572-4002.

Credits

Executive Editor
Jody Lefevere

Acquisitions Editor
Stephanie McComb

Project Editor
Lynn Northrup

Technical Editor
Galen Gruman

Copy Editor
Lynn Northrup

Production Editor
Barath Kumar Rajasekaran

Manager, Content Development & Assembly
Mary Beth Wakefield

Vice President, Professional Technology Strategy
Barry Pruett

About the Author

Guy Hart-Davis is the author of *Teach Yourself VISUALLY MacBook, 3rd Edition; Teach Yourself VISUALLY iPad, 4th Edition; Teach Yourself VISUALLY iPhone 6s; Teach Yourself VISUALLY Android Phones and Tablets, 2nd Edition; Teach Yourself VISUALLY Apple Watch; Teach Yourself VISUALLY Samsung Galaxy S6; Teach Yourself VISUALLY iMac, 3rd Edition; iMac Portable Genius, 4th Edition;* and *iWork Portable Genius, 2nd Edition*.

Author's Acknowledgments

My thanks go to the many people who turned my manuscript into the highly graphical book you are holding. In particular, I thank Stephanie McComb for asking me to write the book, and Jody Lefevere for acting as executive editor for the book project; Lynn Northrup for keeping me on track and skillfully editing the text; Galen Gruman for reviewing the book for technical accuracy and contributing helpful suggestions; and SPi Global for laying out the book.

How to Use This Book

Who This Book Is For

This book is for the reader who has never used this particular technology or software application. It is also for readers who want to expand their knowledge.

The Conventions in This Book

1 Steps

This book uses a step-by-step format to guide you easily through each task. **Numbered steps** are actions you must do; **bulleted steps** clarify a point, step, or optional feature; and **indented steps** give you the result.

2 Notes

Notes give additional information — special conditions that may occur during an operation, a situation that you want to avoid, or a cross reference to a related area of the book.

3 Icons and Buttons

Icons and buttons show you exactly what you need to click to perform a step.

4 Tips

Tips offer additional information, including warnings and shortcuts.

5 Bold

Bold type shows command names, options, and text or numbers you must type.

6 Italics

Italic type introduces and defines a new term.

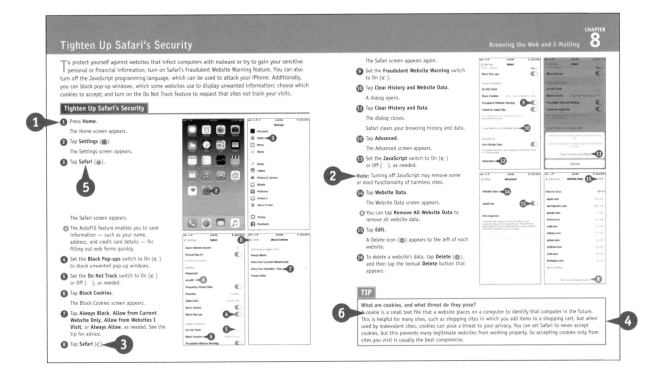

Table of Contents

Chapter 3　Using Voice, Accessibility, and Continuity

Chapter 4　Setting Up Communications

Table of Contents

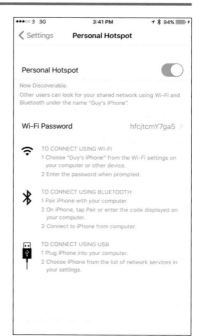

| Chapter 6 | Networking and Social Networking |

Chapter 7 Working with Apps

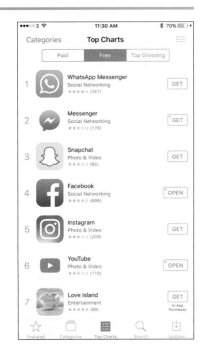

Chapter 8 Browsing the Web and E-Mailing

Table of Contents

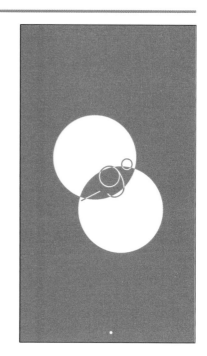

Chapter 11 Working with Photos and Video

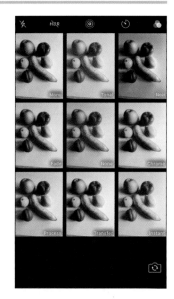

Chapter 12 Advanced Features and Troubleshooting

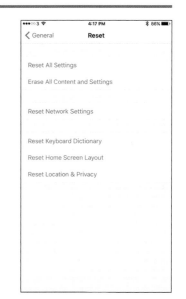

CHAPTER 1

Getting Started with Your iPhone

In this chapter, you set up your iPhone to work with your computer or iCloud. You choose items to sync and learn to use the iPhone interface.

Identify and Compare the iPhone Models

The iPhone is a series of hugely popular smartphones designed by Apple. As of this writing, Apple sells five iPhone models that differ in size, power, and price. This section explains the five models, their common features, and their differences to enable you to distinguish them and choose among them.

Understanding the Five iPhone Models

As of this writing, Apple sells five iPhone models:

- iPhone 7 and iPhone 7 Plus, introduced in 2016. The iPhone 7 Plus is physically larger than the iPhone 7.
- iPhone 6s and iPhone 6s Plus, introduced in 2015. The iPhone 6s Plus is physically larger than the iPhone 6s.
- iPhone SE, introduced in 2016.

Understanding the Common Features of the iPhone Models

Each iPhone comes with the Apple EarPods headset, which incorporates a remote control and a microphone. For the iPhone 7 models, the Apple EarPods headset connects via the Lightning connector, whereas for earlier iPhone models, the headset connects via the headphone socket. Each iPhone includes a USB power adapter and a Lightning-to-USB cable. The iPhone 7 models also include a Lightning to 3.5mm Headphone Jack Adapter for connecting analog headphones via the Lightning port. Each iPhone uses a nano-SIM card to connect to cellular networks and has a Touch ID fingerprint reader.

Each iPhone runs iOS 10, the latest operating system from Apple, which comes with a suite of built-in apps, such as the Safari web browser and the Mail e-mail app.

The iPhone 7 models come in five colors: jet black, which is glossy; black, which is matte; silver; gold; and rose gold. The iPhone 6 models and the iPhone SE come in four colors: gold, silver, space gray, and rose gold.

The iPhone 7 models have a 12-megapixel main camera on the back and a 7-megapixel camera on the front. The iPhone 7 Plus also includes a second camera model to enable optical zoom and other features. The iPhone 6s models have a 12-megapixel main camera on the back and a 5-megapixel camera on the front. The iPhone SE has a 12-megapixel main camera and a 1.2-megapixel front camera.

Compare the iPhone 7 Models with the iPhone 6s Models

The two iPhone 7 models, the iPhone 7 and the iPhone 7 Plus, have faster processors than the corresponding iPhone 6s models, the iPhone 6s and the iPhone 6s Plus. Although each model has a 12-megapixel main camera, the cameras on the iPhone 7 models are better than those on the iPhone 6s model, because they have improvements such as wider apertures — to gather light faster — and optical image stabilization.

The iPhone 7 models have a new design of Home button that features haptic feedback to simulate being pressed without moving. The iPhone 6s models have a physical Home button that actually presses in.

The iPhone 7 models have stereo speakers, whereas the iPhone 6s models have only mono speakers. The iPhone 6s models have a 3.5mm headphone socket, but the iPhone 7 models do not.

The iPhone 7 is the same size as the iPhone 6s but a little lighter, and the iPhone 7 Plus is the same size as the iPhone 6s Plus but a fraction lighter. However, the different layout of speakers and the removal of the headphone socket on the iPhone 7 models mean that only some accessories designed for iPhone 6s models will work with the corresponding iPhone 7 models.

Compare the iPhone Plus Models with the Regular Models

The iPhone 7 Plus and the iPhone 6s Plus are physically larger than the iPhone 7 and the iPhone 6s and have higher-definition screens that may enable you to see greater detail in photos and other high-definition content.

As well as being larger, the iPhone Plus models are somewhat heavier than the regular models; but if you are deciding between the Plus model and the regular model, your main consideration is likely to be whether the device will fit comfortably in your hand and your pocket or purse.

The iPhone 7 Plus has a dual-camera module on the back rather than a single-camera module, as the other models have. One camera as a 28mm wide-angle lens, while the other has a 56mm telephoto lens to provide optical zoom, which gives higher image quality than the digital zoom provided by enlarging pixels via software.

The iPhone 7 models and the iPhone 6s Plus have optical image stabilization to minimize camera shake; the iPhone 6s does not have optical image stabilization. If you shoot many photos and videos, you may find this feature useful.

continued ▶

Apart from physical size, you should consider the storage capacity of the iPhone model you are thinking of buying. Having more storage enables you to install more apps and carry more music, movies, and other files with you. Having plenty of storage is especially important for shooting videos with your iPhone.

Compare the iPhone SE with the iPhone 7 and iPhone 7 Plus Models

The iPhone SE is physically smaller than the iPhone 7 models and the iPhone 6s models. Its 4-inch screen has lower resolution than the screens on the larger models, but it has a powerful A9 processor, as do the iPhone 6s models.

While the rear camera on the iPhone SE has the same 12-megapixel resolution as the camera on the iPhone 7 models and iPhone 6 models, the front camera on the iPhone SE has relatively low 1.2-megapixel resolution.

The iPhone 7 models, iPhone 6s models, and the iPhone SE all have a Near Field Communication (NFC) chip that enables you to use the Apple Pay service to make payments from your iPhone.

Evaluate iPhone Storage Capacity

The iPhone models are available with different amounts of storage capacity. The diagram shows sample amounts of contents.

The iPhone 7 and iPhone 7 Plus come in 32GB, 128GB, and 256GB capacities.

The iPhone 6S and iPhone 6S Plus come in 32GB and 128GB capacities.

The iPhone SE comes in 16GB and 64GB capacities.

Higher capacities command substantially higher prices, so you must decide how much you are prepared to spend. Generally speaking, higher-capacity devices get more use in the long run and are worth the extra cost.

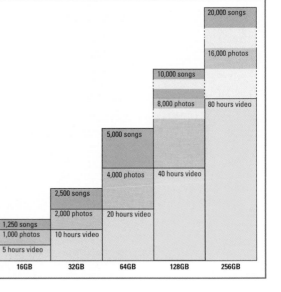

Understanding the 3D Touch Feature

The iPhone 7 models and iPhone 6 models include a feature called 3D Touch that provides shortcuts to content and to frequently used actions. 3D Touch uses force sensors in the screen to detect when you press the screen rather than just tapping it. For example, you can press an app icon on the Home screen to display actions for that app. For instance, press **Maps** (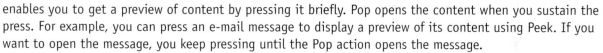) to display the pop-up menu for the Maps app. You can then tap a button in the Maps Destinations box to get directions to upcoming appointments, tap **Mark My Location** to mark your location, tap **Send My Location** to share your location with a contact, or tap **Search Nearby** to search for businesses or other places near you.

3D Touch uses two actions, Peek and Pop. Peek enables you to get a preview of content by pressing it briefly. Pop opens the content when you sustain the press. For example, you can press an e-mail message to display a preview of its content using Peek. If you want to open the message, you keep pressing until the Pop action opens the message.

Understanding the Live Photos Feature

All the current iPhone models include a feature called Live Photos that enables you to capture short sections of video before and after a still photo. After capturing the Live Photo, you can make the video segments play by tapping and holding the photo.

You can view your Live Photos on other Apple devices, such as your iPad or your Mac. You can also use a Live Photo as the wallpaper for your iPhone's lock screen.

Meet Your iPhone's Hardware Controls

After unboxing your iPhone, connect it to its charger and charge the battery fully. Then turn your iPhone on and meet its hardware controls: the Power/Sleep button, the Ringer On/Off switch, the Volume Up button, and the Volume Down button, and the Home button below the screen. If the store or carrier has not inserted a SIM card in the iPhone, you will need to insert a suitable card yourself (see the tip for details).

Meet Your iPhone's Hardware Controls

1 Press and hold the Power/Sleep button for a couple of seconds.

Note: The Power/Sleep button is on the right side of the iPhone 7 models and iPhone 6s models and on the top of the iPhone SE.

As the iPhone starts, the Apple logo appears on the screen.

Above the iPhone's screen are:

A The front-facing camera.

B The receiver speaker, which plays phone calls into your ear when you hold the iPhone up to your face.

C Below the iPhone's screen is the Home button, which you press to display the Home screen.

At the bottom of the iPhone are:

D The microphones.

E The Lightning connector.

F The speakers.

Note: The bottom edge of the iPhone 6s models and the iPhone SE has a mono speaker on the right and a 3.5mm headphone socket on the left, looking from the front.

2 Turn the iPhone so that you can see its left side.

3 When you want to turn the ringer off, move the Ringer On/Off switch to the rear so that the orange background appears.

Note: Turn the ringer off when you do not want the iPhone to disturb you or the peace. Move the Ringer On/Off switch back to the front when you want to turn the ringer back on.

4 Press the Volume Up (+) button to increase the ringer volume.

Note: When the Camera app is displayed, you can press the Volume Up (+) button to take a picture with the camera.

5 Press the Volume Down (−) button to decrease the ringer volume.

6 When the lock screen appears, press **Home**.

The iPhone unlocks, and the Home screen appears.

TIP

How do I insert a SIM card in my iPhone?
If the store or carrier has not inserted a SIM card, insert the SIM removal tool in the SIM hole on the right side of the iPhone. If you do not have a SIM removal tool, straighten out the end of a small paperclip and use that instead. Push gently until the tray pops out, and then pull it with your fingernails. Insert the SIM in the tray, and then push the tray in fully.

Download, Install, and Set Up iTunes

To sync your iPhone with your computer, you use Apple's iTunes application. iTunes comes preinstalled on every Mac but not on PCs; to get iTunes for Windows, you download it from the Apple website and then install it on your PC.

If you do not have a computer, or you do not want to sync your iPhone with your computer, you can set up and sync your iPhone using Apple's iCloud service, as described in "Set Up Your iPhone as New Using iCloud," later in this chapter.

Download, Install, and Set Up iTunes

1 On your PC, open the web browser. This example uses the Microsoft Edge browser on Windows 10.

2 Click the Address box, type **www.apple. com/itunes/download**, and then press Enter.

The Download iTunes Now web page appears.

3 Click the check boxes (☑ changes to ☐) unless you want to receive e-mail from Apple.

4 Click **Download now**.

5 When the download finishes, click **Run** in the pop-up panel that appears.

The iTunes installation begins, and the Welcome to iTunes dialog opens.

6 Click **Next**, and then follow the steps of the installer.

Note: You must accept the license agreement to install iTunes.

The Installation Options screen appears.

7 Click **Add iTunes shortcut to my desktop** (☑ changes to ☐) unless you want this shortcut.

8 Click **Use iTunes as the default player for audio files** (☑ changes to ☐) if you do not want to use iTunes as the default audio player.

9 Click **Automatically Update iTunes and Other Apple Software** (☑ changes to ☐) if you do not want automatic updates.

10 Click **Install**.

Note: If the User Account Control dialog opens, make sure that the Program Name is iTunes and the Verified Publisher is Apple Inc. Then click **Yes**.

The Congratulations screen appears.

11 Click **Open iTunes after the installer exits** (☑ changes to ☐) if you do not want iTunes to launch automatically when you close the installer.

12 Click **Finish**.

The installer closes.

Unless you chose not to open iTunes automatically, iTunes opens.

TIPS

Should I allow Apple to install updates automatically on my PC?
If this is your own PC, installing updates automatically is usually helpful. The updates may include fixes to bugs or vulnerabilities, new features, or both.

How do I set up iTunes on a Mac?
If you have not run iTunes already, click **iTunes** (♫) on the Dock. If the Dock contains no iTunes icon, click **Launchpad** (⊘) on the Dock, and then click **iTunes** (♫) on the Launchpad screen. The iTunes Setup Assistant launches. Follow the steps to set up iTunes.

Begin Setup and Activate Your iPhone

Before you can use your iPhone, you must set it up and activate it. First, you choose your language, specify your country or region, connect to the Internet through either a Wi-Fi network or the cellular network, and choose whether to use Location Services. You then activate the iPhone, registering it with Apple's servers. After this first stage of setup, you choose whether to set up the iPhone as a new iPhone, restore it from an iCloud backup, or restore it from an iTunes backup.

Begin Setup and Activate Your iPhone

Note: If you are upgrading from an existing iPhone, see Chapter 12 for instructions on turning off Find My iPhone, backing up the iPhone fully, and resetting it.

1. Turn on the iPhone by pressing and holding the Power/Sleep button until the Apple logo appears on-screen.

2. When the initial iPhone screen appears, press **Home**.

   The iPhone unlocks and begins the setup routine.

   The Language screen appears.

3. Tap the language you want to use.

   The Select Your Country or Region screen appears.

4. Tap your country or region.

   The Choose a Wi-Fi Network screen appears.

5. Tap the wireless network you want to use.

   A. If your Wi-Fi network does not appear because it does not broadcast its network name, tap **Choose Another Network**. You can then type the network's name.

   B. If your Wi-Fi network does not appear because it is out of range, tap **Use Cellular Connection**.

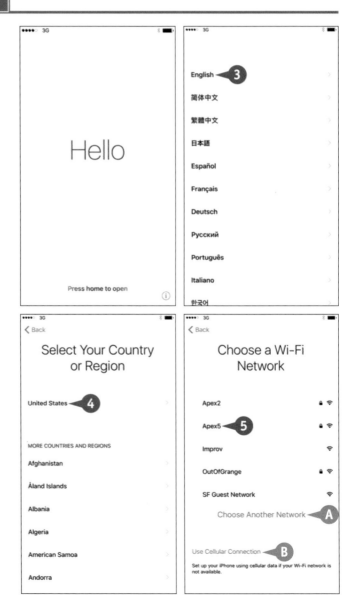

The Enter Password screen appears.

6 Type the password.

7 Tap **Join**.

Your iPhone joins the wireless network and connects to the Internet.

The Location Services screen appears.

8 Tap **Enable Location Services** or **Disable Location Services**, as needed. See the tip for advice.

The Touch ID screen appears.

9 Tap **Continue** and follow the prompts to scan your fingerprint for the Touch ID security mechanism.

The Create a Passcode screen appears.

10 Type a six-digit passcode, and then repeat it on the Re-Enter Your Passcode screen.

C You can tap **Passcode Options** to create a custom alphanumeric code or a four-digit code instead.

The Apps & Data screen appears.

11 Tap the appropriate button:

D Tap **Restore from iCloud Backup** to set up your iPhone using a backup stored in iCloud. See the section "Set Up Your iPhone from an iCloud Backup," later in this chapter.

E Tap **Restore from iTunes Backup** to set up your iPhone using a backup stored on your computer. See the section "Set Up Your iPhone from iTunes," later in this chapter.

F Tap **Set Up as New iPhone** to set up your iPhone from scratch using iCloud. See the next section, "Set Up Your iPhone as New Using iCloud."

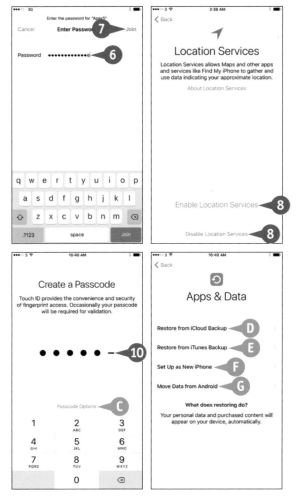

G Tap **Move Data from Android** to use the Move to iOS app to move data from an Android device.

 TIP

Should I enable Location Services?

Normally, enabling Location Services is helpful because it lets apps such as Maps determine your exact location. Using Location Services does mean that your iPhone continually tracks your location, but this is something the cellular network does anyway for cell phones. For privacy, open the Location Settings screen in the Settings app and turn off the switch for any app you do not want to track you.

Set Up Your iPhone as New Using iCloud

If you want to use your iPhone without syncing it to your computer, set it up using Apple's iCloud online service. With this approach, you sync your data to your account on iCloud, from which you can access it using other iOS devices, a Mac, or a web browser on any computer.

To set up a new iPhone to use iCloud, follow the instructions in the previous section to begin setup, and then continue with the instructions in this section.

Set Up Your iPhone as New Using iCloud

① Begin setup as explained in the previous section, "Begin Setup and Activate Your iPhone."

② On the Apps & Data screen, tap **Set Up as New iPhone**.

The Apple ID screen appears.

Ⓐ You can tap **Don't have an Apple ID or forgot it?** to create a new Apple ID or get a reminder about your existing Apple ID.

Ⓑ You can tap **About Apple ID and Privacy** to see information about privacy concerns.

③ Tap **Apple ID** and type your Apple ID.

④ Tap **Password** and type your password.

⑤ Tap **Next**.

The Terms and Conditions screen appears.

⑥ Read the terms and conditions, and tap **Agree** if you want to proceed.

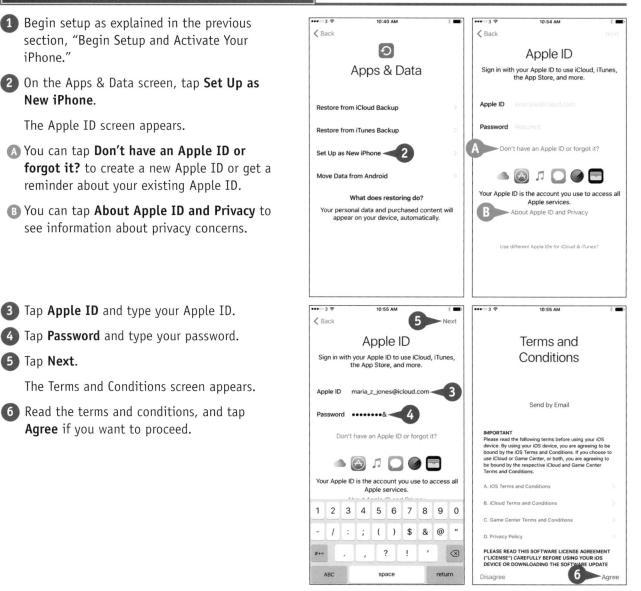

The Apple Pay screen appears.

7 Tap **Next**.

The Add Card screen appears.

8 Point the rear camera lens at your credit card or debit card.

The setup routine recognizes the card details.

C You can tap **Enter Card Details Manually** if the recognition fails or is inaccurate.

D You can tap **Set Up Later in Wallet** to skip adding a card.

The Card Details screen appears.

E You can correct the card details if necessary.

9 Tap **Next** and follow the prompt to set up your card with Apple Pay.

The iCloud Keychain screen appears.

F You can tap **Don't Restore Passwords** if you do not want to restore your passwords from iCloud to your iPhone.

10 Tap **Use iCloud Security Code**.

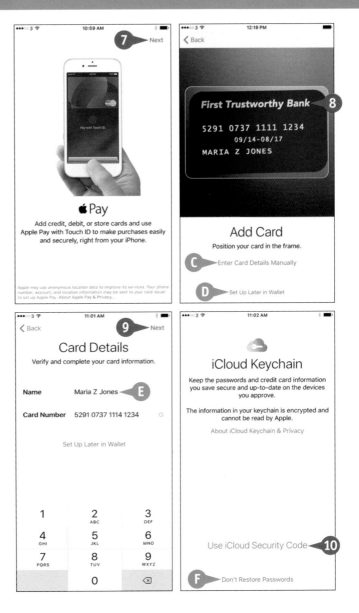

TIP

What is Siri and should I enable it?
Siri is Apple's voice-driven assistant, which enables you to interact with your iPhone by voice. Many people find Siri useful, but if you do not, you can turn Siri off at any time. See Chapter 3 for instructions on using and customizing Siri.

continued ▶

When you set up your iPhone using iCloud, use an e-mail address that you intend to keep for the long term. This is especially important if you use the same e-mail address for the Apple ID that you use for the App Store; each app you buy is tied to that e-mail address, so if you change the address, you will need to authenticate again for each app update.

Set Up Your iPhone as New Using iCloud (continued)

The iCloud Security Code screen appears.

11 Type your security code.

The iPhone verifies the security code with Apple's servers.

The Verification Code screen appears.

12 Type the verification code sent to your trusted phone number.

The iPhone checks that the verification code is correct.

The Siri screen appears.

13 Tap **Set Up Siri** and follow the prompts to set up Siri's voice recognition.

G You can tap **Turn On Siri Later** if you do not want to turn on Siri now.

Note: You can turn Siri on or off at any point after setup.

The Diagnostics screen appears.

Note: To learn which details the diagnostics and usage reports contain, tap **About Diagnostics & Privacy**.

Note: The Diagnostics screen may include buttons such as Automatically Send and Don't Send instead of Continue.

14 Tap **Continue**.

The App Analytics screen appears.

15 Tap **Share with App Developers** if you want to share usage statistics and crash data with the developers of the apps you use. Otherwise, tap **Don't Share**.

The Display Zoom screen appears.

16 Tap **Standard** or **Zoomed** to choose which view to use.

The Display Zoom screen appears.

H You can tap **Standard** or **Zoomed** to switch between the views and decide which you prefer.

17 Tap **Next**.

The Welcome to iPhone screen appears.

18 Tap **Get Started**.

The Home screen appears, and you can begin using your iPhone.

Why should I use iCloud Keychain?

iCloud Keychain gives you an easy way to store your passwords and credit card information securely on your iPhone, other iOS devices, or Mac. Instead of having to remember the password for each website, or look at a credit card when you need to enter its details, you can have iCloud Keychain automatically provide the details.

iCloud Keychain encrypts your data, but you must use a complex passcode to keep it secure. A standard four-digit numeric passcode is not strong enough to keep your iCloud Keychain secure against serious attacks.

Set Up Your iPhone from an iCloud Backup

If you have used an iPhone or other iOS device before, you can set up your iPhone by restoring from an iCloud backup. This backup can be from either another iPhone or iOS device or from the same iPhone.

When you restore your iPhone from an iCloud backup, you choose which backup to use — normally, the most recent one. iOS automatically restores your settings, downloads your apps from the App Store, and then installs them on the iPhone.

Set Up Your iPhone from an iCloud Backup

1 Begin setup as explained in the section "Begin Setup and Activate Your iPhone," earlier in this chapter.

2 On the Apps & Data screen, tap **Restore from iCloud Backup**.

The iCloud Sign In screen appears.

3 Type your Apple ID.

4 Type your password.

5 Tap **Next**.

The Terms and Conditions screen appears.

6 Tap **Agree**.

The Choose Backup screen appears.

7 Tap the backup you want to use.

iOS restores the backup to your iPhone.

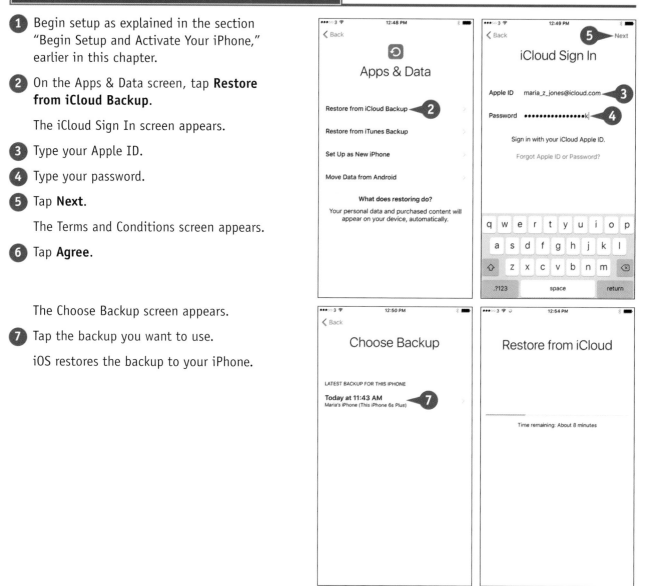

The Update Complete screen appears.

8 Tap **Continue**.

The Location Services screen appears.

9 Tap **Enable Location Services** or **Disable Location Services**, as needed.

Note: If the Apple Pay screen appears, tap **Next** to add a payment card, and then follow the prompts for adding it; you can tap **Enter Card Details Manually** if the data recognition fails. Tap **Set Up Later in Wallet** if you prefer to add a payment card later.

The iCloud Keychain screen appears.

10 Tap **Use iCloud Security Code** and follow the prompts to authenticate your identity.

The Siri screen appears.

11 Tap **Set Up Siri** and follow the prompts to set up Siri's voice recognition.

A You can tap **Turn On Siri Later** if you do not want to turn on Siri now.

Note: You can turn Siri on or off at any point after setup.

The Welcome to iPhone screen appears.

12 Tap **Get Started**.

The Home screen appears, and you can start using your iPhone.

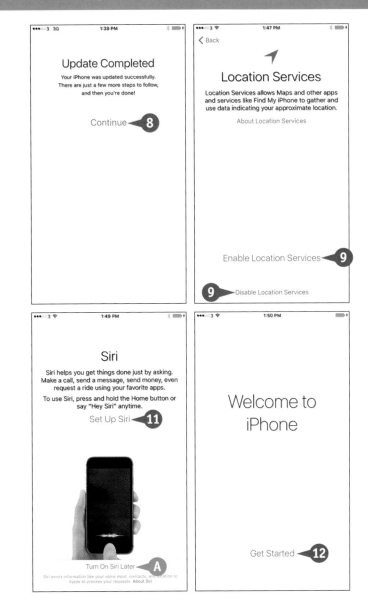

TIP

Which iPhone backup should I use?

Normally, it is best to use the most recent backup available for this iPhone or for the iPhone whose backups you are using. But sometimes you may find a problem exists with the latest backup. In this case, try the previous backup.

Set Up Your iPhone from iTunes

Instead of setting up your iPhone using iCloud, as described in the previous two sections, you can set it up using iTunes. You can either restore an iTunes backup to the device or set up the iPhone from scratch using iTunes.

When setting up your iPhone for the first time, you can restore it from an iTunes backup of another iPhone — for example, your previous iPhone. If you have already set up this iPhone, you can restore it from its own backup.

Set Up Your iPhone from iTunes

1 Begin setup as explained in the section "Begin Setup and Activate Your iPhone," earlier in this chapter.

2 On the Apps & Data screen, tap **Restore from iTunes Backup**.

The Connect to iTunes screen appears.

3 Connect your iPhone to your computer via the USB cable.

On your computer, iTunes opens or becomes active.

The Welcome to Your New iPhone screen appears.

4 Make sure the **Restore from this backup** radio button is selected (◉).

5 Click the pop-up menu button (◉) and select the appropriate iPhone from the menu.

6 Click **Continue**.

iTunes restores your iPhone from the backup.

When the restore is complete, your iPhone restarts.

Your iPhone's control screens appear in the iTunes window.

You can now choose sync settings for the iPhone as explained in the next section, "Choose Which Items to Sync from Your Computer."

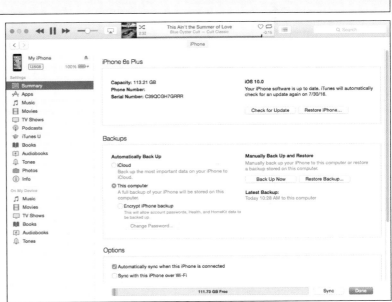

TIP

How do I set up my iPhone from scratch using iTunes?

On the Apps & Data screen, tap **Restore from iTunes Backup**, and then connect your iPhone to your computer via the USB cable. When the Welcome to Your New iPhone screen appears in iTunes on your computer, click **Set up as new iPhone** (○ changes to ◉). Click **Continue**. On the Sync with iTunes screen that appears, click **Get Started**. The iPhone's control screens appear, and you can set up synchronization as described in the next section, "Choose Which Items to Sync from Your Computer."

Choose Which Items to Sync from Your Computer

After specifying that you will use iTunes to sync your iPhone, as explained in the previous section, "Set Up Your iPhone from iTunes," you use the iPhone's control screens in iTunes to choose which items to sync. When setting your sync preferences, start on the Summary tab. Here, you can change your iPhone's name, choose whether to back up the iPhone to iCloud or to your computer, decide whether to encrypt the backup, and set general options for controlling syncing.

Choose Which Items to Sync from Your Computer

Connect Your iPhone and Choose Options on the Summary Tab

1 Connect your iPhone to your computer via the USB cable.

The iTunes window appears.

2 If your iPhone's control screens do not automatically appear, click **iPhone** (📱) on the navigation bar at the top of the screen.

Note: Your iPhone appears in iTunes with either a default name or the name you have given it.

The iPhone's control screens appear.

3 Click **Summary** if the Summary screen is not already displayed.

The Summary screen appears.

4 To change the iPhone's name, click the existing name, type the new name, and press Enter or Return.

5 In the Automatically Back Up area, click **iCloud** (○ changes to ◉) or **This computer** (○ changes to ◉) to specify where to back up your iPhone.

6 If you choose to back up to this computer, click **Encrypt iPhone backup** (☐ changes to ☑).

The Set Password dialog opens.

7 Type a password in the Password box and again in the Verify Password box.

8 On a Mac, click **Remember this password in my keychain** (☐ changes to ☑) if you want to save the password in your keychain.

9 Click **Set Password**.

The Set Password dialog closes.

10 Click **Automatically sync when this iPhone is connected** (☐ changes to ☑) if you want to sync your iPhone automatically when you connect it.

11 Click **Sync only checked songs and videos** (☐ changes to ☑) if you want syncing to omit any song or video whose check box you have deselected (☐).

12 Click **Convert higher bit rate songs to AAC** (☐ changes to ☑) if you want to compress larger songs to fit more on your iPhone. In the pop-up menu, choose the bit rate.

TIP

Should I back up my iPhone to my computer or to iCloud?

If you plan to use your iPhone mostly with your computer, back up the iPhone to the computer. Doing so makes iTunes store a full backup of the iPhone on the computer, so you can restore all the data to your iPhone, or to a replacement iPhone, if necessary. You can also encrypt the backup. To keep your data safe, you must back up your computer as well. For example, you can use Time Machine to back up a Mac.

Backing up your iPhone to iCloud enables you to access the backups from anywhere via the Internet, but make sure your iCloud account has enough storage to contain the backups. An iCloud backup stores less information than an iTunes backup.

continued ▶

iTunes makes it easy to choose which items to sync to your iPhone. By selecting the iPhone in the navigation bar in iTunes, and then clicking the appropriate item in the Settings area of the Source list, you can quickly choose which apps, music, movies, and other items to sync from your computer.

You can sync photos from your computer only if you are not using the iCloud Photos feature. If you have enabled iCloud Photos, your iPhone syncs your photos through iCloud instead.

Choose Which Items to Sync from Your Computer (continued)

Choose Which Apps to Sync

1 Click **Apps**.

A You can click the pop-up menu button (⬍) and choose how to sort the apps: Click **Sort by Name**, **Sort by Kind**, **Sort by Category**, **Sort by Date Added**, or **Sort by Size**, as needed.

2 Click **Install** for each app you want to sync to the iPhone (Install changes to Will Install).

3 Scroll down the screen and click **Automatically install new apps** (☐ changes to ✓) if you want to sync new apps automatically. This is usually helpful.

Choose Which Music to Sync

1 Click **Music**.

2 Click **Sync Music** (☐ changes to ✓).

3 To load a selection of music, click **Selected playlists, artists, albums, and genres** (○ changes to ◉) instead of **Entire music library**.

B Click **Automatically fill free space with songs** (☐ changes to ✓) only if you want to put as much music as possible on your iPhone.

4 Click the check box (☐ changes to ✓) for each playlist, artist, genre, or album to include.

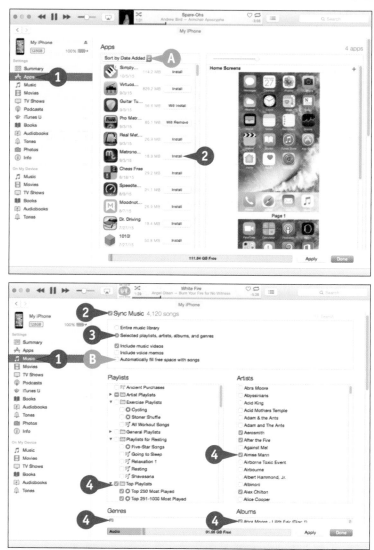

Sync Photos

1. Click **Photos**.

2. Click **Sync Photos** (☐ changes to ☑).

Note: In Windows, click **Sync Photos with** (☐ changes to ☑), and then choose the folder in the drop-down list.

3. Click the pop-up menu button (◆) and choose the source of the photos — for example, **Photos**.

4. Choose which photos to sync. For example, click **Selected albums** (○ changes to ◉), and then choose the albums to include.

Apply Your Changes and Sync

1. Click **Apply** or **Sync**.

Note: The Apply button appears when you have made changes to the items you will sync. Click **Apply** to apply the changes and sync them.

iTunes syncs the items to your iPhone.

C The readout shows you the sync progress.

D If you need to stop the sync, click **Stop** (✕).

When the sync finishes, disconnect your iPhone.

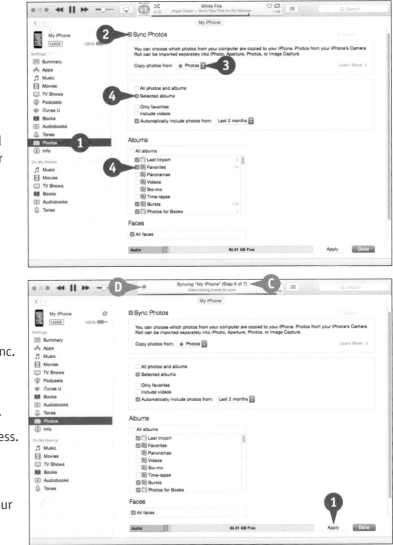

TIP

How can I fit more content on my iPhone?

You cannot install a memory card to increase your iPhone's storage capacity, so you must prune and compress the existing content.

Video, photo, and music files tend to take the most space. For video, remove files you do not need on your iPhone. For photos, if you use iCloud Photo Library, press **Home**, tap **Settings** (⚙), tap **iCloud** (☁), tap **Photos** (✿), and then tap **Optimize iPhone Storage**. For music, click the **Convert higher bit rate songs** check box (☐ changes to ☑) on the Summary tab and choose a low bit rate, such as 128 Kbps, to reduce the size of music files while retaining acceptable audio quality.

Sync Your iPhone with iTunes via Wi-Fi

Instead of syncing your iPhone with iTunes via USB, you can sync it wirelessly or "over the air." You must connect your iPhone and your computer to the same network.

To use wireless sync, you must first enable it in iTunes. You can then have the iPhone sync automatically when connected to a power source and to the same wireless network as the computer. You can also start a sync manually from the iPhone, even if it is not connected to a power source.

Sync Your iPhone with iTunes via Wi-Fi

Set Your iPhone to Sync with iTunes via Wi-Fi

1 Connect your iPhone to your computer with the USB cable.

The iTunes window appears.

2 Click **iPhone** ().

Note: Your iPhone appears in iTunes with the name you gave it.

The iPhone's control screens appear.

3 Click **Summary**.

The Summary screen appears.

4 Click **Sync with this iPhone over Wi-Fi** (☐ changes to ☑).

5 Click **Apply**.

iTunes applies the change.

6 Disconnect your iPhone from your computer.

Perform a Manual Sync via Wi-Fi

1 Press **Home**.

The Home screen appears.

2 Tap **Settings** (⚙).

The Settings screen appears.

3 Tap **General** (⚙).

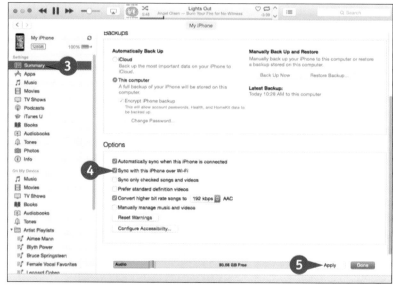

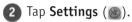

The General screen appears.

4 Tap **iTunes Wi-Fi Sync**.

The iTunes Wi-Fi Sync screen appears.

5 Tap **Sync Now**.

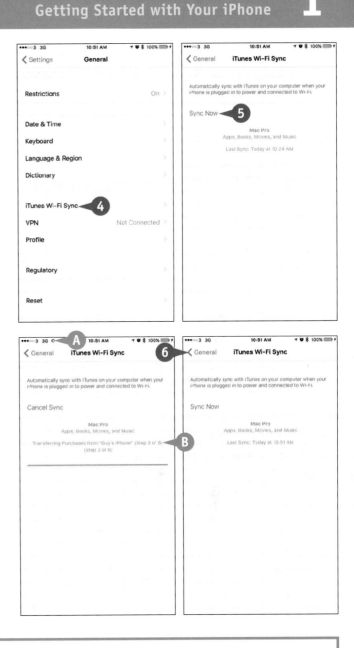

The sync runs.

A The Sync symbol (⟳) appears in the status bar.

B The readout shows which part of the sync is currently running.

6 When the sync completes, tap **General** (〈).

The General screen appears.

TIP

Can I sync my iPhone automatically via Wi-Fi?

Yes. To sync your iPhone automatically via Wi-Fi, connect your iPhone to a power source — for example, the iPhone power adapter. Make sure your computer is on and connected to your network, and that iTunes is running. Your iPhone automatically connects to your computer across the wireless network. iTunes syncs the latest songs, videos, and data.

To avoid interruptions, iTunes may sync your iPhone overnight. This means you need to leave your computer on for automatic syncing to occur, but it is fine for the computer to be asleep.

Explore the Interface and Launch Apps

After you set up your iPhone with iCloud or iTunes, you are ready to start using the device. When you press **Home** to wake the iPhone from sleep, it displays the lock screen. You then unlock the iPhone to reach the Home screen, which contains icons for running the apps installed on the iPhone.

You can quickly launch an app by tapping its icon on the Home screen. From the app, you can return to the Home screen by pressing **Home**. You can then launch another app as needed.

Explore the Interface and Launch Apps

1 Press **Home** with a finger or thumb you have registered for Touch ID, the fingerprint-unlocking feature.

The iPhone's screen lights up.

The lock screen appears momentarily.

The iPhone unlocks.

The Home screen appears.

Note: If you are not using Touch ID, or you press **Home** with a nonregistered finger or thumb, the iPhone prompts you to enter your passcode. After you enter the passcode correctly, the iPhone unlocks, and the Home screen appears.

A The iPhone has two or more Home screens. The gray dots at the bottom of the Home screen show how many Home screens you have. The white dot shows the current Home screen.

2 Tap **Notes** ( ).

The Notes app opens.

Note: If you chose to sync notes with your iPhone, the synced notes appear in the Notes app. Otherwise, the list is empty until you create a note.

3 Tap **New** ( ).

A new note opens, and the on-screen keyboard appears.

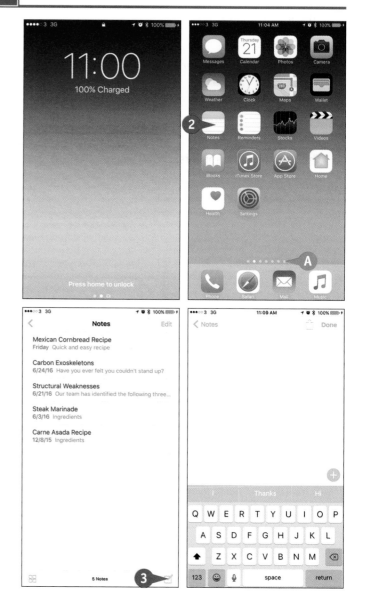

4 Type a short note by tapping the keys.

B If the middle button in the suggestion bar shows the word you want, tap **Spacebar** to accept it. If one of the other buttons shows the right word, tap that button.

5 Tap **Done**.

The on-screen keyboard closes.

6 Tap **Notes** (**<**).

C The Notes list appears, with your note in it.

7 Press **Home**.

The Home screen appears.

8 Tap and drag to the left to display the second Home screen.

Note: You can also tap at the right end of the row of dots on the Home screen to move one screen to the right. Tap at the left end to move one screen to the left.

You can now launch another app by tapping its icon.

9 Press the **Power/Sleep** button.

Your iPhone goes to sleep.

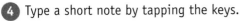

TIP

Where do I get more apps to perform other tasks?
You can find an amazingly wide selection of apps — both free and those you pay for — on Apple's App Store. See Chapter 7 for instructions on finding and downloading the apps you need.

Using Notification Center and Today View

Your iPhone handles many different types of alerts, such as missed phone calls, text messages, and invitations to events such as meetings. Your iPhone integrates these alerts into Notification Center so that you can review them easily.

The iPhone's Today View enables you to view snippets of important and helpful information, such as weather, calendar appointments, and stock updates. You can access Today View either via Notification Center or directly from the Home screen.

Using Notification Center and Today View

Open Notification Center and Deal with Notifications

① Tap at the top of the screen and swipe your finger down.

Notification Center appears.

Note: See the section "Choose Which Apps Can Give Notifications" in Chapter 2 for instructions on customizing notifications.

Ⓐ You can tap **Clear** (⊗) to clear all notifications in a category such as Recent.

② To remove a single notification, swipe it left.

The Clear button appears.

③ Tap **Clear**.

The notification disappears from Notification Center.

④ To go to the app that raised a notification, tap the notification.

The app appears. For example, if you tap the notification for a message, the Messages app appears.

Ⓑ You can take any action needed, such as replying to a message.

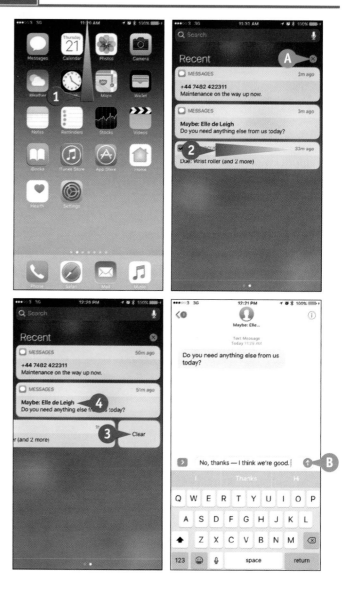

Open Today View

 In Notification Center, swipe right.

C You can also tap the gray dot at the bottom of the screen.

Today View appears.

Note: You can customize the selection of widgets in Today View. See the section "Customize Today View" in Chapter 2 for details.

2 Swipe up.

Other items appear.

D You can tap a widget to go straight to the related app.

E You can tap an item such as a reminder to mark it as done.

3 Drag or swipe up from the bottom of the screen.

Today View closes, and the screen appears that you were using before.

What happens if I receive a notification when my iPhone is locked?

This depends on the type of notification. For most types of notifications, your iPhone displays an alert on the lock screen to alert you to the notification. Unlocking your iPhone while the alert is showing takes you directly to the notification in whatever app it belongs to — for example, to an instant message in the Messages app.

Using Control Center

Control Center puts your iPhone's most essential controls at your fingertips. From Control Center, you can turn Airplane Mode, Wi-Fi, Bluetooth, Do Not Disturb Mode, and Orientation Lock on or off; control music playback and volume and direct your iPhone's audio and video output to AirPlay devices; change the setting for the AirDrop sharing feature; and quickly access the Flashlight, Clock, Calculator, and Camera apps. Control Center appears as a pane that you open by swiping upward from the bottom of the screen.

Using Control Center

Open Control Center

1 Tap and swipe up from the very bottom of the screen.

Control Center opens.

Note: You can open Control Center from most apps and screens. You may find some exceptions — for example, where iOS interprets an upward swipe as an action within the app.

Ⓐ You can tap **AirPlay** (🖵) to connect to an AirPlay device that can mirror the iPhone's screen, such as an Apple TV.

Ⓑ You can tap **Night Shift** (🔅) to turn Night Shift on or off. See Chapter 2 for information on Night Shift.

Control Essential Settings

1 Tap **Airplane Mode** (✈ or ✈) to turn Airplane Mode on (✈) or off (✈).

2 Tap **Wi-Fi** (📶 or 📶) to turn Wi-Fi on (📶) or off (📶).

3 Tap **Bluetooth** (✳ or ✳) to turn Bluetooth on (✳) or off (✳).

4 Tap **Do Not Disturb** (🌙 or 🌙) to turn Do Not Disturb Mode on (🌙) or off (🌙).

5 Tap **Orientation Lock** (🔒 or 🔒) to turn Orientation Lock on (🔒) or off (🔒).

Choose an AirPlay Device for Audio

1 In Control Center, swipe left.

The Audio panel of Control Center appears.

C You can use the audio controls to control playback.

D You can drag the playhead to move through the song.

E You can drag the volume slider to control the volume.

2 Tap **Now Playing On**.

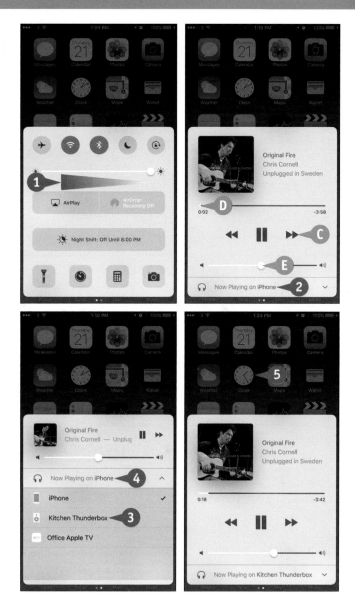

The Now Playing On panel appears.

3 Tap the audio device to use for output.

4 Tap **Now Playing On**.

The Now Playing On panel closes.

5 Tap the screen above Control Center.

Control Center closes.

TIPS

What are the buttons at the bottom of the first panel in Control Center?

Tap **Flashlight** (🔦) to turn on the Flashlight. Tap **Timer** (⏱) to display the Timer screen in the Clock app. Tap **Calculator** (🔢) to display the Calculator app. Tap **Camera** (📷) to display the Camera app.

Can I use Control Center in landscape orientation?

Yes. Simply swipe up from the bottom of the screen in an app that supports the rotated orientation. Control Center has a different landscape layout and takes up the whole screen, but the controls work the same way.

Using 3D Touch

The iPhone's 3D Touch feature enables you to take actions quickly by pressing with your finger on the screen instead of tapping. 3D Touch gives you an alternative way to access some commands in some apps.

Only some apps offer 3D Touch actions, although Apple is encouraging developers to include 3D Touch in their apps. Similarly, only some of the latest iPhone models have 3D Touch.

Understanding Which iPhone Models Have 3D Touch

As of this writing, only the iPhone 7, iPhone 7 Pro, iPhone 6s, and iPhone 6s Plus have 3D Touch. The iPhone SE, although it was introduced after the iPhone 6s and iPhone 6s Plus, does not have 3D Touch.

Understanding 3D Touch's Three Main Features

3D Touch has three main features:

- **Quick Actions**. These are actions you can take by pressing an app's icon on the Home screen or in another location.
- **Peek**. This feature enables you to preview the content of an item, such as an e-mail message or a photo.
- **Pop**. This feature enables you to fully open an item into which you have Peeked.

Using Quick Actions from the Home Screen

3D Touch enables you to take a variety of useful actions directly from the Home screen using the Quick Actions feature. To access Quick Actions on the Home screen, you press the appropriate app's icon and then tap the Quick Action on the menu that opens.

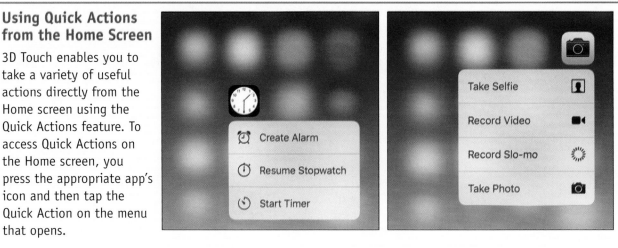

If you press an icon that does not provide any Quick Actions, the screen blinks briefly and your iPhone vibrates, as if to shake its head to say "no."

Understanding How Peek and Pop Work

When using 3D Touch, you normally begin with the Peek action, which opens the Peek panel to give you a preview of the contents of an item. The Peek panel stays open only as long as you keep pressing with the same pressure; when you lift your finger, the Peek panel closes.

Instead of lifting your finger, you can press a little harder to Pop open the item. For example, in Mail, you can 3D-Touch a message to open its Peek panel to look at its contents. You can then 3D-Touch further to Pop the message open for reading, or simply release the 3D Touch to allow the message to close again.

Exploring 3D Touch

This book gives some examples of 3D Touch in cases where it is especially convenient. But there are many other actions you can take with 3D Touch, assuming that your iPhone model supports it.

You can explore 3D Touch further by simply pressing icons or other objects in the user interface and seeing if a Quick Actions menu opens or a Peek panel appears. When you do get the menu or the panel, evaluate whether you will be able to save time by using this feature — and if so, add it to your iPhone repertoire.

Using the Reachability Feature

On large-screen iPhones, iOS provides a feature called Reachability to help you reach the top of the screen when you are using the iPhone one-handed. Reachability is especially useful if you have small hands.

You can turn Reachability on or off in the Settings app. Once it is turned on, you can use it whenever you need it.

Using the Reachability Feature

Turn the Reachability Feature On

1 Press **Home**.

The Home screen appears.

2 Tap **Settings** (⚙).

The Settings screen appears.

3 Tap **General** (⚙).

The General screen appears.

4 Tap **Accessibility**.

The Accessibility screen appears.

5 Toward the bottom of the screen, set the **Reachability** switch to On (⚪).

Use the Reachability Feature

 Press **Home**.

The Home screen appears.

 Double-tap **Home**.

Note: Double-tap **Home** lightly with your finger. Do not double-press **Home**, because that displays the App Switcher instead.

The screen slides down so that its top half is within easy reach.

3 Tap the appropriate button. For example, tap **Photos** (🌸) to launch the Photos app.

The app opens, and you can use it as normal.

4 When you need to reach the top of the screen easily, double-tap **Home**.

The screen slides down.

5 Tap the appropriate button.

The screen resumes its normal appearance.

Note: If you do not tap the screen for a few seconds after activating Reachability, the feature automatically returns the screen to normal.

TIP

How can I make the Home screen icons bigger on a large-screen iPhone?

You can turn on Zoomed view, which makes the Home screen icons and other interface elements appear larger.

Press **Home** and then tap **Settings** (⚙) to display the Settings screen. Tap **Display & Brightness** (🔠) to display the Display & Brightness screen, and then tap **View** in the Display Zoom section. On the Display Zoom screen, tap **Zoomed**, and then tap **Set**.

CHAPTER 2

Personalizing Your iPhone

To make your iPhone work the way you prefer, you can configure its many settings. In this chapter, you learn how to control iCloud sync, notifications, audio preferences, screen brightness, and other key aspects of the iPhone's behavior.

Find the Settings You Need

The iOS operating system includes many settings that enable you to configure your iPhone to work the way you prefer. The central place for manipulating settings is the Settings app, which contains settings for the iPhone's system software, the apps the iPhone includes, and third-party apps you have added. To reach the settings, you first display the Settings screen and then the category of settings you want to configure.

Find the Settings You Need

Display the Settings Screen

1. Press **Home**.

   The Home screen appears.

2. Tap **Settings** (⚙).

   The Settings screen appears.

   A. You can tap **Settings** (🔍) and type a setting name or keyword to locate the setting. You may need to tap the screen and pull down to reveal the Search bar.

   B. The top part of the Settings screen contains settings you are likely to use frequently, such as Airplane Mode, Wi-Fi, and Bluetooth.

3. Tap and drag up to scroll down the screen.

   C. This section contains settings for built-in apps developed by Apple.

4. Tap and drag up to scroll further down the screen. You can also swipe up to move more quickly.

   D. This section contains settings for built-in apps developed by third-party developers.

   E. This section contains settings for apps you install. These apps can be either from Apple or from third-party developers.

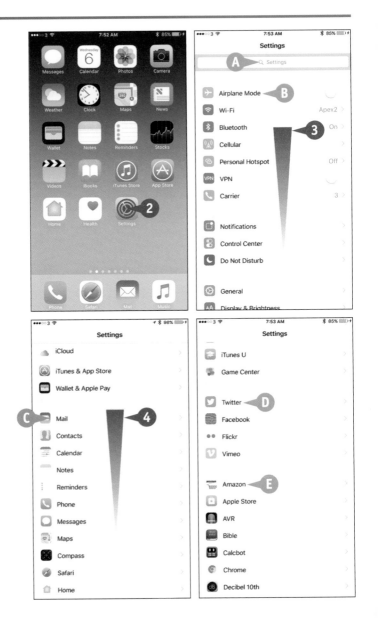

Display a Settings Screen

1 On the Settings screen, tap the button for the settings category you want to display. For example, tap **Sounds** (🔊) to display the Sounds screen.

2 Tap **Settings** (<) when you are ready to return to the Settings screen.

Display the Settings for an App

1 On the Settings screen, tap the button for the app whose settings you want to display. For example, tap **Safari** (🧭) to display the Safari settings.

2 Tap **Settings** (<) when you are ready to return to the Settings screen.

3 Press **Home**.

The Home screen appears again.

Note: When you next open the Settings app, it displays the screen you were last using. For convenience, it is usually best to return to the main Settings screen when you finish choosing settings.

TIP

Why do only some apps have an entry in the Settings app?

The Settings app contains entries for only those apps that have settings you can configure directly through iOS, the iPhone's operating system. Other apps include settings that you configure directly from within the app. This approach is more convenient for apps that have settings you are likely to change frequently while you use the app.

Choose Which iCloud Items to Sync

pple's iCloud service enables you to sync many types of data — such as your e-mail account details, your contacts, and your calendars and reminders — online so you can access them from any of your devices. You can also use the Find My iPhone feature to locate your iPhone when it goes missing. To use iCloud, you set your iPhone to use your Apple ID, and then choose which features to use.

Choose Which iCloud Items to Sync

1 Press **Home**.

The Home screen appears.

2 Tap **Settings** (⚙).

The Settings screen appears.

3 Tap **iCloud** (☁) to display the iCloud screen.

Note: If you have not yet set up iCloud on your iPhone, type your Apple ID and password on the iCloud screen, and then tap **Sign In**. If you do not yet have an Apple ID, tap **Get a Free Apple ID** and follow the prompts.

4 Tap **iCloud Drive** (☁).

The iCloud Drive screen appears.

5 Set the **iCloud Drive** switch to On (⬤) to enable iCloud Drive.

6 Set each app's switch to On (⬤) or Off ( ), as needed.

7 Set the **Use Cellular Data** switch to On (⬤) if you want to transfer data across the cellular connection.

Note: If you set the **Use Cellular Data** switch to On (⬤), monitor your data usage as explained in Chapter 6 to ensure that you do not exceed your data plan.

8 Tap **iCloud** (‹).

The iCloud screen appears again.

9 Tap **Photos** (🌼).

The Photos screen appears.

10 Set the **iCloud Photo Library** switch to On (🔘) to store all your photos in iCloud.

11 Tap **Optimize iPhone Storage** if you need to save space. Tap **Download and Keep Originals** if you prefer to keep original photos on your iPhone.

12 Set the **Upload to My Photo Stream** switch to On (🔘) to upload photos to your photo stream.

13 Set the **iCloud Photo Sharing** switch to On (🔘) to use Photo Sharing.

14 Tap **iCloud** (‹).

The iCloud screen appears again.

15 Set the **Mail** (✉), **Contacts** (👤), **Calendars** (📅), **Reminders** (⁞), **Safari** (🧭), **Notes** (‾), **News** (📰), and **Wallet** (📇) switches to On (🔘) or Off (‾), as needed.

16 Tap **Backup** (☁).

The Backup screen appears.

17 Set the **iCloud Backup** switch to On (🔘).

18 Tap **iCloud** (‹).

19 Tap **Keychain** (📇) to display the Keychain screen, set the **iCloud Keychain** switch to On (🔘), and then follow the prompts to create a security code.

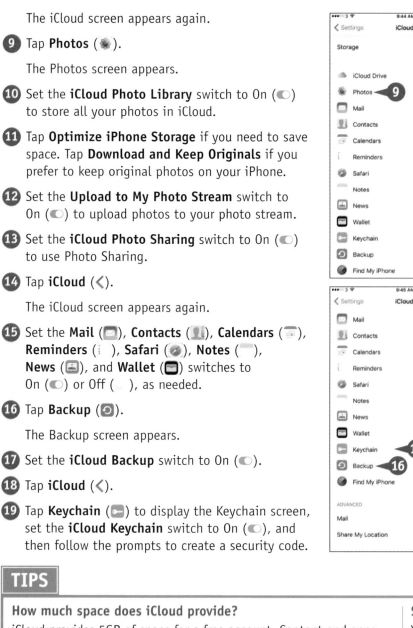

TIPS

How much space does iCloud provide?

iCloud provides 5GB of space for a free account. Content and apps you acquire from Apple do not count against this space, nor do your Photo Stream photos or songs included in iTunes Match — but iCloud Photo Sharing does count. You can buy more space by tapping **Storage**, tapping **Manage Storage** on the Storage screen, and then tapping **Change Storage Plan** on the Manage Storage screen.

Should I turn on Find My iPhone?

Yes. Find My iPhone enables you to locate your iPhone when you misplace it or learn where it is when someone misappropriates it. It also prevents someone else from activating your iPhone on his or her own account.

Choose Which Apps Can Give Notifications

Some iPhone apps can notify you when you have received messages or when updates are available. You can choose which notifications an app gives or prevent an app from showing notifications. You can also control which notifications appear on the lock screen.

iPhone apps use three types of notifications: badges on app icons, banners at the top of the screen, and alert dialogs. See the tip for details.

Choose Which Apps Can Give Notifications

1 Press **Home**.

The Home screen appears.

2 Tap **Settings** (⚙).

The Settings screen appears.

3 Tap **Notifications** (📋).

The Notifications screen appears.

4 Tap the app for which you want to configure notifications. This example uses **Calendar** (📅).

The screen for configuring the app's notifications appears.

5 Set the **Allow Notifications** switch to On (⬤) to enable notifications.

Note: For some apps, all the options appear on the screen for configuring the app's notifications.

6 Tap the button for the notification type you want to configure. This example uses **Upcoming Events**.

The screen for configuring that notification type appears, such as the Upcoming Events screen.

7 Set the **Show in Notification Center** switch to On (⬤) to include these notifications in Notification Center.

8 Tap **Sounds**.

9 Tap the sound you want to use.

Ⓐ You can tap **None** for no sound.

Ⓑ You can tap **Vibration** and choose the vibration pattern for the notification type.

10 Tap the **Back** button (**‹**), such as **Upcoming Events** (**‹**) in this example.

11 Set the **Badge App Icon** switch to On (⬤) to show badges.

12 Set the **Show on Lock Screen** switch to On (⬤) or Off ( ), as needed.

13 Tap **None**, **Banners**, or **Alerts** to choose what alerts to show.

14 Tap the **Back** button (**‹**), such as **Calendar** (**‹**) in this example.

Ⓒ You can configure other notification types, as needed.

15 Tap **Notifications** (**‹**).

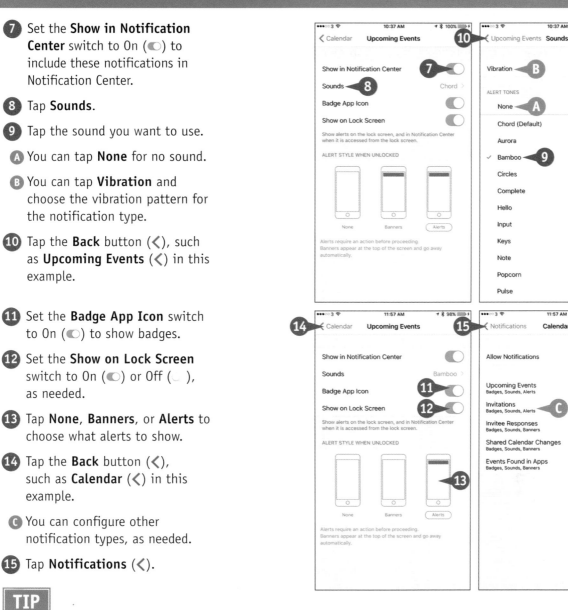

TIP

What are the three kinds of notifications?

A *badge* is a red circle or rounded rectangle that appears on the app's icon on the Home screen and shows a white number indicating how many notifications there are. A *banner* is a pop-up notification that appears briefly at the top of the screen and then disappears automatically. An *alert* is a dialog that appears in front of the running app; you need to dismiss the alert before you can take other actions on your iPhone. Whichever notification type you choose, you can set the **Sounds** switch to On (⬤) to have your iPhone play a sound to get your attention.

Choose Sounds Settings

The Sounds screen in Settings enables you to control what audio feedback your iPhone gives you. You can have the iPhone always vibrate to signal incoming calls, or vibrate only when the ringer is silent. You can set the ringer and alerts volumes, choose your default ringtone and text tone, and choose which items can give you alerts. Your iPhone can play lock sounds to confirm you have locked or unlocked your iPhone. It can also play keyboard clicks to confirm each key press.

Choose Sounds Settings

1 Press **Home**.

The Home screen appears.

2 Tap **Settings** (⚙).

The Settings screen appears.

3 Tap **Sounds** (🔊).

The Sounds screen appears.

4 Set the **Vibrate on Ring** switch to On (🔘) or Off ( ), as needed.

5 Set the **Vibrate on Silent** switch to On (🔘) or Off ( ), as needed.

6 Tap and drag the **Ringer and Alerts** slider to set the volume.

Ⓐ When the **Change with Buttons** switch is On (🔘), you can change the Ringer and Alerts volume by pressing the volume buttons on the side of the iPhone.

7 Tap **Ringtone**.

The Ringtone screen appears.

8 Tap the ringtone you want to hear.

9 Tap **Vibration**.

The Vibration screen appears.

⑩ Tap the vibration pattern you want.

⑪ If you prefer a custom vibration, tap **Create New Vibration** in the Custom area.

The New Vibration screen appears.

⑫ Tap a rhythm.

⑬ Tap **Stop**.

⑭ Tap **Play** to play back the vibration.

⑮ Tap **Save**.

The New Vibration dialog opens.

⑯ Type a name.

⑰ Tap **Save**.

The Vibration screen appears.

⑱ Tap **Back** (〈).

The Ringtone screen appears.

⑲ Tap **Sounds** (〈).

The Sounds screen appears.

⑳ Repeat steps **7** to **19** to set other tones, such as text tones.

㉑ Set the **Lock Sounds** switch to On (◉) or Off ( ), as needed.

㉒ Set the **Keyboard Clicks** switch to On (◉) or Off ( ), as needed.

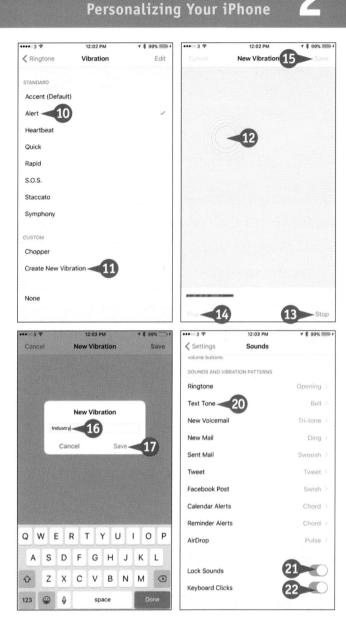

TIP

How do I use different ringtones for different callers?
The ringtone and text tone you set in the Ringtone area of the Sounds screen are your standard tone for phone calls, FaceTime calls, and messaging calls. To set different tones for a contact, press **Home**, tap **Phone** (📞), and then tap **Contacts**. In the Contacts list, tap the contact, tap **Edit**, and then tap **Ringtone**. On the Ringtone screen, tap the ringtone and then tap **Done**. You can also change other settings, such as the Text Tone vibration for the contact. Tap **Done** when you are finished.

Set Display Brightness and Wallpapers

To make the screen easier to see, you can change its brightness. You can also have the iPhone's Auto-Brightness feature automatically set the screen's brightness to a level suitable for the ambient brightness.

To make the screen look good, you can choose which picture to use as the wallpaper that appears in the background. You can use either a static wallpaper or a dynamic, changing wallpaper. You can set different wallpaper for the lock screen and for the Home screen.

Set Display Brightness and Wallpapers

1 Press **Home**.

The Home screen appears.

2 Tap **Settings** (⚙).

The Settings screen appears.

3 Tap **Display & Brightness** (🔠).

4 Tap the **Brightness** slider and drag it left or right to set brightness.

5 Set the **Auto-Brightness** switch to On (◉) or Off ( ), as needed.

6 Set the **Raise to Wake** switch to On (◉) if you want the iPhone to wake up when you raise it.

Ⓐ You can tap **Text Size** to set your preferred text size.

Ⓑ You can set the **Bold Text** switch to On (◉) to make the system text bold.

7 Tap **Settings** (<).

The Settings screen appears again.

8 Tap **Wallpaper** (🖼).

The Wallpaper screen appears.

9 Tap **Choose a New Wallpaper**.

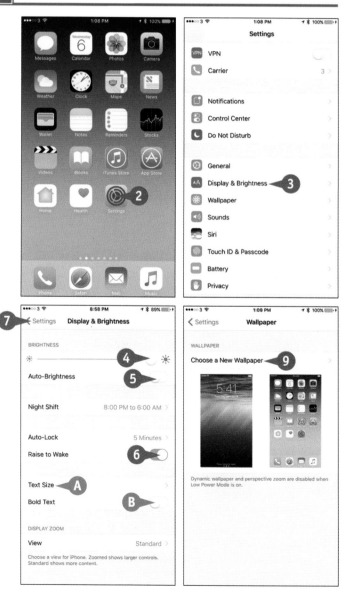

10 Tap **Dynamic**, **Stills**, or **Live** in the Apple Wallpaper area. This example uses **Stills**.

C To choose a picture from a different picture category, tap that category.

11 Tap the wallpaper you want to use.

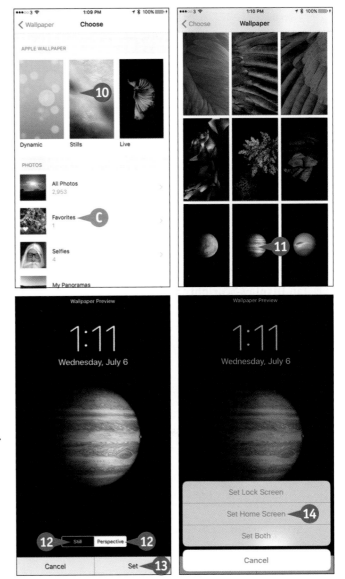

The Wallpaper Preview screen appears.

12 Tap **Still** if you want the image to have no perspective. Tap **Perspective** if you want it to have perspective, as if there is depth between the icons and the wallpaper.

13 Tap **Set**.

14 Tap **Set Lock Screen**, **Set Home Screen**, or **Set Both**. Tap **Cancel** if you do not want to proceed.

15 Press **Home**.

The Home screen appears.

If you changed the Home screen wallpaper, the new wallpaper appears.

Note: To see the lock screen wallpaper, press **Power/Sleep** twice.

TIP

How do I use only part of a picture as the wallpaper?
The Apple wallpapers are the right size for the screen, so you do not need to resize them. But when you use a photo for the wallpaper, you usually need to choose which part of it to display. When you choose a photo as wallpaper, the iPhone displays the Move and Scale screen. Pinch in or out to zoom the photo out or in, and tap and drag to move the picture around. When you have chosen the part you want, tap **Set**.

Configure Night Shift and Display Zoom

Blue light from the screens of devices can prevent or disrupt your body's sleep, so the iPhone includes a feature called Night Shift that reduces blue light from the screen. You can configure Night Shift to run automatically each night, manually enable it until the next day, and adjust the color temperature to look more or less warm.

On large-screen iPhones, you can choose whether to zoom the display in to a larger size or to keep it at the standard size.

Configure Night Shift and Display Zoom

1 Press **Home**.

The Home screen appears.

2 Tap **Settings** (⚙️).

The Settings screen appears.

3 Tap **Display & Brightness** (🔠).

The Display & Brightness screen appears.

4 Tap **Night Shift**.

The Night Shift screen appears.

5 Drag the **Color Temperature** slider along the Less Warm–More Warm axis to set the color temperature you want.

Ⓐ You can set the **Manually Enable Until Tomorrow** switch to On (⚪) to enable Night Shift immediately.

6 Set the **Scheduled** switch to On (⚪) to run Night Shift each night.

7 Tap **From, To**.

The Schedule screen appears.

8 Tap **Sunset to Sunrise** if you want Night Shift to follow sunset and sunrise times for your location; go to step **11**. Otherwise, tap **Custom Schedule**.

9 Tap **Turn On At** and set the time.

10 Tap **Turn Off At** and set the time.

11 Tap **Night Shift** (<).

The Night Shift screen appears.

12 Tap **Display & Brightness** (<).

The Display & Brightness screen appears.

13 Tap **View** in the Display Zoom area.

The Display Zoom screen appears.

14 Tap the unselected tab.

The preview shows the zoom effect.

B You can swipe left or tap a dot to change the preview. The second preview shows Messages. The third preview shows Mail.

15 Tap **Set**.

The Changing Display Zoom Will Restart iPhone dialog opens.

16 Tap **Use Zoomed** or **Use Standard**.

Your iPhone restarts.

The display appears with the zoom effect you chose.

TIP

How does Night Shift know when sunset and sunrise are?
Your iPhone uses Location Services to determine your location, and then looks up the sunset time and sunrise time online. If you disable Location Services, you will need to turn on Night Shift automatically.

Choose Privacy and Location Settings

Your iPhone contains a huge amount of information about you, the people you communicate with, what you do, and where you go. To keep this information safe, you need to choose suitable privacy and location settings.

Privacy settings enable you to control which apps can access your contacts, calendars, reminders, and photos. You can also choose which apps can use your iPhone's location services, and which track the iPhone's location via the Global Positioning System, or GPS.

Choose Privacy and Location Settings

1 Press **Home**.

The Home screen appears.

2 Tap **Settings** ().

The Settings screen appears.

3 Tap **Privacy** ().

Note: To limit how ads can track your iPhone usage, tap **Advertising** at the bottom of the Privacy screen. On the Advertising screen, set the **Limit Ad Tracking** switch to On (⬤). Tap **Reset Advertising Identifier** and then tap **Reset Identifier** in the confirmation dialog.

The Privacy screen appears.

4 Tap the app or service you want to configure. This example uses **Photos** ().

The screen for the app or service appears.

5 Set the switches (⬤ changes to ⬤) to choose which apps can access the item — in this case, your photos.

6 Tap **Privacy** (⟨).

The Privacy screen appears.

7 Configure other apps and services as needed.

8 Tap **Location Services**.

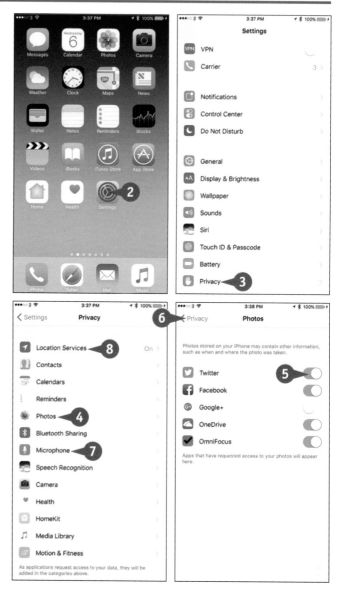

The Location Services screen appears.

9 If you need to turn location services off completely, set the **Location Services** switch to Off ( ). Usually, you would leave it set to On ( ).

10 Tap the app or feature you want to configure.

11 In the Allow Location Access box, tap the appropriate button, such as **While Using the App** or **Never**.

Note: The buttons in the Allow Location Access box vary depending on the app or feature.

12 Tap **Location Services** (〈).

The Location Services screen appears again.

13 Set location access for other apps and features.

14 Tap **System Services**.

The System Services screen appears.

15 Set the switch for each system service to On ( ) or Off ( ), as needed. For example, set the set the **Location-Based iAds** switch to Off ( ) to turn off ads based on your location.

16 Set the **Status Bar Icon** switch to On ( ) to see the Location Services icon in the status bar when an app requests your location.

TIP

Why do some apps need to use Location Services?

Some apps and system services need to use Location Services to determine where you are. For example, the Maps app requires Location Services to display your location, and the Compass service needs your location to display accurate compass information.

If you allow the Camera app to use Location Services, it stores GPS data in your photos. You can then sort the photos by location in applications such as Photos on the Mac. Other apps use Location Services to provide context-specific information, such as information about nearby restaurants. For privacy, review the apps using Location Services and turn off any you prefer not to have this information.

Configure and Use Spotlight Search

Your iPhone can put a huge amount of data in the palm of your hand, and you may often need to search to find what you need.

To make your search results more accurate and helpful, you can configure the Spotlight Search feature. You can turn off searching for items you do not want to see in your search results.

Configure and Use Spotlight Search

Configure Search

1 Press **Home**.

The Home screen appears.

2 Tap **Settings** (⚙).

The Settings screen appears.

3 Tap **General** (⚙).

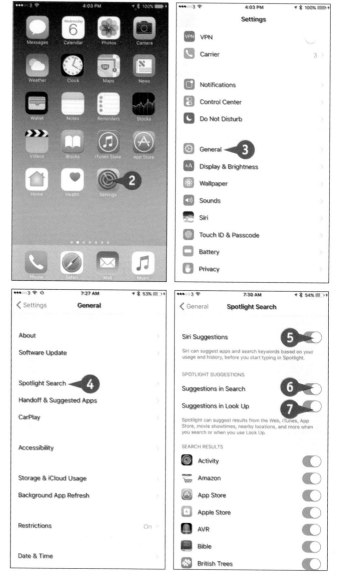

The General screen appears.

4 Tap **Spotlight Search**.

The Spotlight Search screen appears.

5 Set the **Siri Suggestions** switch to On (⬤) if you want to see Siri's suggestions when you search.

6 Set the **Suggestions in Search** switch to On (⬤) if you want to see Spotlight suggestions when you search.

7 Set the **Suggestions in Look Up** switch to On (⬤) if you want to see Spotlight suggestions when you use Look Up.

8 Set each switch to On () or Off ( ) to specify which apps to include in searches and which to exclude.

9 Tap **General** (<).

The General screen appears again.

10 Tap **Settings** (<).

The Settings screen appears again.

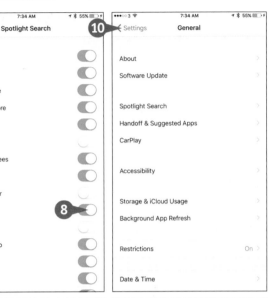

Search for Items Using Spotlight Search

1 Press **Home**.

The Home screen appears.

2 Tap near the top of the screen and pull down.

A The Search panel appears, with the insertion point in it.

Note: You can also start a search by swiping right from the Home screen and then tapping the Search box at the top of the screen.

The keyboard appears.

3 Type your search term.

A list of results appears.

4 Tap the result you want to view.

TIP

Which items should I search?

This depends on what you need to be able to search for. For example, if you do not need to search for music, videos, or podcasts, set the **Music**, **Podcasts**, and **Videos** switches on the Spotlight Search screen to Off (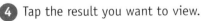) to exclude them from Spotlight searches.

Choose Locking and Control Center Settings

After a period of inactivity whose length you can configure, your iPhone automatically locks itself. It then turns off its screen and goes to sleep to save battery power. Setting your iPhone to lock itself quickly helps preserve battery power, but you may prefer to leave your iPhone on longer so that you can continue work, and then lock your iPhone manually. You can also choose whether to make Control Center accessible from the lock screen and from within apps.

Choose Locking and Control Center Settings

1 Press **Home**.

The Home screen appears.

2 Tap **Settings** (⚙).

The Settings screen appears.

3 Tap **Display & Brightness** (🔠).

Note: If your iPhone is managed by an administrator, you may not be able to set all the options explained here. For example, an administrator may prevent you from disabling automatic locking for security reasons.

The Display & Brightness screen appears.

4 Tap **Auto-Lock**.

The Auto-Lock screen appears.

5 Tap the interval — for example, **1 Minute**.

Note: Choose **Never** for Auto-Lock if you need to make sure your iPhone never goes to sleep. For example, if you are playing music with the lyrics displayed, turning off auto-locking may be helpful.

6 Tap **Display & Brightness** (❮).

The Display & Brightness screen appears again.

7 Tap **Settings** (<).

The Settings screen appears again.

8 Tap **Control Center** (🔲).

Note: Giving yourself access to Control Center from the lock screen is useful, especially if you play music a lot. But it also gives an unauthorized person access to important settings, such as Wi-Fi, without unlocking the iPhone.

The Control Center screen appears.

9 Set the **Access on Lock Screen** switch to On (🔵) or Off ( ), as needed.

10 Set the **Access Within Apps** switch to On (🔵) or Off ( ), as needed.

11 Tap **Settings** (<).

The Settings screen appears again.

TIP

How do I put the iPhone to sleep manually?

You can put the iPhone to sleep at any point by pressing **Power/Sleep** for a moment.

Putting the iPhone to sleep as soon as you stop using it helps to prolong battery life. If you apply a passcode or other means of locking, as discussed in the section "Secure Your iPhone with Touch ID or a Passcode," later in this chapter, putting the iPhone to sleep also starts protecting your data sooner.

Set Up and Use Do Not Disturb Mode

When you do not want your iPhone to disturb you, turn on its Do Not Disturb Mode. You can configure Do Not Disturb Mode to turn on and off automatically at set times each day — for example, on at 10 p.m. and off at 7 a.m. You can turn Do Not Disturb Mode on and off manually from Control Center.

You can allow particular groups of contacts to bypass Do Not Disturb Mode so they can contact you even when Do Not Disturb is on. You can also allow repeated calls to ring when Do Not Disturb is on.

Set Up and Use Do Not Disturb Mode

Configure Do Not Disturb Mode

1 Press **Home**.

The Home screen appears.

2 Tap **Settings** (⚙).

The Settings screen appears.

3 Tap **Do Not Disturb** (🌙).

A You can turn on Do Not Disturb by setting the **Manual** switch to On (⬤).

Note: You can turn Do Not Disturb on and off more easily from Control Center.

4 Set the **Scheduled** switch to On (⬤).

5 Tap **From, To**.

6 Tap **From**.

7 Use the spin wheels to set the From time.

8 Tap **To**.

9 Set the To time.

10 Tap **Do Not Disturb** (⟨).

The Do Not Disturb screen appears again.

11 Tap **Allow Calls From**.

58

The Allow Calls From screen appears.

12 Tap the group you will allow to call you during your quiet hours.

13 Tap **Do Not Disturb** (changes to).

The Do Not Disturb screen appears again.

14 Set the **Repeated Calls** switch to On ( ) or Off ( ), as needed.

15 In the Silence area, tap **Always** or **Only while iPhone is locked**, as needed.

16 Tap **Settings** (<).

The Settings screen appears again.

Turn Do Not Disturb Mode On or Off Manually

1 Press **Home**.

The Home screen appears.

2 Tap and drag up to scroll down the screen.

Control Center opens.

3 Tap **Do Not Disturb** to turn Do Not Disturb on (changes to) or off (changes to).

How can I tell whether Do Not Disturb is on?

When Do Not Disturb is on, a crescent moon symbol appears in the status bar to the left of the battery readout.

How can I allow multiple groups of people to call me when Do Not Disturb is on?

The Allow Calls From screen lets you select only one group. Unless you can put all the relevant contacts into a single group, the best solution is to create a new group and add the existing groups to it. This is easiest to do in your iCloud account by working in a web browser on a computer.

Customize Today View

Today View, which you display by swiping right on the first Home screen, shows a list of widgets to provide you with quick information about the weather, the news, and your time commitments. You can configure Today View by removing widgets you do not need, adding widgets you find useful, and arranging the widgets into the order you find most helpful.

Customize Today View

 Press **Home**.

The Home screen appears.

Note: If the first Home screen does not appear when you press **Home**, press **Home** again to display it.

2 Swipe right.

Today View appears.

3 Swipe up to scroll down to the bottom of the screen.

More items in Today View appear.

4 Tap **Edit**.

The Add Widgets screen appears.

5 Tap **Remove** (⊖) to the left of a widget you want to remove.

60

The textual Remove button appears.

6 Tap **Remove**.

The widget disappears from the list.

7 Swipe up.

The More Widgets list appears.

8 Tap **Add** (⊕) to the left of a widget you want to add to Today View.

The widget appears in the upper list.

9 Tap a widget's handle (☰) and drag up or down to rearrange the widgets.

10 Tap **Done**.

Today View appears, showing the widgets in the order you specified.

How do I get more widgets to add to Today View?

The widgets in Today View come built into apps, so the only way to get more widgets is to install more apps that have widgets.

When choosing an app to add to your iPhone, consider whether the app is one for which a widget in Today View would be useful. If so, look for an app that offers a widget.

Secure Your iPhone with Touch ID or a Passcode

For security, you can lock your iPhone with either Touch ID or a passcode. Touch ID uses your fingerprint to unlock the iPhone quickly and easily; if Touch ID fails, you use the passcode as a backup means of unlocking your iPhone. You can also set your iPhone to automatically erase its data after ten failed passcode attempts. You can also choose between a six-digit passcode — the default — a shorter or longer numeric code, or an alphanumeric code of however many characters you want.

Secure Your iPhone with Touch ID or a Passcode

1 Press **Home**.

The Home screen appears.

2 Tap **Settings** (⚙).

The Settings screen appears.

3 Tap **Touch ID & Passcode** (🔘).

Note: This section shows an iPhone without either Touch ID or a passcode set up. Normally, you would set up either a passcode or Touch ID and a passcode during initial setup.

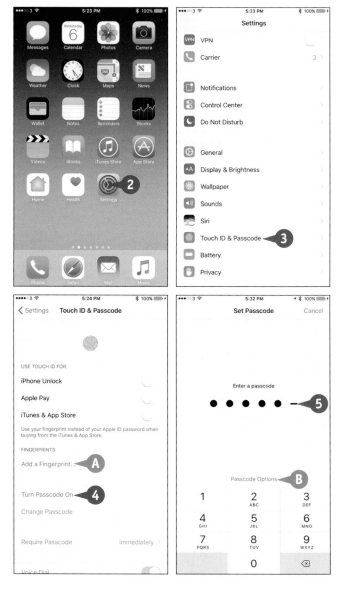

The Touch ID & Passcode screen appears.

Ⓐ To set up Touch ID, tap **Add a Fingerprint** and follow the prompts. You can then set the **iPhone Unlock** switch, the **Apple Pay** switch, and the **iTunes & App Store** switch to On (⚪) or Off ( ), as needed.

4 Tap **Turn Passcode On**.

Ⓑ To change the passcode type, you can tap **Passcode Options** and then tap **Custom Alphanumeric Code**, **Custom Numeric Code**, or **4-Digit Numeric Code**.

5 Type your passcode.

The iPhone displays the message *Verify Your New Passcode*.

6 Type the passcode again.

The Touch ID & Passcode screen appears.

7 Tap **Require Passcode**.

The Require Passcode screen appears.

8 Tap the button for the length of time you want — for example, **Immediately** or **After 1 minute**.

Note: After you apply a fingerprint, the only choice on the Require Passcode screen is Immediately.

9 Tap **Touch ID & Passcode** (<).

The Touch ID & Passcode screen appears.

10 Set the **Voice Dial** switch to On (●○) or Off ( ), as needed.

11 In the Allow Access When Locked area, set the switches to On (●○) or Off ( ), as needed.

Note: Allowing access to Wallet when your iPhone is locked enables you to make payments and reach boarding passes and similar documents more quickly when you need them.

12 If you want the iPhone to erase all its data after ten failed passcode attempts, set the **Erase Data** switch to On (●○).

The iPhone displays a confirmation dialog.

13 Tap **Enable**.

TIPS

Which type of passcode should I use?
The default, a six-digit numeric passcode, provides reasonably good security and is easy to enter. But if you need strong security, choose **Custom Numeric Code** and use 12 or more digits. For extra-strong security, choose **Custom Alphanumeric Code** and create a passcode of 12 or more characters, including upper- and lowercase letters, numbers, and symbols.

What Require Passcode setting should I choose?
Choose **Immediately** for greatest security. Choose **After 1 minute** for good security but more convenience.

Configure Restrictions and Parental Controls

Like any other computer that can access the Internet, the iPhone can reach vast amounts of content not suitable for children or business contexts. You can restrict the iPhone from accessing particular kinds of content. You can use the restrictions to implement parental controls — for example, preventing the iPhone's user from buying content in apps or watching adult-rated movies.

Configure Restrictions and Parental Controls

1 Press **Home**.

The Home screen appears.

2 Tap **Settings** (⚙).

The Settings screen appears.

3 Tap **General** (⚙).

The General screen appears.

4 Tap **Restrictions**.

The Restrictions screen appears.

5 Tap **Enable Restrictions**.

The Set Passcode screen appears.

Note: The passcode you set to protect restrictions is different from the passcode you use to lock the iPhone. Do not use the same code.

6 Type the passcode.

Note: The iPhone shows dots instead of your passcode digits in case someone is watching.

The iPhone displays the Set Passcode screen again, this time with the message *Re-enter Your Restrictions Passcode*.

7 Type the passcode again.

8 In the Allow area, set each switch to On (⬤) or Off (⬡), as needed.

9 Scroll down to the Allowed Content area.

10 If you need to change the country used for rating content, tap **Ratings For**. On the Ratings For screen, tap the country, and then tap **Restrictions** (〈).

Ⓐ You can tap **Password Settings** to choose whether to require a password for each purchase or only after a 15-minute interval, and whether to require a password for free downloads.

11 Choose settings for Music, Podcasts, News & iTunes U, Movies, TV Shows, Books, Apps, Siri, and Websites. For example, tap **Movies**.

The Movies screen appears.

12 Tap the highest rating you will permit.

13 Tap **Restrictions** (〈).

14 Set the **In-App Purchases** switch to Off (⬡) to prevent the user from making in-app purchases. See the first tip.

15 Choose other settings in the Privacy area.

16 Choose settings for Accounts, Cellular Data Use, Background App Refresh, and Volume Limit.

17 Set the **Multiplayer Games** switch, the **Adding Friends** switch, and the **Screen Recording** switch to On (⬤) or Off (⬡), as needed.

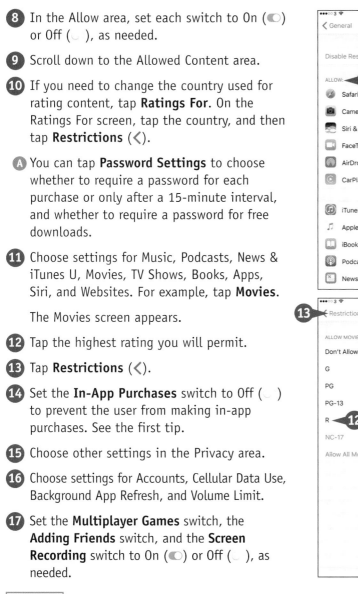

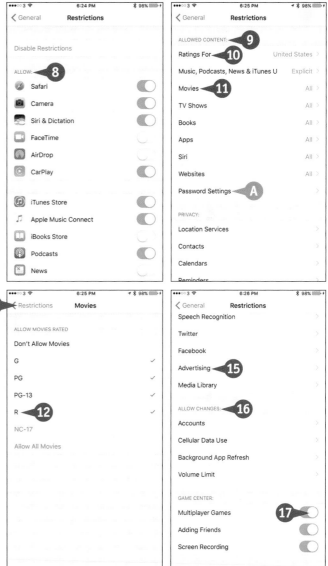

TIPS

What are in-app purchases?

In-app purchases are items you can buy directly from within apps. These are a popular and easy way for developers to sell extra features for apps, especially low-cost apps or free apps. They are also an easy way for the iPhone's user to spend money.

What do the Privacy settings in Restrictions do?

The Privacy settings in Restrictions enable you to control which apps can access the iPhone's location information, contacts, and other apps, and whether the user can change the settings.

Set Up Family Sharing

Apple's Family Sharing feature enables you to share purchases from Apple's online services with other family members. You can also share photos and calendars, and you can use the Find My iPhone feature to find your iOS devices and Macs when they go missing.

This section assumes that you are the Family organizer, the person who gets to set up Family Sharing; invite others to participate; and pay for the content they buy on the iTunes Store, the iBooks Store, and the App Store.

Set Up Family Sharing

1 Press **Home**.

The Home screen appears.

2 Tap **Settings** (⚙).

The Settings screen appears.

3 Tap **iCloud** (☁).

The iCloud screen appears.

4 Tap **Set Up Family Sharing** (☁).

The Family Sharing screen appears.

5 Tap **Get Started**.

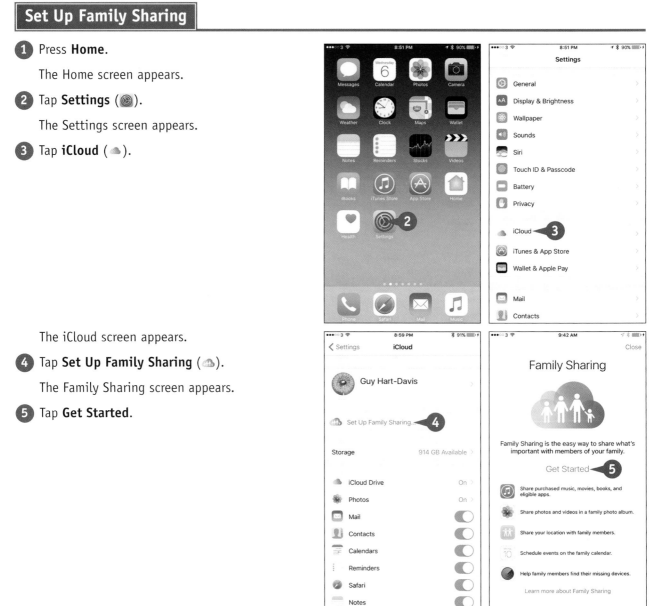

The Family Setup screen appears.

Ⓐ You can tap **add photo** and then either tap **Take Photo** to take a photo with your iPhone's camera or tap **Choose Photo** to select an existing photo for your profile.

Ⓑ You can tap **Not *Name* or want to use a different ID?** to use a different Apple ID for the account.

⑥ Tap **Continue**.

The Share Purchases screen appears.

⑦ Type your password.

⑧ Tap **Next**.

The Payment Method screen appears.

⑨ Verify that iOS has identified the means of payment you want to use.

⑩ Tap **Continue**.

The Share Your Location With screen appears.

⑪ Tap **Share Your Location** or **Not Now**, as appropriate.

The Family screen appears.

⑫ Tap **iCloud**.

The iCloud screen appears.

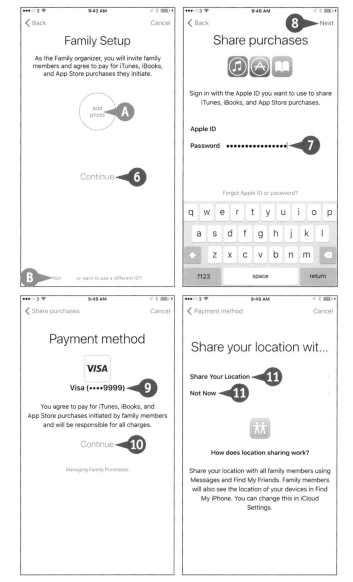

How do I turn off Family Sharing?

① Press **Home**.

② Tap **Settings** (⚙).

③ Tap **iCloud** (☁).

④ Tap **Family** (👪).

⑤ Tap the button with your name and "Organizer" on it.

⑥ Tap **Stop Family Sharing** at the bottom of your profile screen.

Add Family Members to Family Sharing

After setting up the basics of Family Sharing, you can add your family members to the group. You can either send an invitation to a family member to join the group or ask her to enter her Apple ID and password on your iPhone to join immediately.

If you send an invitation, the family member can join at a time of her choosing by using her own iPhone, iPad, iPod touch, or computer.

Add Family Members to Family Sharing

Add a Family Member to Family Sharing

1 Press **Home**.

The Home screen appears.

2 Tap **Settings** (⚙).

The Settings screen appears.

3 Tap **iCloud** (☁).

The iCloud screen appears.

4 Tap **Family** (☁).

The Family screen appears.

5 Tap **Add Family Member**.

The first Add Family Member screen appears.

6 Start typing the name.

A list of matches appears.

7 Tap the appropriate match.

The second Add Family Member screen appears.

Ⓐ If the family member is not present, tap **Send an Invitation**. iOS sends the invitation.

8 If the family member is present, tap **Ask *Name* to Enter Password**.

The Enter Password screen appears.

9 Ask the family member to enter the password.

Note: In some cases, the family member may need to type the full username as well as the password for verification.

10 Tap **Next**.

The Share Purchases screen appears.

11 Verify that the correct account appears.

Ⓑ If the account is wrong, tap **Change Account** and follow the prompts.

12 Tap **Next**, and then agree to the terms and conditions for sharing.

iOS adds the family member to Family Sharing.

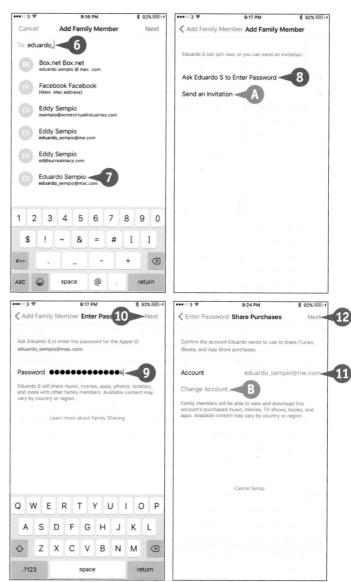

TIPS

How many people can I add to Family Sharing?

Family Sharing works for up to six people, so you can add five other people to your account.

How do I control who can approve purchase requests from Family Sharing members?

On the Family screen in the Settings app, tap the name of the adult involved. The profile screen for the adult appears. Set the **Parent/ Guardian** switch to On (⬤) to enable the adult to approve Ask to Buy requests.

Choose Date, Time, and International Settings

To keep yourself on time and your data accurate, you need to make sure the iPhone is using the correct date and time.

To make dates, times, and other data appear in the formats you prefer, you may need to change the iPhone's International settings.

Choose Date, Time, and International Settings

Choose Date and Time Settings

1. Press **Home**.

   The Home screen appears.

2. Tap **Settings** (⚙).

   The Settings screen appears.

3. Tap **General** (⚙).

The General screen appears.

4. Tap **Date & Time**.

   The Date & Time screen appears.

5. Set the **24-Hour Time** switch to On (⚪) if you want to use 24-hour times.

6. To set the date and time manually, set the **Set Automatically** switch to Off ( ).

7. Use the controls to set the date and time.

8. Tap **General** (<).

   The General screen appears.

Choose International Settings

1 From the General screen, tap **Language & Region**.

The Language & Region screen appears.

A The Region Format Example area shows examples of the time, date, currency, and number formats for the current region.

2 Tap **iPhone Language**.

The iPhone Language screen appears.

3 Tap the language you want to use.

4 Tap **Done**.

The Language & Region screen appears.

5 Tap **Region**.

The Region screen appears.

6 Tap the region you want.

7 Tap **Done**.

The Language & Region screen appears.

TIP

How does my iPhone set the date and time automatically?

Your iPhone sets the date and time automatically by using time servers, computers on the Internet that provide date and time information to computers that request it. The iPhone automatically determines its geographical location so it can request the right time zone from the time server.

CHAPTER 3

Using Voice, Accessibility, and Continuity

Your iPhone includes the Siri personal assistant, helpful accessibility features, and integration with your Mac and Apple Watch via the Continuity feature.

Give Commands with Siri

Often, speaking is even easier than using your iPhone's touch screen — especially when you are out and about or on the move. The powerful Siri feature enables you to take essential actions by using your voice to tell your iPhone what you want. Siri requires a fast Internet connection because the speech recognition runs on servers in Apple's data center.

You can use Siri either with the iPhone's built-in microphone or with the microphone on a headset. Unless you are in a quiet environment, or you hold your iPhone close to your face, a headset microphone typically gives you much better results than the built-in microphone.

Open Siri

From the Home screen or any app, press **Home** or the headset clicker button for several seconds. If you have chosen to allow Siri access when your iPhone is locked, you can also activate Siri while the lock screen is displayed.

The Siri screen appears. A tone indicates that Siri is ready to take your commands. If you enable the "Hey Siri" feature in the Settings app, you can also activate Siri by saying "Hey Siri."

Send an E-Mail Message

Say "E-mail" and the contact's name, followed by the message. Siri creates an e-mail message to the contact and enters the text. Review the message, and then tap **Send** to send it.

If you prefer, you can start the message by saying "E-mail" and the contact's name, and then pausing. Siri then prompts you for the subject and text of the message in turn.

Set an Alarm

Say "Set an alarm for 4:30 a.m." and check the alarm that Siri displays.

You can turn the alarm off by tapping its switch (changes to).

You can ask a question such as "Which alarms do I have set?" to make Siri display a list of your alarms.

Set a Reminder for Yourself

Say "Remind me" and the details of what you want Siri to remind you of. For example, say "Remind me to take my iPad to work tomorrow morning." Siri listens to what you say and creates a reminder. Check what Siri has written. If the reminder is correct, simply leave it; if not, tap **Remove** and then try again.

Send a Text Message

Say "Tell" and the contact's name. When Siri responds, say the message you want to send. For example, say "Tell Maria Jones" and then "I'm stuck in traffic, so I'll be about 10 minutes late to the meeting. Please start without me." Siri creates a text message to the contact, enters the text, and sends the message when you say "Send" or tap **Send.**

You can also say "tell" and the contact's name followed immediately by the message. For example, "Tell Bill Sykes the package will arrive at 10 a.m."

Set Up a Meeting

Say "Meet with" and the contact's name, followed by brief details of the appointment. For example, say "Meet with Don Williamson at noon on Friday for lunch." Siri listens and warns you of any scheduling conflict. Siri then sends a meeting invitation to the contact if it finds an e-mail address, and adds the meeting to your calendar after you tap **Confirm** or say "Confirm."

Dictate Text Using Siri

One of Siri's strongest features is the capability to transcribe your speech quickly and accurately into correctly spelled and punctuated text. Using your iPhone, you can dictate into any app that supports the keyboard, so you can dictate e-mail messages, notes, documents, and more. To dictate, simply tap the microphone icon (🎤), speak after Siri beeps, and then tap **Done**.

To get the most out of dictation, it is helpful to know the standard terms for dictating punctuation, capitalization, symbols, layout, and formatting.

Insert Punctuation

To insert punctuation, use standard terms: "comma," "period" (or "full stop"), "semicolon," "colon," "exclamation point" (or "exclamation mark"), "question mark," "hyphen," "dash" (for a short dash, –), or "em dash" (for a long dash, —). You can also say "asterisk" (*), "ampersand" (&), "open parenthesis" and "close parenthesis," "open bracket" and "close bracket," and "underscore" (_).

For example, say "buy eggs comma bread comma and cheese semicolon and maybe some milk period nothing else exclamation point" to enter the text shown here.

Insert Standard Symbols

To insert symbols, use these terms: "at sign" (@), "percent" (%), "greater than" (>) and "less than" (<), "forward slash" (/) and "backslash" (\), "registered sign" (®), and "copyright sign" (©).

For example, say "fifty-eight percent forward slash two greater than ninety-seven percent forward slash three" to enter the computation shown here.

Insert Currency Symbols

To insert currency symbols, say the currency name and "sign." For example, say "dollar sign" to insert $, "cent sign" to insert ¢, "euro sign" to insert €, "pound sterling sign" to insert £, and "yen sign" to insert ¥.

For example, say "convert dollar sign two hundred to UK pounds sterling" to enter the calculation shown here.

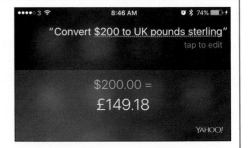

Control Layout

You can control text layout by creating new lines and new paragraphs as needed. A new paragraph enters two line breaks, creating a blank line between paragraphs. To create a new line, say "new line." To create a new paragraph, say "new paragraph."

For example, say "dear Anna comma new paragraph thank you for the parrot period new paragraph it's the most amazing gift I've ever had period" to enter the text shown here.

Control Capitalization

You can apply capitalization to the first letter of a word or to a whole word. You can also switch capitalization off temporarily to force lowercase:

Say "cap" to capitalize the first letter of the next word.

Say "caps on" to capitalize all the words until you say "caps off."

Say "no caps" to prevent automatic capitalization of the next word — for example, "no caps Monday" produces "monday" instead of "Monday."

Say "no caps on" to force lowercase of all words until you say "no caps off."

For example, say "give the cap head cap dining cap table a no caps french polish period" to enter the text shown here.

Insert Quotes and Emoticons

To insert double quotes, say "open quotes" and "close quotes." To insert single quotes, say "open single quotes" and "close single quotes." To enter standard emoticons, say "smiley face," "frown face," and "wink face."

For example, say "she said comma open quotes I want to go to Paris next summer exclamation point close quotes" to enter the text shown here.

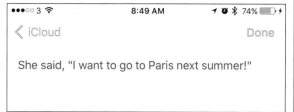

Gather and Share Information with Siri

You can use Siri to research a wide variety of information online — everything from sports and movies to restaurants worth visiting or worth avoiding. You can also use Siri to perform hands-free calculations. When you need to share information quickly and easily, you can turn to Siri. By giving the right commands, you can quickly change your Facebook status or post on your wall. Similarly, you can send tweets on your Twitter account.

Find Information About Sports

Launch Siri and ask a question about sports. For example:

"Siri, when's the next White Sox game?"

"Did the Lakers win their last game?"

"When's the end of the NBA season?"

"Can you show me the roster for the Maple Leafs?"

Find Information About Movies

Launch Siri and ask a question about movies. For example:

"Siri, where is the movie *Central Intelligence* playing in Indianapolis?"

"What's the name of Blake Lively's latest movie?"

"Who's the star of *Me Before You*?"

"Is *Independence Day Resurgence* any good?"

Find a Restaurant

Launch Siri, and then tell Siri what type of restaurant you want. For example:

"Where's the best Mexican food in Palo Alto?"

"Where can I get sushi in Albuquerque?"

"Is there a brewpub in Minneapolis?"

"Is there any dim sum within 50 miles of here?"

Address a Query to the Wolfram Alpha Computational Knowledge Engine

Launch Siri, and then say "Wolfram" and your query. For example:

"Wolfram, what is the cube of 27?"

"Wolfram, minus 20 centigrade in Kelvin."

"Wolfram, tangent of 60 degrees."

"Wolfram, give me the chemical formula for hydrogen peroxide."

Update Your Facebook Status or Post a Comment on Your Wall

Launch Siri and give the appropriate command:

"Update my Facebook status," and then give details when Siri prompts you.

"Post on my Facebook wall," and then dictate the post when Siri prompts you.

If the post turns out to your liking, tap **Post**.

Send a Tweet

Launch Siri, and then say "Tweet" and the text of the tweet. Siri displays a preview of the tweet, including the number of characters remaining.

When you are satisfied with the tweet, tap **Send**.

Configure Siri to Work Your Way

To get the most out of Siri, spend a few minutes configuring Siri. You can set the language Siri uses and choose when Siri should give you voice feedback. You can also decide whether to use the Raise to Speak option, which activates Siri when you raise your iPhone to your face.

Most important, you can tell Siri which contact record contains your information, so that Siri knows your name, address, phone numbers, e-mail address, and other essential information.

Configure Siri to Work Your Way

 Press **Home**.

The Home screen appears.

② Tap **Settings** (⚙).

The Settings screen appears.

③ Tap **Siri** (🔘).

The Siri screen appears.

④ Set the **Siri** switch to On (🔘).

⑤ Set the **Access on Lock Screen** switch to On (🔘) if you want to use Siri from the lock screen.

 Set the **Allow "Hey Siri"** switch to On (🔘) if you want to be able to activate Siri by saying "Hey Siri!"

⑦ Tap **Language**.

The Language screen appears.

⑧ Tap the language you want to use.

⑨ Tap **Siri** (‹).

The Siri screen appears again.

 Tap **Siri Voice**.

80

The Siri Voice screen appears.

11 In the Accent box, tap the accent you want Siri to use. For example, for English (United States), you can tap **American**, **Australian**, or **British**.

12 In the Gender box, tap **Male** or **Female**, as needed.

13 Tap **Siri** (<).

The Siri screen appears again.

14 Tap **Voice Feedback**.

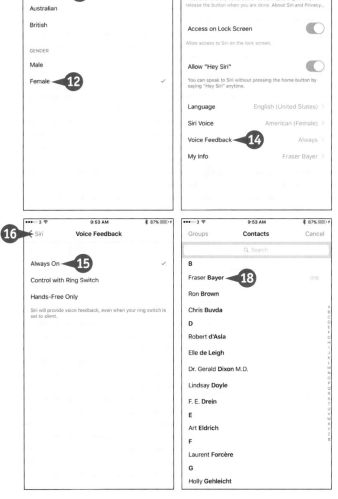

The Voice Feedback screen appears.

15 Tap **Always On**, **Control with Ring Switch**, or **Hands-Free Only**, as needed.

16 Tap **Siri** (<).

The Siri screen appears again.

17 Tap **My Info**.

The Contacts screen appears, showing either the All Contacts list or the groups you have selected.

Note: If necessary, click Groups to display the Groups screen, select the groups you need, and then tap **Done**.

18 Tap the contact record that contains your information.

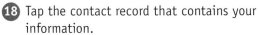

TIP

Does Apple store the details of what I ask Siri?

Yes, but not in a way that will come back to haunt you. When you use Siri, your iPhone passes your input to servers in Apple's data center in North Carolina, USA, for processing. The servers analyze your request and tell Siri how to respond to it. Apple's data center stores the details of your request and may analyze them to determine what people use Siri for and work out ways of making Siri more effective. Apple does not associate your Siri data with other data Apple holds about you — for example, the identity and credit card data you used to pay for iTunes Match.

Set Up VoiceOver to Identify Items On-Screen

If you have trouble identifying the iPhone's controls on-screen, you can use the VoiceOver feature to read them to you. VoiceOver changes your iPhone's standard finger gestures so that you tap to select the item whose name you want it to speak, double-tap to activate an item, and flick three fingers to scroll.

VoiceOver can make your iPhone easier to use. Your iPhone also includes other accessibility features, which you can learn about in the next section, "Configure Other Accessibility Features."

Set Up VoiceOver to Identify Items On-Screen

1 Press **Home**.

The Home screen appears.

2 Tap **Settings** ( ).

The Settings screen appears.

3 Tap **General** ( ).

The General screen appears.

4 Tap **Accessibility**.

The Accessibility screen appears.

5 Tap **VoiceOver**.

Note: You cannot use VoiceOver and Zoom at the same time. If Zoom is on when you try to switch VoiceOver on, your iPhone prompts you to choose which of the two to use.

6 Set the **VoiceOver** switch to On (changes to).

7 Tap **VoiceOver Practice**.

A selection border appears around the button, and VoiceOver speaks its name.

8 Double-tap **VoiceOver Practice**.

The VoiceOver Practice screen appears.

9 Practice tapping, double-tapping, triple-tapping, swiping, and flicking. VoiceOver identifies each gesture and displays an explanation.

10 Tap **Done** to select the button, and then double-tap **Done**.

11 Swipe up with three fingers.

The screen scrolls down.

12 Tap **Speaking Rate** to select it, and then swipe up or down to adjust the rate. Swiping up or down is the VoiceOver gesture for adjusting the slider.

13 Set the **Speak Hints** switch to On ( ) if you want VoiceOver to speak hints about using VoiceOver.

14 Tap **Typing Feedback** to select it, and then double-tap.

15 In the Software Keyboards area, tap and then double-tap the feedback type you want: **Nothing, Characters**, **Words**, or **Characters and Words**.

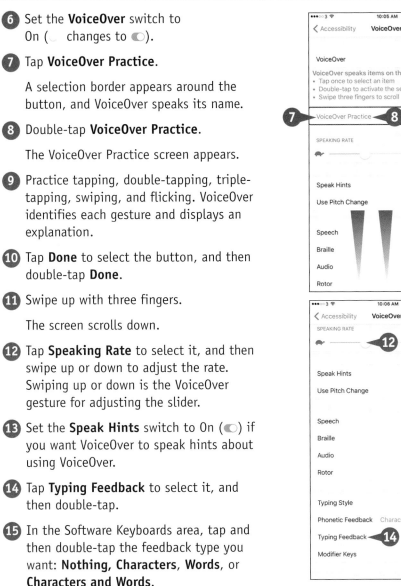

Is there an easy way to turn VoiceOver on and off?

Yes. You can set your iPhone to toggle VoiceOver on or off when you press **Home** three times in rapid sequence. At the bottom of the Accessibility screen, tap **Accessibility Shortcut** to display the Accessibility Shortcut screen. In the Triple-Click the Home Button For list, tap **VoiceOver**, placing a check mark next to it. Tap **Accessibility** (<) to return to the Accessibility screen.

Configure Other Accessibility Features

If you have trouble using your iPhone in its default configuration, explore the other accessibility features that your iPhone offers apart from VoiceOver.

To help you see the screen better, iOS provides a full-featured zoom capability. After turning on zooming, you can display the Zoom Controller to give yourself easy control of zoom, choose the zoom region, and set the maximum zoom level. You can then triple-tap the screen to zoom in and out quickly.

Configure Other Accessibility Features

Display the Accessibility Screen and Configure Zoom Settings

1 Press **Home**.

The Home screen appears.

2 Tap **Settings** (⚙).

The Settings screen appears.

3 Tap **General** (⚙).

The General screen appears.

Note: Apart from the accessibility features explained in this section, your iPhone supports physical accessibility features such as Switch Control and AssistiveTouch. Switch Control enables you to control your iPhone through a physical switch you connect to it. AssistiveTouch lets you use an adaptive accessory to touch the screen.

4 Tap **Accessibility**.

The Accessibility screen appears.

5 Tap **Zoom**.

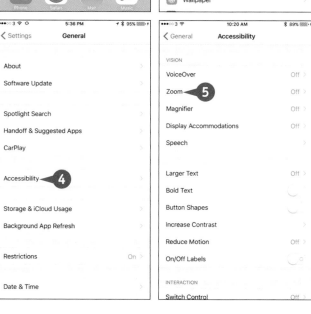

84

The Zoom screen appears.

6 Set the **Zoom** switch to On (changes to ⬤).

Ⓐ The Zoom window appears if the Zoom Region is set to Window Zoom.

7 Set the **Follow Focus** switch to On (⬤) to make the zoomed area follow the focus on-screen.

8 Set the **Smart Typing** switch to On (⬤) to make iOS switch to Window Zoom when a keyboard appears, so that text is zoomed but the keyboard is regular size.

9 Set the **Show Controller** switch to On (⬤).

Ⓑ The Zoom Controller (⬤) appears.

10 Tap **Idle Visibility** and set the visibility percentage for the Zoom Controller when it is idle.

11 Tap **Zoom Region**.

The Zoom Region screen appears.

12 Tap **Full Screen Zoom** or **Window Zoom**, as needed.

13 Tap **Zoom** (ᐸ).

The Zoom screen appears.

14 Drag the **Maximum Zoom Level** slider to set the maximum zoom level, such as 8×.

15 Tap **Accessibility** (ᐸ).

The Accessibility screen appears.

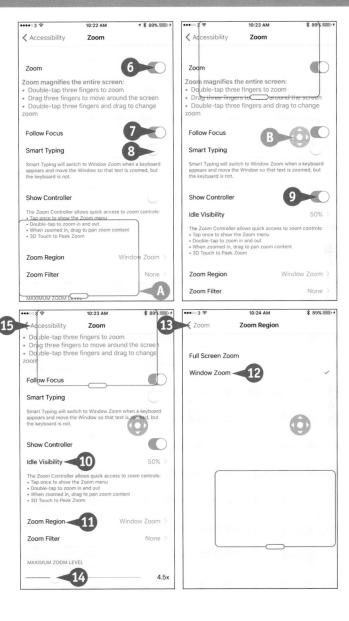

 TIP

Is there an easy way to turn the Zoom feature on and off?
Yes. You can set your iPhone to toggle Zoom on or off when you press **Home** three times in rapid sequence. At the bottom of the Accessibility screen, tap **Accessibility Shortcut** to display the Accessibility Shortcut screen. In the Triple-Click the Home Button For list, tap **Zoom**, placing a check mark next to it, and then tap **Accessibility** (ᐸ). You can also use the Home triple-press to toggle the VoiceOver feature, the Invert Colors feature, the Grayscale feature, the Switch Control feature, or the AssistiveTouch feature.

continued ▶

Your iPhone includes several "display accommodations" to make the screen easier to view. These accommodations include inverting the screen colors entirely, reducing the white point to lessen the intensity of bright colors, and applying color filters for grayscale or for the protanopia, deuteranopia, or tritanopia color blindnesses.

You can also configure visual interface accessibility settings to make items easier to see. For example, you can set a larger text size, apply shading around text-only buttons, reduce the transparency of items, and darken colors.

Configure Other Accessibility Features (continued)

Configure Display Accommodations

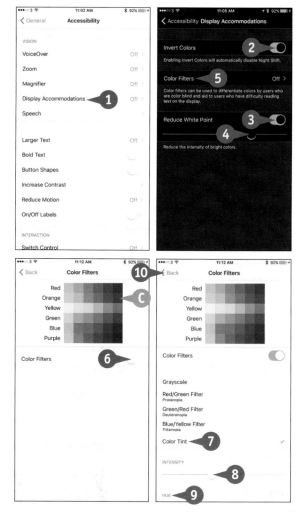

1 On the Accessibility screen, tap **Display Accommodations**.

The Display Accommodations screen appears.

2 Set the **Invert Colors** switch to On (⬤) if you want to invert the colors so that white changes to black and so forth, as in this example.

Note: Enabling the Invert Colors feature disables the Night Shift feature.

3 Set the **Reduce White Point** switch to On (⬤) if you want to reduce the intensity of bright colors.

4 Drag the slider to adjust the white point.

5 Tap **Color Filters**.

The Color Filters screen appears.

C The color chart displays colors using the filtering you apply.

6 Set the **Color Filters** switch to On (⬤).

The list of color filters appears.

7 Tap the filter you want to apply: **Grayscale**, **Red/Green Filter**, **Green/Red Filter**, **Blue/Yellow Filter**, or **Color Tint**.

8 If the Intensity slider appears, drag it to adjust the intensity.

9 For Color Tint, drag the **Hue** slider to adjust the hue.

10 Tap **Back** (<).

Configure Visual Interface Accessibility Settings

1 On the Accessibility screen, tap **Larger Text**.

The Larger Text screen appears.

2 Set the **Larger Accessibility Sizes** switch to On (changes to).

3 Drag the slider to set the text size.

4 Tap **Accessibility** (<).

The Accessibility screen appears.

Ⓓ You can set the **Bold Text** switch to On () to make text appear bold. You must restart your iPhone to effect this change.

Ⓔ You can set the **Button Shapes** switch to On () to make shapes appear around buttons, as on the General button at the top of the left screen.

5 Tap **Increase Contrast**.

The Increase Contrast screen appears.

6 Set the **Reduce Transparency** switch to On () or Off ( ), as needed.

7 Set the **Darken Colors** switch to On () or Off ( ), as needed.

8 Tap **Accessibility** (<).

The Accessibility screen appears again.

9 Tap **Reduce Motion**; set the **Reduce Motion** switch on the Reduce Motion screen to On () or Off ( ), as needed; and then tap **Accessibility** (<).

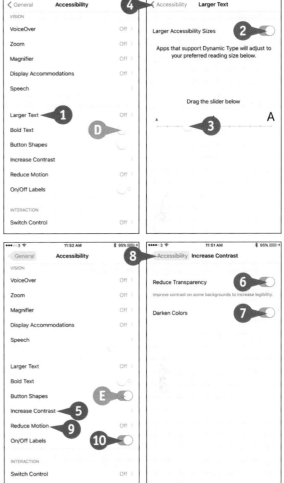

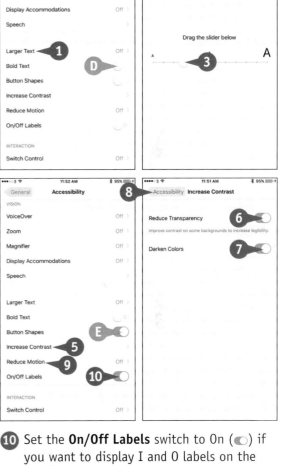

10 Set the **On/Off Labels** switch to On () if you want to display I and O labels on the switches.

TIPS

How do I set up a hearing aid with my iPhone?
Tap **Hearing Devices** on the Accessibility screen to display the Hearing Devices screen. Here you can pair a hearing aid that conforms to the Made for iPhone standard; for other hearing aids, work on the Bluetooth screen, as for other Bluetooth devices.

What does the Reduce Motion switch do?
Set the **Reduce Motion** switch to On () if you want to reduce the amount of movement that occurs when you tilt the iPhone when displaying a screen such as the Home screen, where the icons appear to float above the background.

continued ▶

Your iPhone includes a suite of interaction features designed to make it easier for you to interact with the touch screen and other hardware components, such as the accelerometers that detect and analyze the device's movements. Changes you can make include setting the tap-and-hold duration and the repeat interval, adjusting the pressure needed for 3D Touch, and configuring the double- and triple-click speed for the Home button. You can also choose your default audio device for call audio.

Configure Other Accessibility Features (continued)

Configure Interaction Accessibility Features

1. On the Accessibility screen, tap **Touch Accommodations**.

   The Touch Accommodations screen appears.

2. Set the **Touch Accommodations** switch to On (⬤) to enable touch accommodations.

3. Set the **Hold Duration** switch to On (⬤) if you need to adjust the hold duration.

Note: If the Important dialog opens, warning you that Touch Accommodations changes iPhone-control gestures, tap **OK**.

4. Tap **+** or **−** to set the Hold Duration.

5. Set the **Ignore Repeat** switch to On (⬤) if your iPhone detects false repeat touches.

6. Tap **+** or **−** to set the Ignore Repeat interval.

7. In the Tap Assistance box, tap **Off**, **Use Initial Touch Location**, or **Use Final Touch Location**, as needed.

8. Tap **Accessibility** (<).

9. Tap **3D Touch**.

F. You can set the **3D Touch** switch to Off ( ) to disable 3D Touch.

10. Drag the **3D Touch Sensitivity** slider to Light, Medium, or Firm, as needed.

G. Press the image to test the 3D Touch setting.

11. Tap **Accessibility** (<).

The Accessibility screen appears again.

12 Tap **Shake to Undo**.

The Shake to Undo screen appears.

13 Set the **Shake to Undo** switch to Off ( ) if the feature undoes actions by accident.

14 Tap **Accessibility** (**‹**).

The Accessibility screen appears again.

H If you want to disable all vibration, tap **Vibration**, set the **Vibration** switch on the Vibration screen to Off ( ), and then tap **Accessibility** (**‹**).

15 Tap **Call Audio Routing**.

The Call Audio Routing screen appears.

16 Tap the audio output device you want to use for phone calls and FaceTime audio calls — for example, tap **Bluetooth Headset**.

17 Tap **Accessibility** (**‹**).

The Accessibility screen appears again.

18 Tap **Home Button**.

The Home Button screen appears.

19 Tap **Default**, **Slow**, or **Slowest** to set the double-click speed.

20 Tap **Accessibility** (**‹**).

The Accessibility screen appears again.

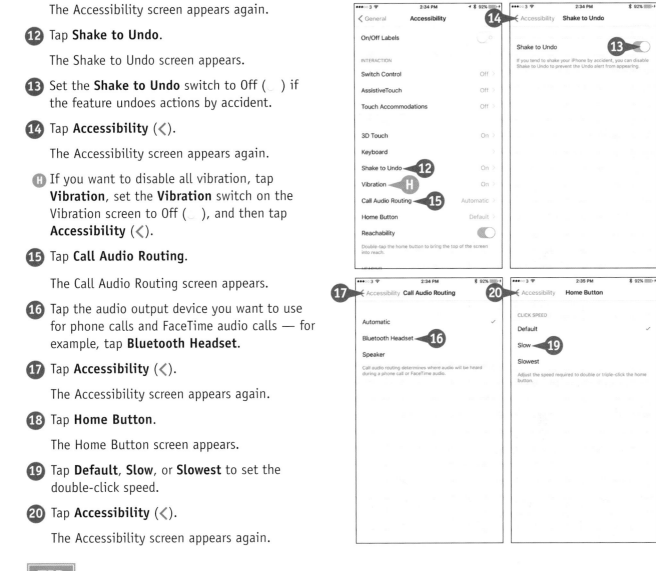

TIP

What are the Speech accessibility settings?

You can have your iPhone speak selected text to you when you tap the nearby Speak button. You can also make your iPhone speak all the text on-screen by swiping down with two fingers from the top.

To enable these features, tap **Speech** on the Accessibility screen and then set the **Speak Selection** switch or the **Speak Screen** switch to On ( ). Tap **Voices** to choose the speaking voice and drag the **Speaking Rate** slider to set the speaking speed. To have your iPhone speak what you type, tap **Typing Feedback** and then choose settings on the Typing Feedback screen.

Using Your iPhone with Your Mac

If you have a Mac, you can enjoy the impressive integration that Apple has built into iOS and the Mac's operating system, now called macOS but formerly called OS X. Apple calls this integration Continuity. Continuity involves several features including Handoff, which enables you to pick up your work or play seamlessly on one device exactly where you have left it on another device. For example, you can start writing an e-mail message on your Mac and then complete it on your iPhone.

Understanding Which iPhone Models and Mac Models Can Use Continuity

To use Continuity, your iPhone must be running iOS 8, iOS 9, iOS 10, or a later version. Your Mac must be running Yosemite, El Capitan, Sierra, or a later version. Your Mac must have Bluetooth 4.0 hardware. In practice, this includes a Mac mini or MacBook Air from 2011 or later, a MacBook Pro or iMac from 2012 or later, a Mac Pro from 2013 or later, or a MacBook from 2015 or later.

Enable Handoff on Your iPhone

To enable your iPhone to communicate with your Mac, you need to enable the Handoff feature. Press **Home** to display the Home screen, tap **Settings** (⚙) to open the Settings app, tap **General** (⚙) to display the General screen, and then tap **Handoff & Suggested Apps**. On the Handoff & Suggested Apps screen, set the **Handoff** switch to On (⬤) and then set the switches in the Suggested Apps list to On (⬤) or Off ( ). You may prefer to set only the **Installed Apps** switch to On (changes to ⬤) at first until you see how useful you find Handoff.

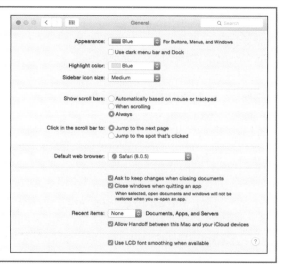

Enable Handoff on Your Mac

You also need to enable Handoff on your Mac. To do so, click on the menu bar and then click **System Preferences** to open the System Preferences window. Click **General** to display the General pane. Click **Allow Handoff between this Mac and your iCloud devices** (☐ changes to ☑). You can then click **System Preferences** on the menu bar and click **Quit System Preferences** to quit System Preferences.

Make and Take Phone Calls on Your Mac

When you are using your Mac within Bluetooth range of your iPhone, Continuity enables you to make and take phone calls on your Mac instead of your iPhone. For example, when someone calls you on your iPhone, your Mac displays a call window automatically, and you can pick up the call on your Mac.

Send and Receive Text Messages from Your Mac

Your Mac can already send and receive messages via Apple's iMessage service, but when your iPhone's connection is available, your Mac can send and receive messages directly via Short Message Service (SMS) and Multimedia Messaging Service (MMS). This capability enables you to manage your messaging smoothly and tightly from your Mac.

Using Your iPhone with Your Apple Watch

Apple Watch puts timekeeping, notifications, and other essential information directly on your wrist. Apple Watch is an accessory for the iPhone — it requires an iPhone to set it up, to provide apps and data, and to give access to the cellular network and the Internet.

Apple Watch works with iPhone 5 and later models — as of this writing, the iPhone 5c, iPhone 5s, iPhone 6, iPhone 6 Plus, iPhone 6s, iPhone 6s Plus, iPhone SE, iPhone 7, and iPhone 7 Plus.

Pair Your Apple Watch with Your iPhone

You must pair Apple Watch with your iPhone before you can use the devices together. Press and hold the **side button** on Apple Watch until the Apple logo appears, and then wait while Apple Watch finishes starting up.

On your iPhone, press **Home** to display the Home screen, and then tap **Watch** (⬤) to open the Watch app. Tap **Start Pairing**, and then follow the prompts to hold Apple Watch up to your iPhone's rear camera so that the Watch app can recognize the pattern on the Apple Watch screen.

When the Your Apple Watch Is Paired screen appears, tap **Set Up Apple Watch** and complete the setup routine.

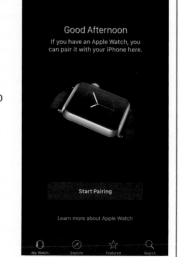

Configure Your Apple Watch Using Your iPhone

The Watch app on your iPhone enables you to configure your Apple Watch. On your iPhone, press **Home** to display the Home screen, tap **Watch** (⬤) to open the Watch app, and then tap **My Watch** (⬛) to display the My Watch screen.

From here, you can choose a wide range of settings. For example, you can tap **App Layout** (⬛) to configure the layout of the apps on your Apple Watch's screen, or you can tap **Notifications** (⬛) to choose which notifications you receive on your Apple Watch.

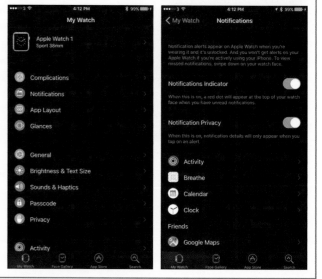

Install Apps on Your Apple Watch

The Watch app on your iPhone enables you to install apps on your Apple Watch — and remove them if necessary.

When you install an iPhone app that has a companion app for Apple Watch, the app's name appears on the My Watch screen. Tap the app's name to display the app's screen. You can then set the **Show App on Apple Watch** switch to On ( changes to ⬤) to install the app.

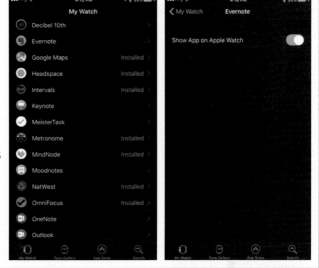

Receive Notifications on Your Apple Watch

When you receive a notification from an app you have permitted to raise notifications, your Apple Watch displays an icon showing the app and other information, such as the sender of an e-mail message. You can tap the notification to view its details.

Receive Calls on Your Apple Watch

When you receive a phone call, it rings on both your Apple Watch and your iPhone. You can tap **Accept** () to pick up the call on Apple Watch or tap **Decline** (⬤) to decline the call, sending it to voicemail.

CHAPTER 4

Setting Up Communications

In this chapter, you learn how to add your e-mail accounts to the Mail app and control how Mail displays your messages. This chapter also shows you how to control the way your iPhone displays your contacts, import contacts from a SIM card, choose options for your calendars, and set up Wallet and Apple Pay.

Set Up Your Mail Accounts

Usually, you set up your iCloud account while going through the initial setup routine for your iPhone. But if you have other e-mail accounts, you can set them up as explained in this section.

To set up an e-mail account, you need to know the e-mail address and password, as well as the e-mail provider. You may also need to know the addresses of the mail servers the account uses. For Microsoft Exchange, you must know the domain name as well.

Set Up Your Mail Accounts

1 Press **Home**.

The Home screen appears.

2 Tap **Settings** (⚙).

The Settings screen appears.

Note: If you have not yet set up an e-mail account on the iPhone, you can also open the Add Account screen by tapping **Mail** on the iPhone's Home screen.

3 Tap **Mail** (✉).

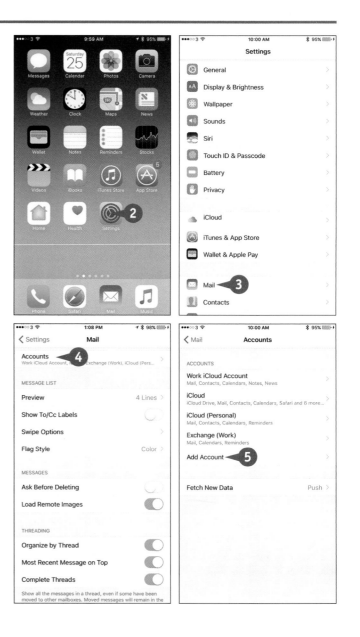

The Mail screen appears.

4 Tap **Accounts**.

The Accounts screen appears.

5 Tap **Add Account**.

Note: Some account types have fields other than those shown here. For example, some accounts include a field for entering your name the way you want it to appear on outgoing messages. Some include a field for changing the description displayed for the account.

The Add Account screen opens.

6 Tap the kind of account you want to set up. For example, tap **Google**.

The screen for setting up that type of account appears.

A You can tap **More options** and then tap **Create New Account** to create a new account.

7 Tap **Enter your email** and type the e-mail address.

8 Tap **Next**.

The Password screen appears.

9 Type your password and tap **Next**.

10 If another security screen appears, such as the 2-Step Verification screen shown here, enter the required information and tap **Next**.

The configuration screen for the account appears.

11 Make sure the **Mail** switch is set to On (◯).

12 Set the **Contacts** switch, **Calendars** switch, **Notes** switch, and any other switches to On (◯) or Off ( ), as needed.

13 Tap **Save**.

The account appears on the Mail screen.

TIP

How do I set up a Hotmail account?

Hotmail is one of the services that Microsoft has integrated into its Outlook.com service. Tap **Outlook.com** on the Add Account screen and then fill in your e-mail address and password on the Outlook screen that appears. On the Let This App Access Your Info? Screen, tap **Yes**. Verify your password again if prompted. After Mail verifies the account, set the **Mail** switch, **Contacts** switch, **Calendars** switch, and **Reminders** switch to On (◯) or Off ( ), as needed, and then tap **Save**.

Control How Your E-Mail Appears

In the Mail app, you can choose how many lines to include in message previews, decide whether to display the To and Cc label, and control whether Mail prompts you before deleting a message. You can change the minimum font size. You can also choose whether to load remote images in messages; whether to mark e-mail addresses outside a particular domain, such as that of your company or organization; and whether to increase the indentation on messages you reply to or forward.

Control How Your E-Mail Appears

① Press **Home**.

The Home screen appears.

② Tap **Settings** (⚙).

The Settings screen appears.

③ Tap **Mail** (✉).

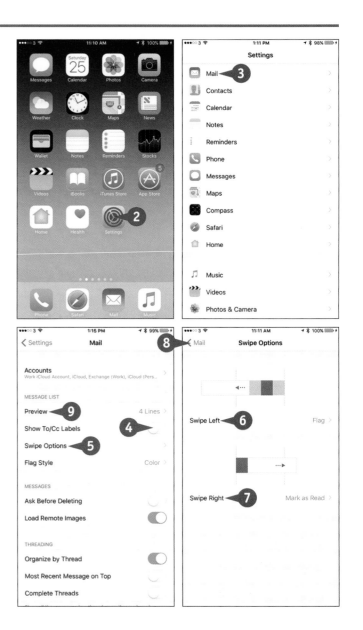

The Mail screen appears.

④ Set the **Show To/Cc Label** switch to On (⬤) or Off (   ), as needed.

⑤ Tap **Swipe Options**.

The Swipe Options screen appears.

⑥ Tap **Swipe Left**; tap **None**, **Mark as Read**, **Flag**, or **Move Message**; and then tap **Swipe Options** (‹).

⑦ Tap **Swipe Right**; tap **None**, **Mark as Read**, **Flag**, **Move Message**, or **Archive**; and then tap **Swipe Options** (‹).

⑧ Tap **Mail** (‹).

The Mail screen appears again.

⑨ Tap **Preview**.

The Preview screen appears.

10 Tap the number of preview lines you want.

11 Tap **Mail** (<).

12 Tap **Flag Style**, tap **Color** or **Shape** to control how message flags appear, and then tap **Mail** (<).

13 Set the **Ask Before Deleting** switch to On (●) or Off ( ), as needed.

14 Set the **Load Remote Images** switch to On (●) or Off ( ), as needed.

15 Tap **Mark Addresses**.

The Mark Addresses screen appears.

16 In the Mark Addresses Not Ending With box, type the domain name of your company or organization, such as surrealmacs.com.

17 Tap **Mail** (<).

The Mail screen appears again.

18 Tap **Increase Quote Level**.

The Increase Quote Level screen appears.

19 Set the **Increase Quote Level** switch to On (●) or Off ( ), as needed.

20 Tap **Mail** (<).

21 Tap **Settings**.

TIPS

Why might I want to turn off Load Remote Images?

Loading a remote image lets the sender know that you have opened the message. When Mail requests the remote image, the server that provides the image can log the date and time and your Internet connection's IP address, which reveals your approximate location.

What is Always Bcc Myself useful for?

Most e-mail services automatically put a copy of each message you send or forward into a folder with a name such as Sent. If your e-mail service does not use a Sent folder, set the **Always Bcc Myself** switch to On (●) to send a bcc copy of each message to yourself for your records.

Organize Your E-Mail Messages by Threads

The Mail app gives you two ways to view e-mail messages. You can view the messages as a simple list, or you can view them with related messages organized into *threads*, which are sometimes called *conversations*.

Having Mail display your messages as threads can help you navigate your Inbox quickly and find related messages easily. You may find threading useful if you tend to have long e-mail conversations, because threading reduces the number of messages you see at once.

Organize Your E-Mail Messages by Threads

Set Mail to Organize Your Messages by Thread

1 Press **Home**.

The Home screen appears.

2 Tap **Settings** (⚙).

The Settings screen appears.

3 Tap **Mail** (✉).

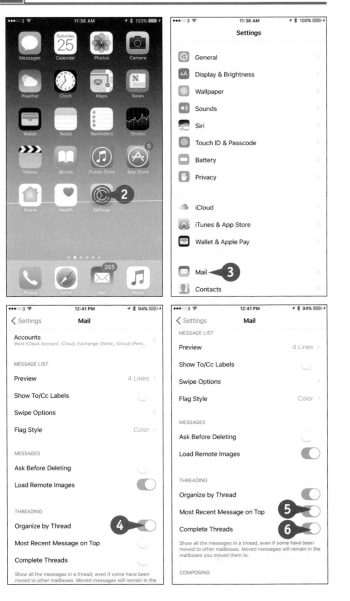

The Mail screen appears.

4 Set the **Organize by Thread** switch to On (◯).

5 Set the **Most Recent Message on Top** switch to On (◯) if you want the newest message in each thread to appear at the top of the screen. This option is often helpful for keeping up with your messages.

6 Set the **Complete Threads** switch to On (◯) if you want each thread to show all its messages, even if you have moved some to other mailboxes. This option is usually helpful.

Read Messages Organized into Threads

1 Press **Home**.

The Home screen appears.

2 Tap **Mail** ().

The Mailboxes screen appears.

Note: If Mail displays the contents of a mailbox, tap **Back** (**<**) to return to the Mailboxes screen.

3 Tap the mailbox you want to open.

The Inbox for the account appears.

Ⓐ Two chevrons on the right indicate a thread.

4 Tap the thread.

The Thread screen appears, showing the thread. The screen's title shows the number of messages in the thread.

5 Tap the message you want to display.

Is there a quick way to enter my name and information at the end of a message?

Yes. You can create one or more e-mail signatures, which are sections of predefined text that Mail can insert at the end of messages. From the Home screen, tap **Settings** (⚙), and then tap **Mail** (✉). Scroll down to the Composing section and tap **Signature** to display the Signature screen. Tap **All Accounts** to use the same signature for each account, or tap **Per Account** to use a different signature for each account. Then type the text to use.

Set Your Default E-Mail Account

If you set up two or more e-mail accounts on your iPhone, make sure that you set the right e-mail account to be the default account. The default account is the one from which the Mail app sends messages unless you choose another account, so choosing the appropriate account is important.

You can quickly set your default e-mail account on the Mail screen in the Settings app.

Set Your Default E-Mail Account

1 Press **Home**.

The Home screen appears.

2 Tap **Settings** (⚙).

The Settings screen appears.

3 Tap **Mail** (✉).

The Mail screen appears.

4 In the Composing section, tap **Default Account**.

The Default Account screen appears.

5 Tap the account you want to make the default.

6 Tap **Mail** (<).

Note: To change the e-mail account for a new message, tap **From**, and then tap the address on the list that appears at the bottom of the screen.

Control How Your Contacts Appear

To swiftly and easily find the contacts you need, you can set your iPhone to sort and display the contacts in your preferred order. Your iPhone can sort contacts either by first name, putting Abby Brown before Bill Andrews, or by last name, putting Bill Andrews before Abby Brown. Your iPhone can display contacts either as first name followed by last name or last name followed by first name. You can also configure short names preferences for contacts.

Control How Your Contacts Appear

1 Press **Home**.

The Home screen appears.

2 Tap **Settings** (⚙).

The Settings screen appears.

3 Tap **Contacts** (👤).

The Contacts screen appears.

4 In the Contacts section, tap **Sort Order** or **Display Order**, depending on which order you want to set. This example uses Sort Order.

The Sort Order screen or the Display Order screen appears.

5 Tap **First, Last** or **Last, First**, as needed.

6 Tap **Contacts** (‹).

The Contacts screen appears again.

7 Tap **Short Name**.

The Short Name screen appears.

8 Set the **Short Name** switch to On (⬤).

9 Tap **First Name & Last Initial**, **First Initial & Last Name**, **First Name Only**, or **Last Name Only** to specify the format for short names.

10 Set the **Prefer Nicknames** switch to On (⬤) or Off ( ), as needed.

11 Tap **Contacts** (‹).

The Contacts screen appears again.

Import Contacts from a SIM Card

If you have stored contacts on a SIM card, such as contacts from your previous phone, you can import them into your iPhone. If the SIM card is the same size as the iPhone's SIM card, you can insert the SIM card in the iPhone temporarily and import the contacts. Another approach is to insert the iPhone's SIM card in an unlocked cell phone, copy the contacts to the SIM card, and then put the SIM card back in the iPhone.

Import Contacts from a SIM Card

1 Press **Home**.

The Home screen appears.

2 Tap **Settings** ().

The Settings screen appears.

3 Tap **Contacts** (📇).

The Contacts screen appears.

4 In the Contacts section, tap **Import SIM Contacts**.

5 If the Import SIM Contacts to Account dialog appears, tap the account in which you want to put the contacts.

Your iPhone imports the contacts from the SIM.

A Set the **Contacts Found in Apps** switch to On ( ) if you want your iPhone to suggest creating contacts from names and data found in e-mail messages, incoming calls, or contact data.

Choose Default Alert Options for Calendar Events

Your iPhone enables you to sync your calendars via iCloud and other online services. To help keep on schedule, you can set default alert times for calendar events. You can set a different alert time for each type of event — for example, 15 minutes' notice for a regular event and a week's notice for a birthday. You can also turn on the Time to Leave feature to make the Calendar app allow travel time based on your location and current traffic.

Choose Default Alert Options for Calendar Events

1 Press **Home**.

The Home screen appears.

2 Tap **Settings** (⚙).

The Settings screen appears.

3 Tap **Calendar** (📅).

The Calendar screen appears.

A Set the **Location Suggestions** switch to On (⬤) if you want Calendar to suggest locations for events.

B Set the **Events Found in Apps** switch to On (⬤) if you want your iPhone to suggest creating events from apparent event data found in apps such as Mail and Messages.

4 Tap **Default Alert Times**.

The Default Alert Times screen appears.

5 Tap the event type for which you want to set the default alert time. For example, tap **Events**.

The Events screen, Birthdays screen, or All-Day Events screen appears.

6 Tap the amount of time for the alert.

7 Tap **Default Alert Times** (‹).

The Default Alert Times screen appears again.

8 Set default alert times for other event types by repeating steps **5** to **7**.

9 Set the **Time to Leave** switch to On (⬤) if you want Calendar to suggest leave times based on your location and current traffic information.

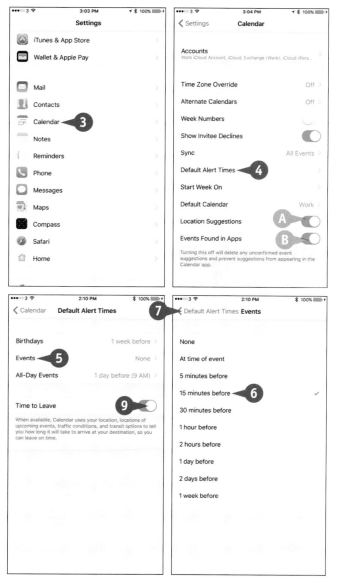

Choose Your Default Calendar and Time Zone

When you use multiple calendars on your iPhone, set your default calendar, the calendar that receives events you create outside any specific calendar. For example, if you have a Work calendar and a Home calendar, you might set the Home calendar as the default calendar.

If you travel to different time zones, use the Time Zone Override feature to specify the time zone in which to show event dates and times. Otherwise, Calendar uses the time zone for your current location.

Choose Your Default Calendar and Time Zone

1 Press **Home**.

The Home screen appears.

2 Tap **Settings** ().

The Settings screen appears.

3 Tap **Calendar** ().

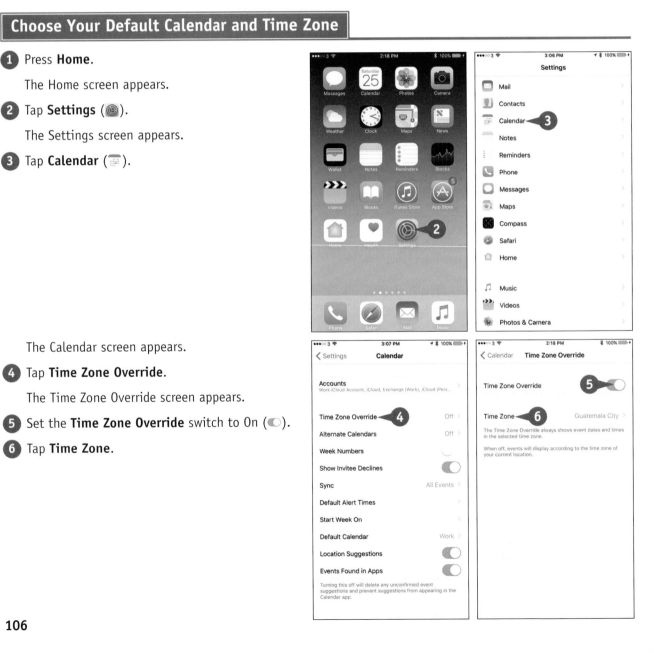

The Calendar screen appears.

4 Tap **Time Zone Override**.

The Time Zone Override screen appears.

5 Set the **Time Zone Override** switch to On ().

6 Tap **Time Zone**.

The Time Zone screen appears.

7 Type the first letters of a city in the time zone.

8 Tap the search result you want.

The Time Zone Override screen appears again, now showing the city you selected.

9 Tap **Calendar** (<).

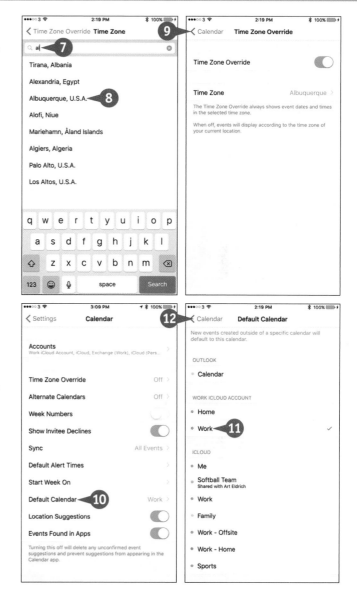

The Calendar screen appears again.

10 Tap **Default Calendar**.

The Default Calendar screen appears.

11 Tap the calendar you want to make the default.

12 Tap **Calendar** (<).

The Calendar screen appears again.

TIP

Where do I control which calendars the Calendar app displays?

You choose the calendars in the Calendar app, not in the Settings app. Press **Home** to display the Home screen, tap **Calendar** (🗓), and then tap **Calendars**. On the Calendars screen, tap to place a check mark on each calendar you want to show. Tap to remove a check mark from a calendar you want to hide. Tap **Done** when you finish.

Set Up and Use Wallet and Apple Pay

Your iPhone enables you to make payments using the Apple Pay system and the Wallet app on your iPhone. Apple Pay can be faster and more convenient than paying with cash. It can also be more secure than paying with a credit card or debit card.

Understanding Apple Pay and Wallet

Apple Pay is Apple's electronic-payment and digital-wallet service. After setting up Apple Pay with one or more credit cards or debit cards, you can make payments using your iPhone either at contactless payment terminals or online. If you have an Apple Watch, you can use Apple Pay on that device as well.

Wallet is the app you use on your iPhone to manage Apple Pay and the digital documents you want to carry with you, such as airline tickets or store rewards cards.

Set Up Wallet

Press **Home** to display the Home screen, and then tap **Wallet** (▣) to open the Wallet app.

If you have not yet set up a credit card or debit card, tap **Add Credit or Debit Card** in the Pay area of the Wallet screen. Follow the prompts to add a card to Wallet. You can add the card either by lining it up within an on-screen frame and using the camera to recognize it or by typing in the details manually. Complete the card registration by selecting the correct billing address. For some cards, you may need to contact the card provider to confirm you are setting up Apple Pay.

If you have already added a card, you can add another by tapping **Add Card** (⊕) in the upper-right corner of the screen.

After you add cards, they appear at the top of the Wallet screen.

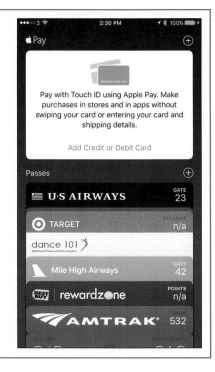

Set Apple Pay to Use Touch ID

After setting up Apple Pay, you can set your iPhone to use Touch ID instead of your Apple ID password for buying items. Touch ID enables you to authenticate yourself and approve a purchase by placing one of your registered fingers on the Home button. This is much more convenient than typing a password, especially when you are shopping in the physical world rather than online.

To set your iPhone to use Touch ID for Apple Pay, press **Home** to display the Home screen, and then tap **Settings** (⬤) to display the Settings screen. Tap **Touch ID & Passcode** (⬛) to display the Touch ID & Passcode screen, and then set the **Apple Pay** switch to On (⬤).

Make a Payment with Apple Pay

Now that you have set up Apple Pay and configured your iPhone to use it, you can make payments by bringing your iPhone close to the contact area on a payment terminal.

When the Near Field Communication (NFC) chips make contact, a tone sounds. Your iPhone then displays details of the transaction and prompts you to confirm it by placing your finger on the Home button so that it can verify your fingerprint.

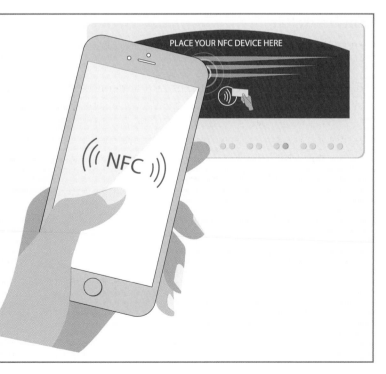

CHAPTER 5

Making Calls and Messaging

You can make calls by holding your iPhone to your face, by using the speakerphone, or by using a headset. You can also make calls using Favorites and recent numbers, send and receive text and multimedia messages, and chat using the FaceTime feature.

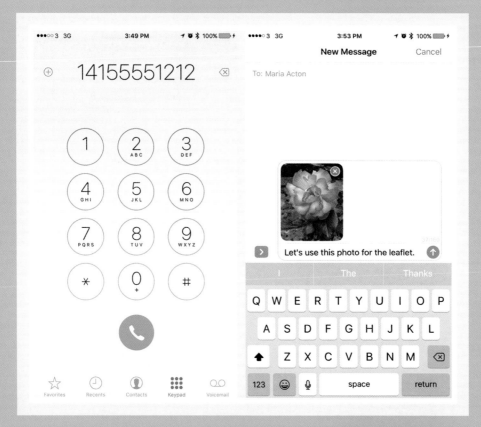

Make Phone Calls

With your iPhone, you can make phone calls anywhere you have a connection to the cellular network. You can dial a phone number using the iPhone's keypad, but you can place calls more easily by tapping the appropriate phone number for a contact, using the Phone app's Recents screen, using the Favorites list, or using Siri. When other people near you need to be able to hear the call, you can switch on your iPhone's speaker; otherwise, you can use the headset for privacy.

Make Phone Calls

Open the Phone App

1 Press **Home**.

The Home screen appears.

2 Tap **Phone** ().

The Phone app opens and displays the screen you used last — for example, the Contacts screen.

A Your phone number appears at the top of the Contacts list for quick reference.

Note: You can dial a call by activating Siri and speaking the contact's name or the number. See Chapter 3 for instructions on using Siri.

Dial a Call Using the Keypad

1 Tap **Keypad** (changes to).

The Keypad screen appears.

Note: On the Keypad screen, you can tap **Call** ( ) without dialing a number to display the last number dialed.

2 Tap the number keys to dial the number.

B You can tap **Add to Contacts** (⊕) to add this number to your Contacts list.

C If you dial a number similar to a contact's number, the Maybe readout suggests the contact.

3 Tap **Call** ( ).

Your iPhone makes the call.

4 Tap **End** ( ) when you are ready to end the call.

Dial a Call to a Contact

1 Tap **Contacts** (👤 changes to 👤).

The Contacts list appears.

2 Tap the contact you want to call.

The contact's info appears.

3 Tap **Call** (📞).

Note: You can also place a call to a phone number that the iPhone has identified — for example, by tapping an underlined phone number on a web page or in an e-mail message.

The Call panel opens.

4 Tap the number you want to call.

Your iPhone places the call.

5 When you are ready to end the call, tap **End** (📞).

Your iPhone ends the call.

The Call Ended screen appears for a moment.

The screen from which you placed the call appears — for example, the Contacts screen.

Note: To end a call for which you are using the headset, press the clicker button.

TIPS

Can I use the iPhone as a speaker phone?

Yes. Tap **speaker** (🔊 changes to 🔊) on the screen that appears while you are making a phone call. The iPhone starts playing the phone call through the speaker on the bottom instead of the small speaker at the top. Tap **speaker** (🔊 changes to 🔊) to switch off the speaker.

What is Dial Assist?

Dial Assist is a feature that automatically determines the correct local prefix or international prefix when you place a call. To turn Dial Assist on or off, press **Home**, tap **Settings** (⚙️), tap **Phone** (📞), and then set the **Dial Assist** switch to On (🔘) or Off ( ).

Instead of using the headset that came with your iPhone, you can use a Bluetooth headset. Similarly, you can use a car kit with a Bluetooth connection when using your iPhone in your vehicle.

You must first pair the Bluetooth headset or car kit with your iPhone, as discussed in Chapter 6.

Using a Wireless Headset or Car Kit

1 Turn on the wireless headset or connection and make sure it works.

2 Press **Home**.

The Home screen appears.

3 Tap **Phone** (📞).

The Phone app opens.

4 Dial the call as usual using one of the techniques described in this chapter. For example, tap **Contacts**, tap the contact, tap **Call** (📞), and then tap the appropriate phone number.

Note: You can also tell Siri to place the call for you.

Your iPhone places the call.

The Audio dialog opens.

5 Tap the headset or other device you want to use.

The Audio dialog closes.

A You can tap **audio** (🔊) to display the Audio dialog and switch to another audio device.

Note: If you are playing audio or video on a Bluetooth headset when you receive a call, your iPhone automatically pauses the audio or video and plays the ringtone on the headset.

Mute a Call or Put a Call on Hold

When you are on a call, you may need to mute your iPhone's microphone so that you can confer with people near you without the person at the other end of the phone call hearing.

You may also need to put a call on hold so that you can make another call or take a break from the call.

Mute a Call or Put a Call on Hold

1 Establish the phone call as usual. For example, call a contact.

2 Tap **mute** (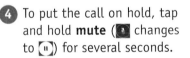 changes to 🔵).

The iPhone mutes the call.

3 When you are ready to unmute the call, tap **mute** again (🔵 changes to ●).

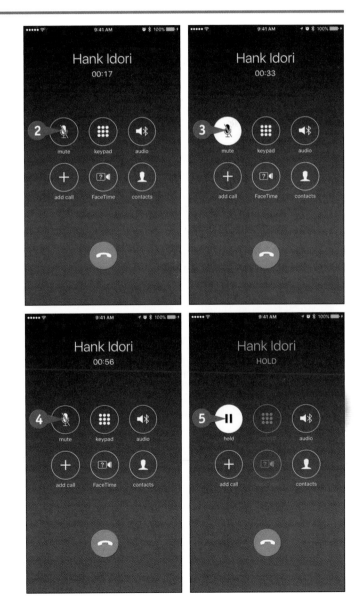

The iPhone turns off muting.

4 To put the call on hold, tap and hold **mute** (● changes to ⏸) for several seconds.

The iPhone puts the call on hold.

Note: After placing a call on hold, you can make another call if necessary.

5 When you are ready to take the call off hold, tap **hold** (⏸ changes to ●).

Make a Conference Call

As well as making phone calls to one other phone at a time, your iPhone can make calls to multiple phones. To make a conference call, you call the first participant, and then add each other participant in turn. During a conference call, you can talk in private to individual participants. You can also drop a participant from the call.

Make a Conference Call

1 Press **Home**.

The Home screen appears.

2 Tap **Phone** (📞).

The Phone app opens.

3 Tap **Contacts** (👤 changes to 🔵).

The Contacts screen appears.

4 Tap the contact you want to call first.

The contact's record appears.

5 Tap **Call** (📞) on the phone number to use.

Note: You can also add a contact to the call by using Favorites, Recents, or Keypad.

Your iPhone establishes the call.

6 Tap **add call** (➕).

The Contacts screen appears.

7 Tap the contact you want to add.

The contact's record appears.

8 Tap **Call** (📞).

The Call dialog opens.

9 Tap the phone number to use.

Ⓐ The iPhone places the first call on hold and makes the new call.

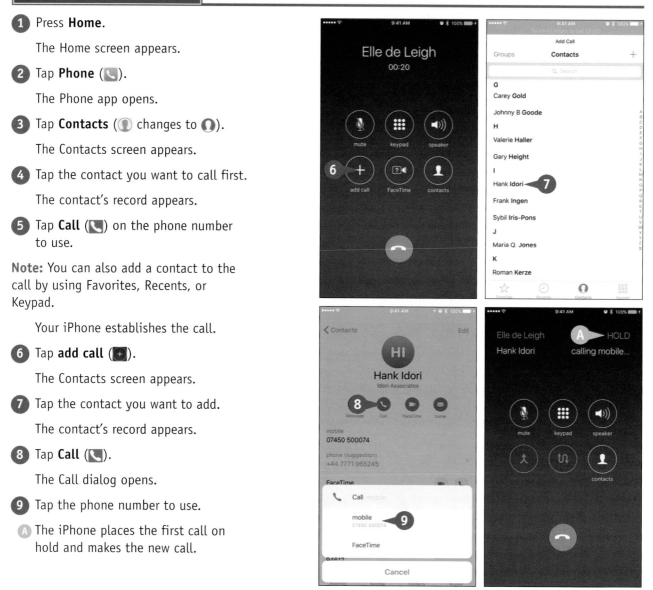

10 Tap **merge calls** ().

The iPhone merges the calls and displays the participants' names at the top of the screen. You can now speak to both participants.

Ⓑ You can add more participants by tapping **add call** (⊕), specifying the contact or number, and then merging the calls.

11 To speak privately to a participant, tap **Information** (ⓘ).

The Conference screen appears, showing a list of the participants.

12 Tap **Private** next to the participant.

The iPhone places the other caller or callers on hold.

Ⓒ You can tap **swap** (⟲) to swap the caller on hold and the active caller.

13 When you are ready to resume the conference call, tap **merge calls** (🤵).

The iPhone merges the calls, and all participants can hear each other again.

14 When you finish the call, tap **End** (☎).

The iPhone ends the call.

TIPS

How do I drop a participant from a conference call?
Tap **Information** (ⓘ) to display the Conference screen, and then tap **End** next to the participant you want to drop.

How many people can I add to a conference call?
This depends on your carrier, not on your iPhone. Ask your carrier what the maximum number of participants can be.

Save Time with Call Favorites and Recents

You can dial phone numbers easily from your Contacts list, but you can save time and effort by using the Favorites and Recents features built into the Phone app.

Favorites are phone numbers that you mark as being especially important to you. Recents are phone numbers you have called and received calls from recently.

Save Time with Call Favorites and Recents

Add a Contact to Your Favorites List

1 Press **Home**.

The Home screen appears.

2 Tap **Phone** ().

The Phone app opens.

3 Tap **Contacts** (changes to).

The Contacts list appears.

4 Tap the contact you want to add.

The contact's record appears.

5 Tap **Add to Favorites**.

The Add to Favorites dialog opens.

6 Tap the heading for the type of favorite you want to add. This example uses **Call**.

The list of phone numbers for the contact appears.

7 Tap the phone number you want to add to your Favorites list.

The Add to Favorites dialog closes, and the iPhone creates a favorite for the contact.

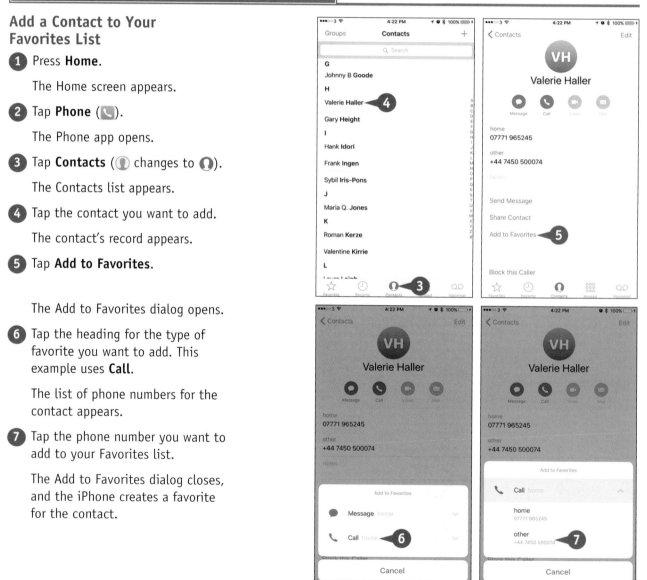

Call a Favorite

1 In the Phone app, tap **Favorites**
(☆ changes to ★).

The Favorites list appears.

2 Tap the Favorite you want to call.

Your iPhone places the call.

A To display the contact's record, tap
Information (ⓘ) instead of tapping the
contact's button. You can then tap a
different phone number for the contact
if necessary.

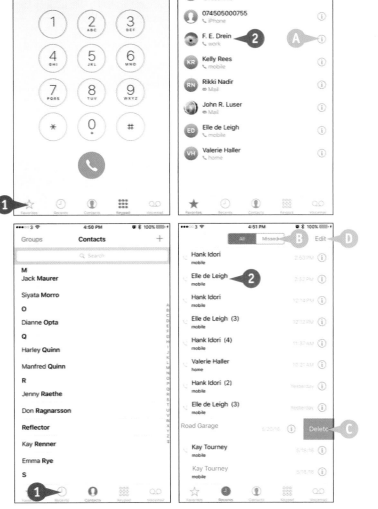

Call a Recent

1 In the Phone app, tap **Recents**
(🕐 changes to 🕐).

The Recents screen appears. Red entries
indicate calls you missed.

B Tap **Missed** if you want to see only recent
calls you missed.

2 Tap the recent you want to call.

Your iPhone places the call.

C You can delete a recent by swiping its
button left and then tapping the textual
Delete button.

D If you want to clear the Recents list, tap
Edit and then tap **Clear**. In the dialog that
opens, tap **Clear All Recents**.

TIP

How do I remove a contact from my Favorites?
Tap **Favorites** to display the Favorites list, and then tap **Edit**. Tap **Delete** (⊖) next to the contact, and
then tap the textual **Delete** button. You can also rearrange your favorites by tapping the handle (▤) and
dragging up or down. Tap **Done** when you have finished changing your favorites.

Send Text and Multimedia Messages

Your iPhone can send instant messages using the Short Message Service, abbreviated SMS; the Multimedia Messaging Service, MMS; or Apple's iMessage service. An SMS message consists of only text, whereas an MMS message can contain text, videos, photos, sounds, or other data. An iMessage can contain text, multimedia content, emoji, animations, handwriting, or other features. The Messages app automatically chooses the appropriate type — SMS, MMS, or iMessage — for the messages you create and the ways you send them.

Send Text and Multimedia Messages

1 Press **Home**.

The Home screen appears.

2 Tap **Messages** (⬜).

The Messages screen appears.

3 Tap **New Message** (✏️).

Note: Before sending an SMS or MMS message, make sure the recipient's phone number can receive such messages. Typically, you do not receive an alert if the message cannot be delivered.

The New Message screen appears.

4 Tap **Add Contact** (⊕).

The Contacts list appears.

5 Tap the contact to whose phone you want to send the message.

Note: If the contact's record contains multiple phone numbers, Messages displays the contact record. Tap the phone number to use.

120

The contact's name appears in the To field of the New Message screen.

6 Tap the text field.

The text field expands, and the More button appears.

7 Tap in the text field, and then type your message.

8 Tap **More** (>).

The other buttons reappear.

9 To add a photo, tap **Photo** (📷).

The Photo dialog opens.

A You can tap **Take Photo** (⭕) to take a photo.

B You can tap **Switch Cameras** (📷) to switch between the front and rear cameras.

10 Tap a recent photo to add it. Scroll left to view recent other photos.

C You can tap **Back** (<) and tap **Photo Library** to select a photo from your photo library.

D The photo appears in the message.

11 Tap **Send** (↑).

Messages sends the message and the photo.

How can I respond quickly to an instant message?
When Messages displays a notification for an instant message, tap the notification to display the Text Message box. You can then type a reply and tap **Send** to send it.

Is there another way to send a photo or video?
Yes. You can start from the Camera app or the Photos app. Select the photo or video you want to share, and then tap **Share** (⬆). On the Share sheet, tap **Message**. Your iPhone starts an MMS message containing the photo or video. You can then address and send the message.

Using Emoji and iMessage Features

The Messages app makes it easy to include *emoji* — graphical characters — in your messages. You can send emoji to users of most instant-messaging services, not just to iMessage users.

When you are sending a message to another user of the iMessage service, you can also use a wide range of features that are not available for SMS messages and text messages. These features include stickers, handwriting and sketches, animations, and Digital Touch, which enables you to send a pattern of taps or your heartbeat. You can also respond quickly to a message by using the Tapback feature.

Add Emoji to Messages

The Messages app makes it easy to add emoji to your messages. After typing text, tap **Emoji** (☺) on the keyboard. Messages highlights with color any words in the message that you can replace with emoji; tap a word to insert the corresponding emoji icon, such as 👍 for "great!"

You can also insert other emoji manually by tapping them on the emoji keyboard. Tap the buttons at the bottom of the screen, or simply scroll the emoji panel left or right, to browse the available emoji.

Send a Handwritten Message or Sketch

To send a handwritten message or sketch, tap **New** (✐) to begin a new message. Address the message to an iMessage user, and then tap **Digital Touch** (💗) to display the Digital Touch controls.

Tap **Expand** (◣) to expand the panel to full screen, tap the color you want, and then write or draw what you want to send. Tap **Send** (⬆) to send the message.

Send a Message with Effect

To send a message with effect, write the text for the message, and then tap and hold **Send** (⬆). The Send with Effect screen appears. At the top of the screen, tap **Bubble** if you want to send a bubble with an effect such as Slam or Invisible Ink, and then tap the button for the effect; a preview then plays. To send text with a full-screen effect, tap **Screen** at the top of the screen, and then swipe left or right to reach the effect you want; again, a preview plays. When you are ready to send the message, tap **Send** (⬆).

Send Heartbeats or Taps

To send heartbeats or taps, tap **New** (✎) to begin a new message. Address the message to an iMessage user, and then tap **Digital Touch** (💬) to display the Digital Touch controls.

To send a heartbeat, tap and hold with two fingers on the screen. Messages displays a heartbeat graphic and sends a heartbeat; you do not need to tap Send (⬆).

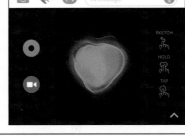

Respond Quickly Using the Tapback Feature

iMessage enables you to respond quickly to an incoming message by tapping and holding it. The Tapback panel opens, and you can tap the icon you want to send as an instant response.

Share the Music You Are Listening To

With iMessage, you can quickly share links to the music you are enjoying on Apple Music. Tap **New** (✎) to begin a new message, and then address the message to an iMessage user. Tap **Digital Touch** (💬) to display the Digital Touch controls. Tap **Apps** (Ⓐ) to display the Apps panel. Swipe left or right if necessary to display the Music panel, and then tap the item you want to share. A button for the item appears in the message box. Type any explanatory or exhortatory text needed, and then tap **Send** (⬆).

Manage Your Instant Messages

essages is great for communicating quickly and frequently with your nearest and dearest and with your colleagues, so it may not take long before the interface is so full of messages that it becomes hard to navigate.

To keep your messages under control, you can forward messages to others and delete messages you do not need to keep. You can either delete messages from a conversation, leaving the conversation's other messages, or delete the entire conversation.

Manage Your Instant Messages

Delete an Entire Conversation

1 Press **Home**.

The Home screen appears.

2 Tap **Messages** (⬜).

The Messages screen appears.

3 Tap **Edit**.

The Messages screen switches to Edit Mode.

4 Tap the **selection button** (⬤ changes to ✓) for each conversation you want to delete.

The Delete button appears.

5 Tap **Delete**.

Messages deletes the conversation.

Ⓐ You can also delete a conversation by swiping it to the left and then tapping **Delete**.

6 When you finish deleting conversations, tap **Done**.

Messages turns off Edit Mode.

Forward or Delete One or More Messages from a Conversation

1 On the Messages screen, tap the conversation that contains the message or messages you will forward.

The conversation appears.

Note: You can tap in a conversation and slide your finger left to display the time of each message.

2 Tap and hold a message.

A dialog opens.

3 Tap **More**.

A selection button (⃝) appears to the left of each message.

4 Tap the **selection button** (⃝ changes to ✅) for each message you want to affect.

5 Tap **Forward** (⮕).

Messages starts a new message containing the message or messages you selected.

Ⓑ Instead of forwarding the selected messages, you can tap **Delete** (🗑) to delete them from the conversation.

Ⓒ You can also tap **Delete All** to delete all the messages.

6 Address the message.

7 Type any extra text needed.

8 Tap **Send** (⬆) to send the message.

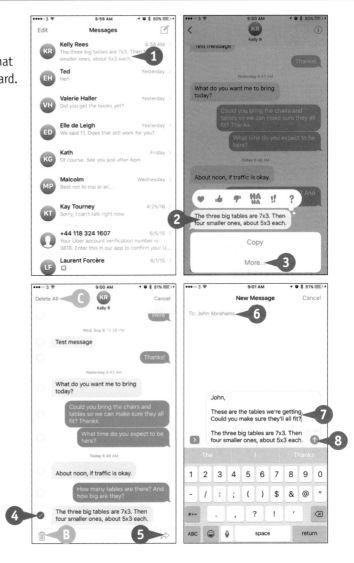

TIP

Can I resend a message?

Yes, you can resend a message in either of these ways:

- If a red icon with an exclamation point appears next to the message, the message has not been sent. Tap the icon to try sending the message again.

- If the message has been sent, you can forward it as described in this section. Alternatively, tap and hold the message text, and then tap **Copy** to copy it. Tap and hold in the message text field, and then tap **Paste** to paste the text. Tap **Send** to send the message.

Choose Settings for Messages

essages includes many settings that you can configure to control the way the app looks and behaves. These settings include whether to send messages as SMS if the iMessage service is unavailable, whether to use MMS messaging, and how long to keep messages.

A key setting is whether to send read receipts for the messages you receive. You can turn read receipts on or off for Messages as a whole, but you can also make exceptions for individual contacts.

Choose Settings for Messages

1 Press **Home**.

The Home screen appears.

2 Tap **Settings** (⚙).

The Settings screen appears.

3 Tap **Messages** (○).

The Messages screen appears.

4 Set the **iMessage** switch to On (○) to use the iMessage service.

5 Set the **Show Contact Photos** switch to On (○) to display contact photos.

6 Set the **Send Read Receipts** switch to On (○) or Off ( ) to control whether Messages sends read receipts for all messages.

7 Tap **Text Message Forwarding**.

The Text Message Forwarding screen appears.

8 Set the switch to On (○) for each Mac or device you want to allow to send text messages via the iPhone.

9 Tap **Messages** (<).

The Messages screen appears again.

10 Set the **Send as SMS** switch to On (○) to send iMessage messages as SMS or MMS messages when iMessage is unavailable.

11 Tap **Send & Receive**.

The iMessage screen appears.

12 Verify that this list shows the correct phone number and address.

13 Tap the phone number or e-mail address from which to start new conversations.

14 Tap **Messages** (**<**).

The Messages screen appears again.

15 Set the **MMS Messaging** switch to On (●) to enable MMS messaging.

16 Set the **Show Subject Field** switch to On (●) or Off ( ), as needed.

17 Set the **Character Count** switch to On (●) or Off ( ), as needed.

18 Tap **Keep Messages**.

The Keep Messages screen appears.

19 Tap **30 Days**, **1 Year**, or **Forever**, as needed.

20 Tap **Messages** (**<**).

The Messages screen appears again.

21 Set the **Filter Unknown Senders** switch to On (●) if you want to keep messages from unknown senders separate.

22 Tap **Expire** and choose **After 2 Minutes** or **Never** for audio messages.

23 Set the **Raise to Listen** switch to On (●) or Off ( ).

24 Tap **Expire** and choose **After 2 Minutes** or **Never** for video messages.

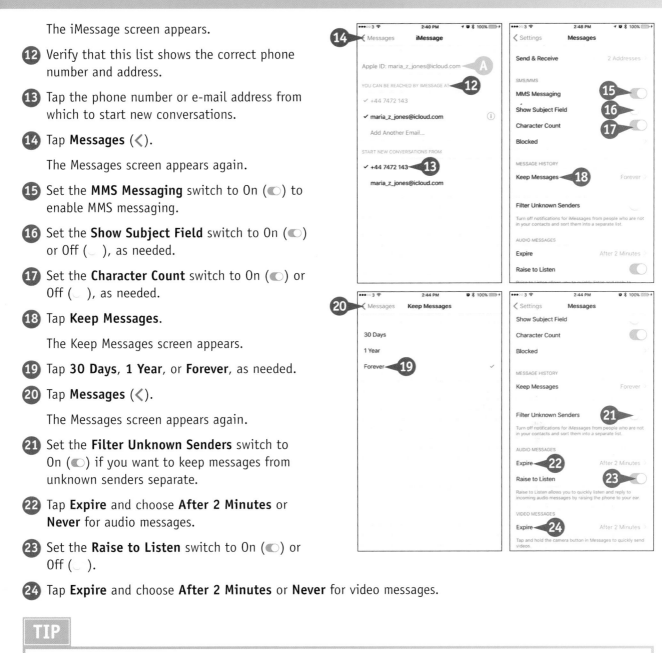

TIP

How do I control read receipts for individual contacts?

First, on the Messages screen in the Settings app, set the **Send Read Receipts** switch to On (●) or Off ( ) to control whether Messages sends read receipts by default.

Next, in the Messages app, open a message to or from the appropriate contact. Tap **Info** (ⓘ) to display the Details screen. Set the **Send Read Receipts** switch to On (●) or Off ( ), as needed, and then tap **Done**.

Block and Unblock Senders

essages enables you to block any sender from whom you do not want to receive communications. You can implement blocking from the Messages app or from the Phone app. Whichever app you start from, blocking the contact prevents you from receiving notifications when the contact phones or messages you.

You can review your list of blocked senders and unblock any sender from whom you want to receive messages again.

Block and Unblock Senders

Block a Sender from the Messages App

1 Press **Home**.

The Home screen appears.

2 Tap **Messages** (⬤).

The Messages screen appears.

Note: If the screen for a contact appears, tap **Back** (❮) to display the Messages screen.

3 Tap a conversation with the contact you want to block.

The conversation opens.

4 Tap **Info** (ⓘ).

The Details screen appears.

5 Tap the contact's name.

The contact record opens.

6 Tap **Block this Caller**.

A confirmation dialog opens.

7 Tap **Block Contact**.

View Your Blocked List and Unblock Senders

1 Press **Home**.

The Home screen appears.

2 Tap **Settings** (⚙️).

The Settings screen appears.

3 Tap **Messages** (💬).

The Messages screen appears.

4 In the SMS/MMS section, tap **Blocked**.

The Blocked screen appears, showing the list of contacts you have blocked.

Ⓐ You can tap **Add New** to display the contacts screen, and then tap the contact you want to block. Blocking the contact blocks all the means of contact, but you can then unblock any means of contact you wish to allow.

5 To unblock a means of contact, swipe its button to the left.

The Unblock button appears.

6 Tap **Unblock**.

TIP

How do I block a contact in the Phone app?
In the Phone app, tap **Contacts** (👤 changes to 👤), tap the contact to display the contact record, and then tap **Block this Caller**. In the confirmation dialog that opens, tap **Block Contact**.

Chat Face-to-Face Using FaceTime

B y using your iPhone's FaceTime feature, you can enjoy video chats with any of your contacts who have an iPhone 4 or later, an iPad 2 or later, an iPad mini, a fourth-generation or later iPod touch, or the FaceTime for Mac app.

To make a FaceTime call, you and your contact must both have Apple IDs. Your iPhone must be connected to either a wireless network or the cellular network. Using a wireless network is preferable because you typically get better performance and do not use up your cellular data allowance.

Chat Face-to-Face Using FaceTime

Receive a FaceTime Call

1 When your iPhone receives a FaceTime request, and the screen shows who is calling, aim the camera at your face, and then tap **Accept** ().

The Connecting screen appears.

When the connection is established, your iPhone displays the caller full-screen, with your video inset.

2 Start your conversation.

3 Tap the screen.

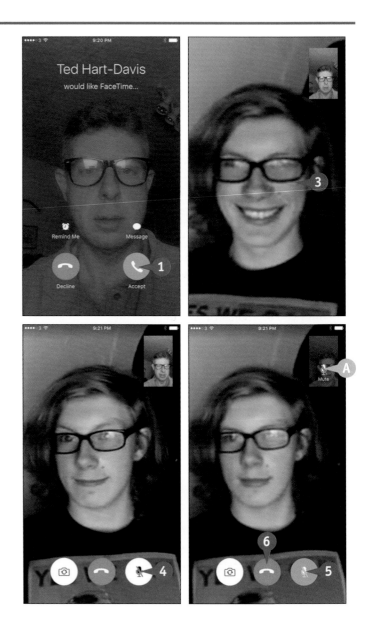

The controls appear.

4 If you need to mute your microphone, tap **Mute** (changes to).

A The Mute icon () appears on your inset video.

5 Tap **Mute** again (changes to) when you want to turn muting off.

6 Tap **End** () when you are ready to end the FaceTime call.

Make a FaceTime Call

1 Press **Home**.

The Home screen appears.

2 Tap **FaceTime** ().

The FaceTime app opens.

3 Tap **Video**.

The Video tab appears.

4 Tap the contact you want to call.

The FaceTime app starts a video call, showing your preview.

5 When your contact answers, smile and speak.

B If you need to show your contact something using the rear-facing camera, tap **Switch Cameras** (📷).

6 When you are ready to end the call, tap **End** (📞).

TIP

Are there other ways of starting a FaceTime call?

Yes. Here are two easy ways to start a FaceTime call:

- Ask Siri to call a contact via FaceTime. For example, press and hold **Home** to summon Siri, and then say "FaceTime John Smith."
- During a phone call, tap **Video** (📹).

CHAPTER 6

Networking and Social Networking

You can control which cellular and wireless networks your iPhone uses and enjoy social networking wherever you go.

Using Airplane Mode

Normally, you will want to keep your iPhone connected to the cellular network so that you can make or receive phone calls and access the Internet. But when you do not need or may not use the cellular network, you can turn on the iPhone's Airplane Mode feature to cut off all connections.

Turning on Airplane Mode turns off Wi-Fi and Bluetooth connections as well, but you can also turn Wi-Fi and Bluetooth on and off separately when you need to.

Using Airplane Mode

① Swipe up from the bottom of the screen.

Control Center opens.

Note: You can open Control Center from within most apps. If you are using an app that blocks Control Center, press **Home** to display the Home screen, and then swipe up to open Control Center.

② Tap **Airplane Mode** ( ).

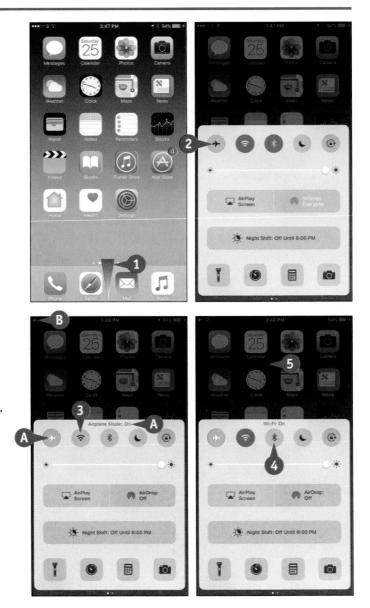

Ⓐ Your iPhone enables Airplane Mode (changes to), turning off all cellular and wireless connections.

Ⓑ An airplane icon appears in the status bar.

③ To turn on Wi-Fi, tap **Wi-Fi** (changes to).

④ To turn on Bluetooth, tap **Bluetooth** (changes to).

⑤ Tap the screen above Control Center.

Control Center closes.

Note: When your iPhone has a wireless network connection, it uses that connection instead of the cellular connection. This helps keep down your cellular network usage and often gives a faster connection.

The Cellular screen appears again.

10 If cellular data is enabled, set each app's switch to On (⬤) or Off (◯), as needed.

11 To see which system services have been using cellular data, tap **System Services**.

The System Services screen appears.

12 Browse the list to identify any services that hog cellular data.

13 Tap **Cellular** (<).

The Cellular screen appears.

14 Tap **Settings** (<).

The Settings screen appears.

15 Tap **General** (⚙).

The General screen appears.

16 Tap **Background App Refresh**.

The Background App Refresh screen appears.

17 Set the **Background App Refresh** switch to On (⬤) or Off (◯), as needed.

18 Assuming you enabled Background App Refresh, set each individual app switch to On (⬤) or Off (◯), as needed.

19 Tap **General** (<).

The General screen appears.

20 Tap **Settings** (<).

The Settings screen appears.

TIP

Which apps should I allow to use Background App Refresh?
Normally, you should restrict Background App Refresh to those apps for which it is important to have updated information immediately available each time you access the app. For example, if you use your iPhone for navigation, getting updated map and GPS information in the background is a good idea, whereas updating magazine subscriptions is usually a waste of cellular data.

Connect Your iPhone to a Different Carrier

Your iPhone's SIM card makes it connect automatically to a particular carrier's network, such as the AT&T network or the Verizon network. If your iPhone is not locked to a particular carrier's network, you can connect the iPhone to a different carrier's network when you go outside the area your carrier covers. For example, if you travel to the United Kingdom, you can connect your iPhone to carriers such as O2, Vodafone, Three, or EE. You may need to change the iPhone's SIM card to connect to another network.

Connect Your iPhone to a Different Carrier

1 Press **Home**.

The Home screen appears.

2 Tap **Settings** (⚙).

The Settings screen appears.

3 Tap **Carrier** (📱).

Note: To connect to a different carrier's network, you may need to set up an account with that carrier or pay extra charges to your standard carrier. You may also need to insert a different SIM card in your iPhone.

The Network Selection screen appears.

4 Set the **Automatic** switch to Off (⬤ changes to ⚪).

The list of available carriers appears.

5 Tap the carrier you want to use.

Note: When you want to switch back to your regular carrier, set the **Automatic** switch on the Network Selection screen to On (⚪ changes to ⬤).

Turn Data Roaming On or Off

When you need to use your iPhone somewhere your carrier does not provide Internet service, you can turn on data roaming, which enables you to access the Internet using other carriers' networks. Data roaming may incur extra charges, especially when you use it in another country, so keep data roaming turned off and turn it on only when you need it. Normally, you will want to use data roaming only when no wireless network connection is available.

Turn Data Roaming On or Off

1 Press **Home**.

The Home screen appears.

2 Tap **Settings** (⚙).

The Settings screen appears.

3 Tap **Cellular** (📶).

The Cellular screen appears.

Ⓐ You can also turn off cellular data altogether by setting the **Cellular Data** switch to Off ( ). Do this when you need to ensure that all apps use Wi-Fi rather than cellular connections.

4 Tap **Cellular Data Options**.

The Cellular Data Options screen appears.

5 Set the **Data Roaming** switch to On (changes to ⚫).

Note: When you need to turn data roaming off again, set the **Data Roaming** switch on the Cellular Data Options screen to Off (changes to).

Connect Bluetooth Devices to Your iPhone

To extend your iPhone's functionality, you can connect devices to it that communicate using the wireless Bluetooth technology.

For example, you can connect a Bluetooth headset and microphone so that you can listen to music and make and take phone calls. Or you can connect a Bluetooth keyboard so that you can quickly type e-mail messages, notes, or documents.

Connect Bluetooth Devices to Your iPhone

Set Up a Bluetooth Device

1. Press **Home**.

   The Home screen appears.

2. Tap **Settings** (⚙).

   The Settings screen appears.

3. Tap **Bluetooth** (🔵).

   The Bluetooth screen appears.

4. Set the **Bluetooth** switch to On (⚪ changes to 🔵).

   The iPhone scans for Bluetooth devices.

5. Turn on the Bluetooth device and make it discoverable.

Note: Read the Bluetooth device's instructions to find out how to make the device discoverable via Bluetooth.

Ⓐ Devices in the My Devices list are already paired with your iPhone. You can tap a device to connect it.

6. Tap the device's button.

B For a device such as a keyboard or a computer, the Bluetooth Pairing Request dialog opens.

7 Type the code on the device.

The iPhone pairs with the device and then connects to it.

C The My Devices list shows the device as Connected. You can start using the device.

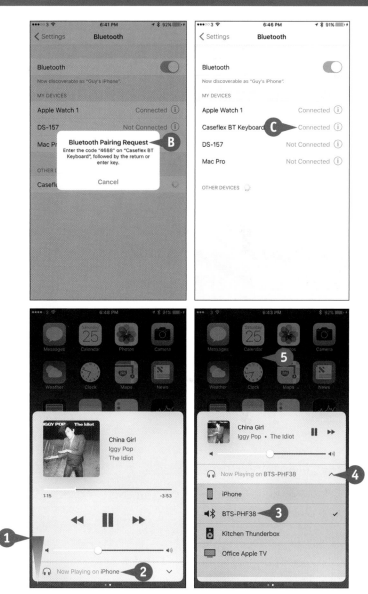

Choose the Device for Playing Audio or Taking a Call

1 Swipe up from the bottom of the screen.

Note: This example uses the Music app.

Control Center opens.

2 Tap **Now Playing on**.

The Now Playing On panel opens.

3 Tap the device you want to use.

4 Tap **Now Playing on**.

The Now Playing On panel closes.

5 Tap the app above Control Center.

Control Center closes.

TIP

How do I stop using a Bluetooth device?

When you no longer need to use a particular Bluetooth device, tell your iPhone to forget it. Press **Home**, and then tap **Settings** (⚙). Tap **Bluetooth** (✷), and then tap **Info** (ⓘ) for the device. On the device's screen, tap **Forget This Device**, and then tap **Forget Device** in the confirmation dialog.

Share Items via AirDrop

AirDrop enables you to share files quickly and easily with iOS devices and Macs near your iPhone. For example, you can use AirDrop to share a photo, a contact record, or an item from Wallet. You can use AirDrop in any app that displays a Share button (⬆).

You can turn AirDrop on when you need it and off when you do not. When AirDrop is on, you can choose between accepting items only from your contacts or from everyone.

Share Items via AirDrop

Turn AirDrop On or Off

1. Swipe up from the bottom of the screen.

   Control Center opens.

   A The readout shows AirDrop's status: *AirDrop: Receiving Off*; *AirDrop: Contacts Only*; or *AirDrop: Everyone*.

2. Tap **AirDrop**.

Note: AirDrop uses Wi-Fi or Bluetooth to transfer files wirelessly without the devices having to be on the same wireless network.

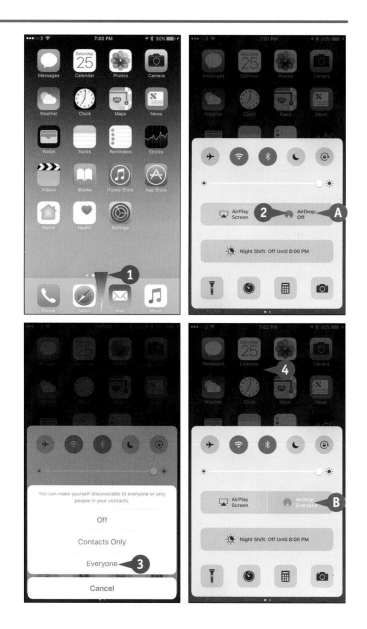

   The AirDrop dialog opens.

3. Tap **Receiving Off**, **Contacts Only**, or **Everyone**, as needed.

   The AirDrop dialog closes.

   B The AirDrop readout shows the AirDrop setting you chose.

4. Tap the screen above Control Center.

   Control Center closes.

Share an Item via AirDrop

1 Open the app that contains the item. For example, tap **Photos** (🌸) on the Home screen.

2 Navigate to the item you want to share. For example, tap a photo to open it.

3 Tap **Share** (📤).

The Share sheet appears.

C In some apps, you can select other items to share at the same time. For example, in Photos, you can select other photos.

4 In the AirDrop area, tap the contact or device you want to send the item to.

Receive an Item via AirDrop

D When someone tries to send you an item via AirDrop, the AirDrop dialog opens.

E You can tap **Cancel** if you do not want to receive the item. You may need to react quickly, because iOS automatically accepts the item.

F Your iPhone stores the item in the appropriate app and displays it if possible. For example, when you receive a photo, the Photos app opens and displays the photo so that you can enjoy it, edit it, delete it, or all three.

TIPS

Which devices can use AirDrop?
AirDrop works on all iPhone, iPad, and iPod touch models that have the Lightning port rather than the older, larger Dock Connector port.

Does AirDrop pose a security threat to my iPhone and data?
AirDrop encrypts files so it can transfer them securely. When using AirDrop, you choose which files — if any — you want to share from your iPhone; other iOS devices and Macs cannot use AirDrop to grab files from your iPhone.

Share Internet Access via Personal Hotspot

Your iPhone can not only access the Internet itself from anywhere it has a suitable connection to the cellular network, but it can also share that Internet access with your computer and other devices. This feature is called *Personal Hotspot*.

For you to use Personal Hotspot, your iPhone's carrier must permit you to use it. Some carriers charge an extra fee per month on top of the standard data plan charge.

Share Internet Access via Personal Hotspot

Set Up Personal Hotspot

1. Press **Home**.

   The Home screen appears.

2. Tap **Settings** (⚙).

   The Settings screen appears.

3. Tap **Personal Hotspot** (📶).

The Personal Hotspot screen appears.

4. Tap **Wi-Fi Password**.

   The Wi-Fi Password screen appears.

5. Tap **Delete** (ⓧ) to delete the default password.

6. Type the password you want to use.

7. Tap **Done**.

The Personal Hotspot screen appears again.

⑧ Set the **Personal Hotspot** switch to On (⚪ changes to 🔵).

The Personal Hotspot screen shows the message *Now Discoverable* and displays information for connecting computers and devices to the hotspot.

You can now connect your computer or other devices.

🅐 The blue bar at the top of the screen shows how many computers or devices are connected to Personal Hotspot.

Stop Using Personal Hotspot

① Press **Home**.

The Home screen appears.

② Tap the Personal Hotspot bar.

The Personal Hotspot screen appears.

③ Set the **Personal Hotspot** switch to Off (🔵 changes to ⚪).

TIP

How else can I connect a PC or Mac to Personal Hotspot?

Usually, you can connect a PC to Personal Hotspot by simply connecting your iPhone to the PC via USB. Windows automatically detects the iPhone's Internet connection as a new network connection and installs any software needed.

Similarly, you can connect a Mac via USB, but you may need to configure the network connection. `Control`+click or right-click **System Preferences** (🖥️) on the Dock and click **Network** on the contextual menu to open the Network preferences pane. In the left pane, click **iPhone USB**. If the Apply button is dark, click **Apply**.

If you cannot get USB to work, connect the computer via Wi-Fi or Bluetooth, if your computer has either of those features.

Connect to Wi-Fi Networks and Hotspots

To conserve your data allowance, use a Wi-Fi network instead of the cell phone network whenever you can. Your iPhone can connect to both private Wi-Fi networks and to public Wi-Fi hotspots.

The first time you connect to a Wi-Fi network, you must provide the network's password. After that, the iPhone stores the password, so you can connect to the network without entering the password again.

Connect to Wi-Fi Networks and Hotspots

Connect to a Network Listed on the Wi-Fi Screen

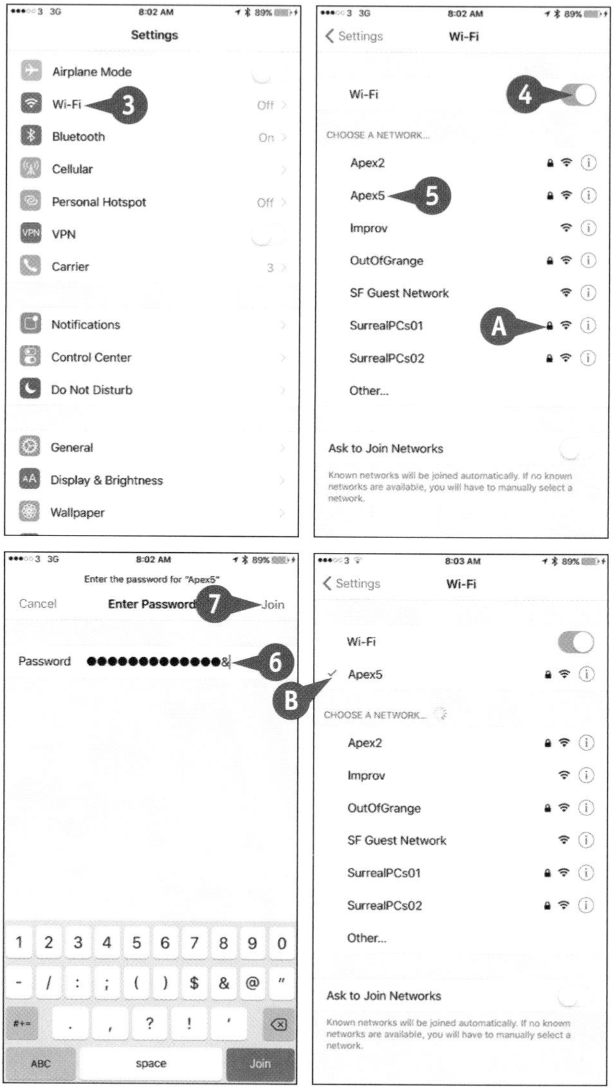

1. Press **Home**.

   The Home screen appears.

2. Tap **Settings** ( ).

   The Settings screen appears.

3. Tap **Wi-Fi** ( ).

   The Wi-Fi screen appears.

4. If Wi-Fi is off, set the **Wi-Fi** switch to On (changes to).

   The Choose a Network list appears.

A. A lock icon ( ) indicates the network has security such as a password.

5. Tap the network you want to connect to.

Note: If the network does not have a password, your iPhone connects to it without prompting you for a password.

Note: When connecting to a Wi-Fi hotspot, you may need to enter login information in Safari. In this case, Safari usually opens automatically and prompts you to log in.

   The Enter Password screen appears.

6. Type the password.
7. Tap **Join**.

   Your iPhone connects to the wireless network.

B. The Wi-Fi screen appears again, showing a check mark (✓) next to the network the iPhone has connected to.

Connect to a Network Not Listed on the Wi-Fi Screen

1 On the Wi-Fi screen, tap **Other**.

The Other Network screen appears.

2 Type the network name.

Note: If the network does not use security, tap **Join**.

C The Wi-Fi signal icons () on the Wi-Fi screen and in the status bar show the strength of the Wi-Fi signals. The more bars that appear, the stronger a signal is.

3 Tap **Security**.

The Security screen appears.

4 Tap the security type — for example, **WPA2**.

5 Tap **Other Network** (<).

The Other Network screen appears.

6 Type the password.

7 Tap **Join**.

Your iPhone joins the network.

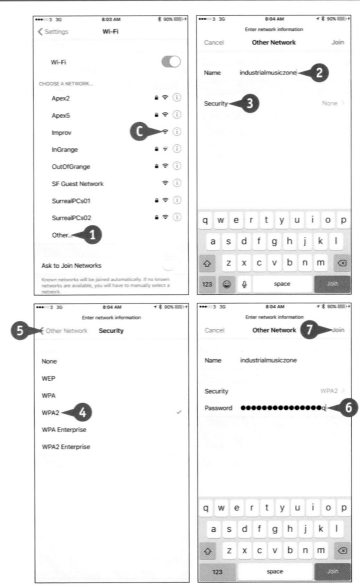

TIPS

What does the Ask to Join Networks switch control?

Your iPhone automatically connects to networks it "knows" — those it has connected to before. Set the **Ask to Join Networks** switch to On () if you want your iPhone to prompt you when unknown networks are available.

How do I stop using a particular wireless network?

Tap **Info** (ⓘ) to the right of the network's name on the Wi-Fi screen. On the network's screen, tap **Forget This Network**. In the dialog that opens, tap **Forget**.

Always forget a Wi-Fi hotspot you will not use again. Forgetting the hotspot helps prevent your iPhone from connecting to a malevolent hotspot that mimics the genuine hotspot.

Set Up Your Social Network Accounts

With built-in support for several types of social networks — including Facebook, Twitter, Flickr, and Vimeo — your iPhone enables you to post updates, photos, and videos to your accounts on these social networks. For example, you can quickly create a Facebook post or a Twitter tweet from the Notifications screen, or you can share a photo from the Photos app or the Camera app.

Before you can use a social network, you must enter the details of your account.

Set Up Your Social Network Accounts

Open the Settings App and Set Up Your Twitter Account

1 Press **Home**.

The Home screen appears.

2 Tap **Settings** (⚙).

The Settings screen appears.

3 Tap **Twitter** (🐦).

The Twitter screen appears.

4 Type your username.

Note: To create a new Twitter account, tap **Create New Account** and follow the resulting screens.

5 Type your password.

6 Tap **Sign In**.

Twitter verifies your username and password, and then sets up your account on the iPhone.

Ⓐ You can tap **Update Contacts** to add Twitter usernames and photos to your Contacts.

7 Set the **Siri** switch to On (⬤) if you want to tweet via Siri.

8 Set the **Twitter** switch to On (⬤) if you want to tweet from the Twitter app.

9 Tap **Settings** (‹).

The Settings screen appears.

148

Set Up Your Facebook Account

 1 On the Settings screen, tap
Facebook ().

The Facebook screen appears.

2 Type your username.

Note: To create a new Facebook account, tap
Create New Account and follow the resulting
screens.

3 Type your password.

4 Tap **Sign In**.

The Sign In screen appears.

5 Tap **Sign In**.

The Facebook screen appears again.

6 Set the **Calendars** switch, the **Contacts**
switch, and the **Facebook** switch to On (○)
or Off (   ), as needed.

7 Tap **Settings**.

The Settings screen for Facebook appears.

8 Tap **Location**; tap **Never**, **While Using the
App**, or **Always**, as needed; and then tap
Facebook (<).

9 Set the **Photos** switch, **Background App
Refresh** switch, **Cellular Data** switch, and
Upload HD switch to On (○) or Off (   ), as
needed.

10 Tap **Facebook** (<).

The Facebook screen appears again.

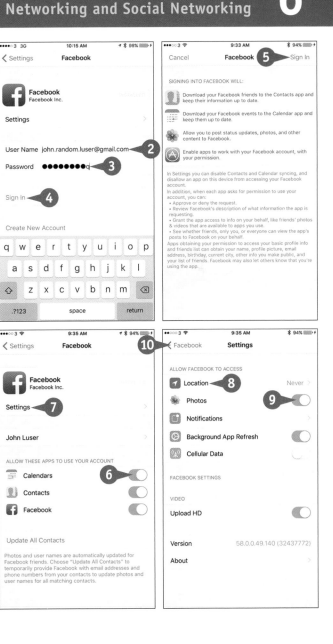

TIP

How do I set up my Flickr account and Vimeo account?

To set up a Flickr account or Vimeo account, tap **Flickr** or **Vimeo** on the Settings screen. If the Install
button appears, the app is not yet installed, so you need to tap **Install** to install it. You can then return to
the Settings screen, type your username and password, and tap **Sign In**.

Share Your Updates Using Twitter

Your iPhone's apps are fully integrated with Twitter, the online microblogging service. You can tweet either by working in the Twitter app itself or by starting from the app that contains the content you want to share.

When you want to send a short text tweet, the Twitter app is usually the easiest way to work. If you need to send a photo, you can start from the Photos app and create a tweet in moments.

Share Your Updates Using Twitter

Send a Text Tweet

1 Press **Home**.

The Home screen appears.

2 Tap **Twitter** (🐦).

Note: If Twitter does not appear on the Home screen, tap **Settings** (⚙), tap **Twitter**, and then tap **Install**.

The Twitter app opens.

3 Tap **New Tweet** (✍).

The New Tweet screen appears.

4 Tap **What's happening?** and type the text of the tweet.

A The readout shows the number of characters left.

Note: You can also tap the microphone icon (🎤) to activate Siri, and then dictate the text of the tweet.

5 Tap **Location** (📍) if you want to add your location to the tweet.

6 Tap **Tweet**.

Twitter posts the tweet to your Twitter account.

Send a Photo Tweet

1 From the Home screen, tap **Photos** ( ).

The Photos app opens.

2 Navigate to the album or other category that holds the photo you want to tweet. For example, tap **All Photos**.

3 Tap the photo to display it.

4 Tap **Share** ( ).

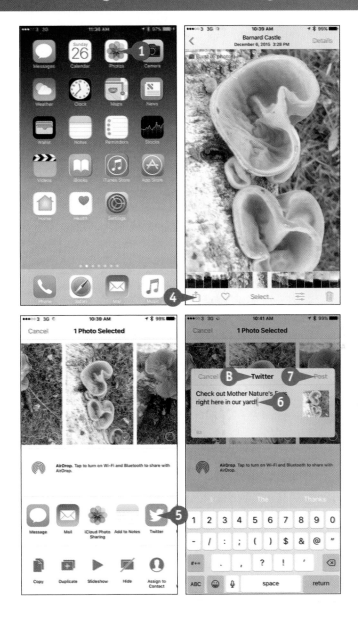

The Share sheet appears.

5 Tap **Twitter** ( ).

B The Twitter dialog opens, showing the tweet with the photo attached.

6 Type the text of the tweet.

7 Tap **Post**.

Your iPhone posts the tweet.

TIPS

How do I read other people's tweets?
To read other people's tweets, use the Twitter app. Press **Home** to display the Home screen, tap **Twitter** ( ), and then tap **Home** (changes to) to catch up on tweets from the Twitter accounts you are following.

How can I send tweets from other apps?
You can use the Share sheet method to send tweets from many apps. The general steps are to open the app, select the item, tap **Share** ( ), and then tap **Twitter** ( ) on the Share sheet. You can then complete the tweet and post it.

Post Updates on Facebook

If you have an account on Facebook, the world's biggest social network, you can post updates directly from your iPhone with a minimum of fuss.

You can work either from within the Facebook app or from apps that contain content suitable for Facebook posts. This section shows an example of posting a status update from the Facebook app and an example of posting a photo from the Photos app.

Post Updates on Facebook

Post an Update Using the Facebook App

1 Press **Home**.

The Home screen appears.

2 Tap **Facebook** ().

Note: If Facebook does not appear on the Home screen, tap **Settings** (⚙), tap **Facebook** (📘), and then tap **Install**.

The Facebook app opens.

3 Tap **Status** (📝).

The Update Status screen appears.

4 Tap **Share With**, the pop-up menu that shows the group set to receive the update.

The Share With screen appears.

5 Tap the appropriate group, such as **Public** or **Friends except acquaintances**.

6 Tap **Done**.

The Update Status screen appears again, now showing the group you chose.

7 Type your update.

8 Tap **Post**.

Post a Photo Update

1 In the Photos app, navigate to the photo you want to post. For example, tap **Albums** and then tap the album that contains the photo.

2 Tap the photo to display it.

3 Tap **Share** (⬆).

The Share sheet appears.

4 Tap **Facebook** (f).

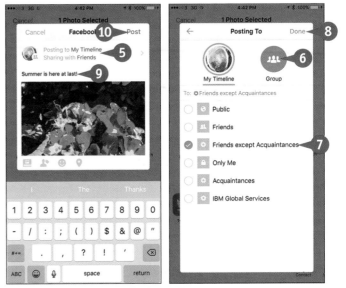

The Facebook dialog opens.

5 Tap **Posting to**.

The Posting To dialog opens.

6 Tap **My Timeline** or **Group**, as needed.

7 If you choose Group, tap the group, such as **Friends** or **Friends except Acquaintances**.

8 Tap **Done**.

The Facebook dialog opens again.

Note: You can take other actions by tapping **Album** (🖼), **Tag Friends** (👥), **What Are You Doing?** (☺), or **Check In** (📍).

9 Type the text for the update.

10 Tap **Post**.

TIP

From what other apps can I post updates to Facebook?

You can post updates to Facebook from any app to which the developer has added Facebook integration. For example, you can post a location from the Maps app or a lecture from iTunes U to Facebook.

To see whether you can post updates to Facebook from an app, tap **Share** (⬆) from the app. If Facebook appears on the Share sheet, you can post an update to Facebook.

CHAPTER 7

Working with Apps

iOS enables you to customize the Home screen, putting the icons you need most right at hand and organizing them into folders. You can switch instantly among the apps you are running, find the apps you need on Apple's App Store, and update and remove apps. You can also work easily with text and take notes.

Customize the Home Screen

From the Home screen, you run the apps on your iPhone. You can customize the Home screen to put the apps you use most frequently within easy reach. You can create further Home screens as needed and move the app icons among them. You can customize the Home screen by working on the iPhone, as described here. If you synchronize your iPhone with a computer, you can use iTunes instead. This is an easier way to make extensive changes, such as changing the order of the Home screens.

Customize the Home Screen

Unlock the Icons for Customization

1 Press **Home**.

The Home screen appears.

2 Swipe left or right to display the Home screen you want to customize.

Ⓐ You can also tap the dots to move from one Home screen to another.

3 Tap and hold the icon you want to move.

Note: You can tap and hold any icon until the apps start jiggling. Usually, it is easiest to tap and hold the icon you want to move, and then drag that icon.

The icons start to jiggle, indicating that you can move them.

Move an Icon Within a Home Screen

1 After unlocking the icons, drag the icon to where you want it.

The other icons move out of the way.

2 When the icon is in the right place, drop it.

Ⓑ The icon stays in its new position.

Move an Icon to a Different Home Screen

1 After unlocking the icons, drag the icon to the left edge of the screen to display the previous Home screen or to the right edge to display the next Home screen.

The previous Home screen or next Home screen appears.

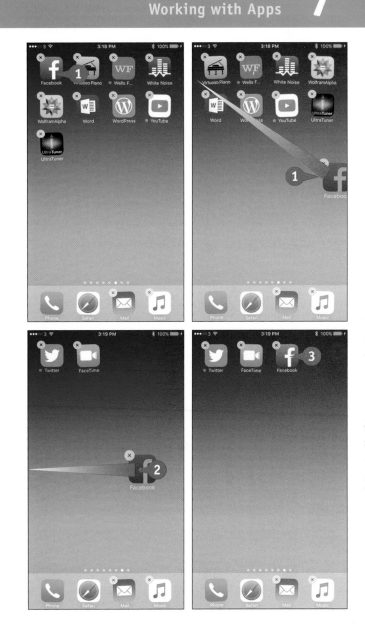

2 Drag the icon to where you want it.

If the Home screen contains other icons, they move out of the way as needed.

3 Drop the icon.

The icon stays in its new position.

Stop Customizing the Home Screen

1 Press **Home**.

The icons stop jiggling.

TIP

How can I put the default apps back into their original Home screen locations?
Press **Home**, tap **Settings** (), and then tap **General** (⚙). Tap and drag up to scroll down the screen, and then tap **Reset**. On the Reset screen, tap **Reset Home Screen Layout**, and then tap **Reset Home Screen** in the dialog that opens. Press **Home** to return to the Home screen.

Organize Apps with Folders

To organize the Home screen, you can arrange the items into folders. The iPhone's default Home screen layout includes a folder named Extras, which contains items such as the Contacts app and the Compass app, but you can create as many other folders as you need. Like the Home screen, each folder can have multiple pages, so you can put many apps in a folder.

Organize Apps with Folders

Create a Folder

1 Display the Home screen that contains the item you want to put into a folder.

2 Tap and hold the item until the icons start to jiggle.

Note: When creating a folder, you may find it easiest to first put both items you will add to the folder on the same screen.

3 Drag the item to the other icon you want to place in the folder you create.

The iPhone creates a folder, puts both icons in it, and assigns a default name based on the genre.

4 Tap **Delete** () in the folder name box.

The folder name is deleted.

The keyboard appears.

5 Type the name for the folder.

6 Tap outside the folder.

The iPhone applies the name to the folder.

7 Press **Home**.

The icons stop jiggling.

Note: You can quickly rename a folder by force-touching it, tapping **Rename**, typing the new name, and then tapping outside the folder.

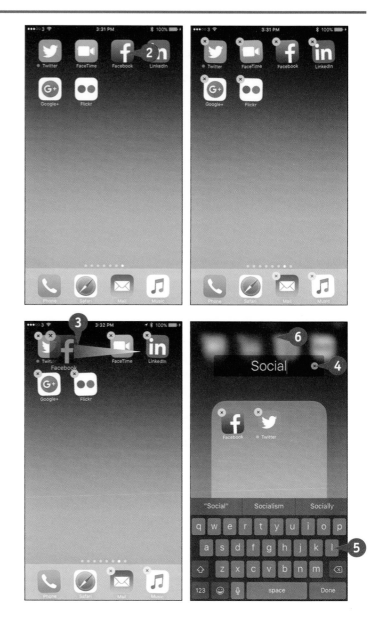

Open an Item in a Folder

1 Display the Home screen that contains the folder.

2 Tap the folder's icon.

The folder's contents appear, and the items outside the folder fade and blur.

3 If necessary, swipe left or right or tap a dot to navigate to another page in the folder.

4 Tap the item you want to open.

The item opens.

Add an Item to a Folder

1 Display the Home screen that contains the item.

2 Tap and hold the item until the icons start to jiggle.

3 Drag the icon on top of the folder and drop it there.

Note: If the folder is on a different Home screen from the icon, drag the icon to the left edge to display the previous Home screen or to the right edge to display the next Home screen.

The item goes into the folder.

4 Press **Home** to stop the icons jiggling.

TIPS

How do I take an item out of a folder?
Tap the folder to display its contents, and then tap and hold the item until the icons start to jiggle. Drag the item out of the folder, drag it to where you want it on the Home screen, and then drop it.

How do I create another page in a folder?
Open the folder, and then tap and hold an item until the icons start jiggling. Drag the item to the right side of the current page. A new page appears automatically.

Switch Quickly from One App to Another

You can run many apps on your iPhone at the same time, switching from one app to another as needed.

You can switch apps by pressing Home to display the Home screen and then tapping the icon for the next app. But the iPhone also has an app-switching screen that enables you to switch quickly from one running app to another running app. From the app-switching screen, you can also easily close one or more running apps.

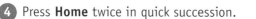

Switch Quickly from One App to Another

1 Press **Home**.

The Home screen appears.

2 Tap the app you want to launch. This example uses **Maps** ( ).

The app's screen appears.

3 Start using the app as usual.

4 Press **Home** twice in quick succession.

Ⓐ The app-switching screen appears, showing a carousel of thumbnails of the open apps.

Ⓑ The icons identify the app thumbnails.

5 Swipe left or right to scroll until you see the app you want.

Note: The last app you used appears on the right side of the app-switching screen. To its right is the Home screen. To its left are the apps you have used most recently.

6 Tap the app.

The app appears.

7 When you are ready to switch back, press **Home** twice in quick succession.

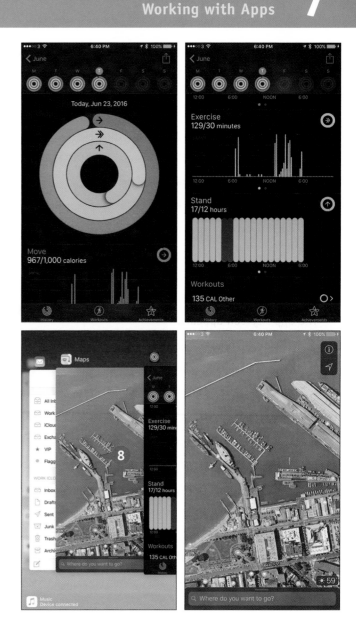

The app-switching screen appears.

8 Scroll left or right as needed, and then tap the app to which you want to return.

The app appears, ready to resume from where you stopped using it.

TIP

How do I stop an app that is not responding?

If an app stops responding, you can quickly close it from the app-switching screen. Press **Home** twice to open the app-switching screen. Scroll to the problem app and then drag it upward so it disappears off the screen. Tap the app you want to use or press **Home** to return to the Home screen.

You can use this move to close any app that you no longer want to use, whether or not it has stopped responding. For example, if an app seems to be devouring battery power, you can use this technique to close it.

Find Apps on the App Store

The iPhone comes with essential apps, such as Safari for surfing the web, Mail for e-mail, and Calendar for keeping track of your schedule. But to get the most out of your iPhone, you will likely need to add other apps.

To get apps, you use the App Store, which provides apps that Apple has approved as correctly programmed, suitable for purpose, and free of malevolent code. Before you can download any apps, including free apps, you must create an App Store account.

Find Apps on the App Store

1 Press **Home**.

The Home screen appears.

2 Tap **App Store** (⊘).

The App Store screen appears.

Usually, the Featured screen appears at first.

3 Tap **Categories** (☐ changes to ☐).

The Categories screen appears.

4 Tap the category you want to see. This example uses the **Productivity** category.

The category's screen appears.

5 Tap and drag to see additional apps in a list, or tap and drag up to see other lists. Then tap **See All** to display your chosen list.

The screen shows the list you chose.

6 Tap the app you want to view.

The app's screen appears.

Note: To understand what an app does and how well it does it, look at the app's rating, read the description, and read the user reviews. Swipe the images to see screen captures from the app.

Ⓐ The Offers Apple Watch App readout indicates the app has a companion app for Apple Watch.

7 Tap the price button or the **Get** button.

The price button or Get button changes to an Install button.

8 Tap **Install**.

Note: If the iPhone prompts you to sign in, type your password and then tap **OK**.

Note: If you have not created an App Store account already, the iPhone prompts you to create one now.

The iPhone downloads and installs the app.

9 Tap **Open**.

The app opens, and you can start using it.

TIP

Why does App Store not appear on the Home screen or when I search for it?

If App Store (⬜) does not appear on the Home screen, and if searching for it does not show a result, the iPhone has restrictions applied that prevent you from installing apps. You can remove these restrictions if you know the restrictions passcode. Press **Home**, tap **Settings** (⚙), and then tap **General** (⚙). Scroll down, and then tap **Restrictions**. Type the passcode on the Enter Passcode screen, and then set the **Installing Apps** switch to On (⬜ changes to ⬤).

Update and Remove Apps

To keep your iPhone's apps running smoothly, you should install app updates when they become available. Most updates for paid apps are free, but you must often pay to upgrade to a new version of the app.

When you no longer need an app you have installed on your iPhone, you can remove it, thus recovering the space it occupied. You can remove some but not all of the built-in apps.

Update and Remove Apps

Update an App

1 Press **Home**.

The Home screen appears.

A The badge on the App Store icon shows the number of available updates.

2 Tap **App Store** (Ⓐ).

The App Store screen appears.

3 Tap **Updates** (⬆).

Note: You can force-touch **App Store** (Ⓐ) on the Home screen and then tap **Update All** on the force-touch panel to update all apps easily.

Note: You can also update apps using your computer. In iTunes, click **Apps** (Ⓐ), click the **Updates** tab, and then click **Update All Apps**. Then connect your iPhone and click **Sync**.

The Updates screen appears.

4 Tap **Update All** to apply all the available updates now.

B You can tap **Update** to update a single app.

C You can tap **Purchased** to display the All Purchases screen. You can then tap **My Purchases** to view the list of apps you have purchased.

From the resulting screen, which shows your name at the top, you can update individual apps or install apps you have bought but not yet installed on this iPhone.

Remove an App from the iPhone

1 Press **Home**.

   The Home screen appears.

2 Display the Home screen that contains the app you want to delete.

3 Tap and hold the item until the icons start to jiggle.

4 Tap **Delete** (⊗) on the icon.

   The Delete dialog appears.

5 Tap **Delete**.

   The iPhone deletes the app, and the app's icon disappears.

6 Press **Home**.

   The icons stop jiggling.

TIP

How do I remove an app using my computer?

Connect your iPhone to your computer. Then, in iTunes on the computer, click **iPhone** (▯), click **Apps** (⚒) in the Source list on the left, and then click **Remove** to the right of the app. Click **Sync** to effect the change.

Cut, Copy, and Paste Text

You can easily type text on your iPhone's keyboard or dictate it using Siri, but if the text already exists, you can copy and paste the text instead. This section demonstrates copying text from an e-mail message and pasting it into a Pages document.

If the text is in a document you can edit, you can either copy the text or cut it. If the text is in a document you cannot edit, you can only copy the text.

Cut, Copy, and Paste Text

Open an App and Copy Text

1 Press **Home**.

The Home screen appears.

Note: This example uses the Mail app, but you can cut, copy, and paste text in many other apps as well.

2 Tap **Mail** (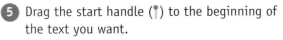).

The Mail app opens.

3 Tap the message you want to open.

The message's contents appear.

4 Double-tap a word in the section of text you want to copy or cut.

The word becomes highlighted.

Selection handles appear around the selection.

Ⓐ The formatting bar appears.

5 Drag the start handle (⌖) to the beginning of the text you want.

6 Drag the end handle (⌖) to the end of the text you want.

7 Tap **Copy**.

Your iPhone places the text on the Clipboard, a hidden storage area.

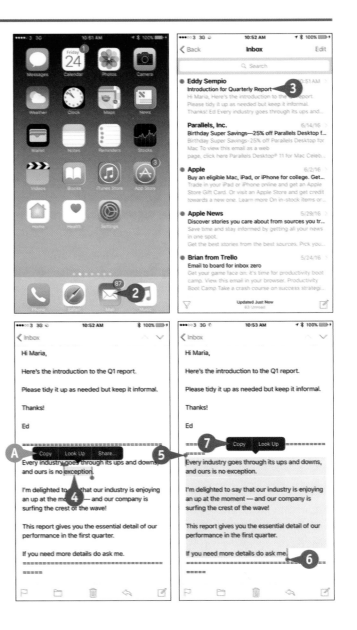

Paste the Content You Have Copied or Cut

1 Press **Home**.

The Home screen appears.

2 Tap the app into which you want to paste the text. This example uses Notes, but you can use many other apps.

The app opens.

3 Create a new document or open an existing document, as needed. For example, in Notes, tap **New** () to create a new note.

The document opens.

4 Tap where you want to paste the text.

The formatting bar opens.

5 Tap **Paste**.

Ⓑ The copied text appears in the document.

TIPS

How many items can I store on the Clipboard?

You can store only one item on the Clipboard at a time. Each item you cut or copy replaces the existing item on the Clipboard. But until you replace the existing item on the Clipboard, you can paste it as many times as needed.

Can I transfer the contents of the Clipboard to my computer?

You cannot transfer the Clipboard's contents directly to your computer, but you can easily transfer it indirectly. For example, paste it into an e-mail message and send it to yourself, or paste it into a note in the Notes app and sync your devices.

Bold, Italicize, Underline, and Replace Text

Some apps enable you to add text formatting such as boldface, underline, and italics to text to make parts of it stand out. For example, you can apply formatting in e-mail messages you create using the Mail app on some e-mail services and in various apps for creating word-processing documents.

To apply formatting, you first select the text, and then choose options from the pop-up formatting bar. Some apps also offer other text commands, such as replacing a word or phrase from a menu of suggestions.

Bold, Italicize, Underline, and Replace Text

Apply Bold, Italics, and Underline

1 Tap and hold the text to which you want to apply bold, italics, or underline.

The formatting bar appears.

2 Tap **Select**.

Part of the text becomes highlighted, and the selection handles appear.

3 Drag the start handle (⌐) to the beginning of the text you want.

4 Drag the end handle (⌐) to the end of the text you want.

5 Tap **B**/**U** on the formatting bar.

The formatting bar displays formatting options.

6 Tap **Bold**, **Italic**, or **Underline**, as needed.

The text takes on the formatting you chose.

7 Tap outside the selected text to deselect it.

Note: Some apps have their own formatting tools, many of which are more extensive than the standard formatting tools shown here.

Note: Some e-mail services and notes services do not support formatting.

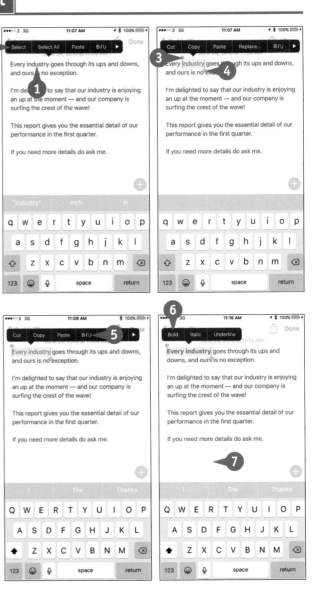

Replace Text with Suggested Words

1 Double-tap the word you want to replace.

Note: You can tap and hold anywhere in the word, and then tap **Select** on the formatting bar to select the word.

The word becomes highlighted and selection handles appear around it.

The formatting bar appears.

2 Tap **Replace**.

The formatting bar displays suggested replacement words.

3 Tap the word with which you want to replace the selected word.

The word you tapped appears in the text.

Note: Tap **More** () to display more commands on the formatting bar. For example, in some apps, you can insert photos and videos.

TIP

What does the Quote Level button on the pop-up formatting bar in Mail do?

Tap **Quote Level** when you need to increase or decrease the quote level of your selected text. You may need to tap **More** (▶) to display the Quote Level button. When you tap Quote Level, the formatting bar displays an Increase button and a Decrease button. Tap **Increase** to increase the quote level, indenting the text more and adding a colored bar to its left, or **Decrease** to decrease the quote level, reducing the existing indent and removing a colored bar.

CHAPTER 8

Browsing the Web and E-Mailing

Your iPhone is fully equipped to browse the web and send e-mail via a Wi-Fi connection or via the cellular network.

Browse the Web with Safari

Your iPhone comes equipped with the Safari app, which enables you to browse the web. You can quickly go to a web page by entering its address in the Address box or by following a link.

Although you can browse quickly by opening a single web page at a time, you may prefer to open multiple pages and switch back and forth among them. Safari makes this easy to do.

Browse the Web with Safari

Open Safari and Navigate to Web Pages

1 Press **Home**.

The Home screen appears.

2 Tap **Safari** ( ).

Safari opens and loads the last web page that was shown.

3 Tap the Address box.

Safari selects the current contents of the Address box, and the keyboard appears.

4 Tap **Delete** ( ) if you need to delete the contents of the Address box.

5 Type the address of the page you want to open.

Ⓐ You can also tap a search result that Safari displays below the Address box.

6 Tap **Go**.

Safari displays the page.

7 Tap a link on the page.

Safari displays that page.

Ⓑ After going to a new page, tap **Back** (<) to display the previous page. You can then tap **Forward** (>) to go forward again.

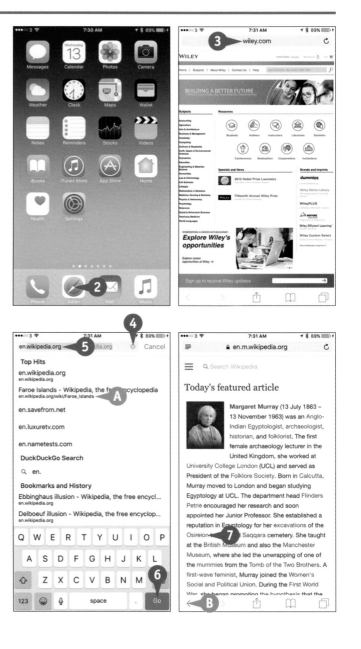

Open Multiple Pages and Navigate Among Them

1 Tap **Pages** (▢).

Safari displays the list of open pages, each bearing a Close button (✕).

ⓒ Below the list of open pages, you can find a list of recent pages you opened on other devices that use the same iCloud account.

2 Tap **New Page** (➕).

Note: In landscape orientation, a large-screen iPhone displays a tab bar at the top of the screen. Tap the tab for the page you want to view.

Safari opens a new page and displays your bookmarks.

3 Tap the Address box, and then go to the page you want.

Note: You can also go to a page by using a bookmark, as described in the next section, "Access Websites Quickly with Bookmarks."

The page appears.

4 To switch to another page, tap **Pages** (▢).

Safari displays the list of pages.

5 Tap the page you want to see.

ⓓ You can tap **Close** (✕) to close a page.

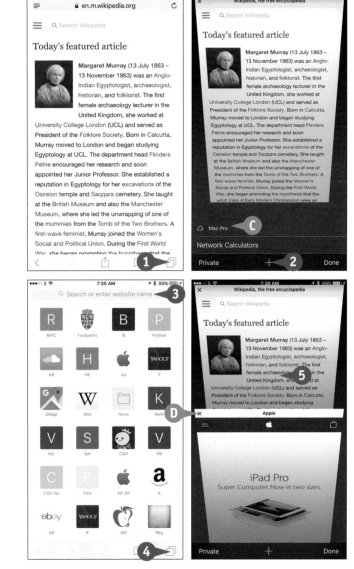

TIPS

How do I search for information?
Tap the Address box to select its current contents, and then type your search terms. Safari searches as you type; you can type further to narrow down the results, and stop as soon as you see suitable results. Tap the result you want to see, and then tap a link on the results page that Safari opens.

How can I return to a tab I closed by mistake?
Tap **Pages** (▢) to display the list of open pages, and then tap and hold **New Page** (➕). On the Recently Closed Tabs screen that appears, tap the tab you want to reopen.

Access Websites Quickly with Bookmarks

Typing web addresses can be laborious, even with the help that the iPhone's keyboard adds, so you will probably want to use bookmarks to access websites you visit often.

By syncing your existing bookmarks from your computer or online account, as described in Chapter 1, you can instantly provide your iPhone with quick access to the web pages you want to visit most frequently. You can also create bookmarks on your iPhone, as discussed in the next section, "Create Bookmarks."

Access Websites Quickly with Bookmarks

Open the Bookmarks Screen

1. Press **Home**.

   The Home screen appears.

2. Tap **Safari** ().

   Safari opens.

3. Tap **Bookmarks** (📖).

   The Bookmarks screen appears.

Note: You can display the Bookmarks screen quickly from the Home screen by 3D-touching **Safari** (⊘) and then tapping **Show Bookmarks** on the Peek panel.

Explore Your History

1. On the Bookmarks screen, tap **History**.

   A list of the web pages you have recently visited appears.

   Ⓐ You can tap a time or a day to display the list of web pages you visited then.

   Ⓑ You can tap **Search History** (🔍) and type search terms to search for particular pages.

2. Tap **Bookmarks** (<) to return to the Bookmarks screen.

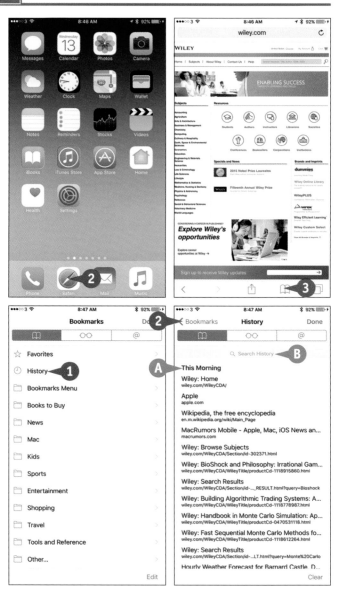

Explore a Bookmarks Category

1 On the Bookmarks screen, tap the bookmarks folder or category you want to see. This example uses the **Mac** folder.

The contents of the folder or category appear. For example, the contents of the Mac folder appear.

2 Tap the **Back** button (**<**) one or more times to go back. The button's name depends on the previous folder — in this case, you would tap **Bookmarks** (**<**).

Open a Bookmarked Page

C You can delete a bookmark by swiping it to the left and then tapping **Delete**.

1 When you find the bookmark for the web page you want to open, tap the bookmark.

D The web page opens.

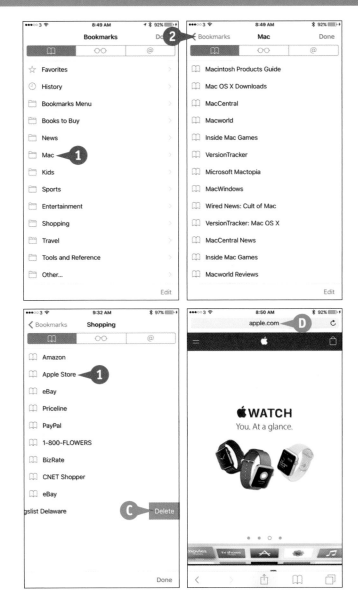

TIP

How can I quickly access a website?

Creating a bookmark within Safari — as discussed in the next section, "Create Bookmarks" — is good for sites you access now and then. But if you access a site frequently, create an icon for it on your Home screen. Open the site in Safari. Tap **Share** (⬆), tap **Add to Home Screen** (➕), type the name on the Add to Home screen, and then tap **Add**. You can then go straight to the page by tapping its icon on the Home screen.

Create Bookmarks

When you want to access a web page again easily, create a bookmark for it. If you have set your iPhone to sync bookmarks with your iCloud account, the bookmark becomes available on your computer or online account as well when you sync.

If you create many bookmarks, it is usually helpful to create multiple folders in which you can organize the bookmarks. You can create folders easily on the iPhone and choose the folder in which to store each bookmark.

Create a Bookmark

1 Press **Home**.

The Home screen appears.

2 Tap **Safari** ().

Safari opens and displays the last web page you were viewing.

3 Navigate to the web page you want to bookmark.

4 Tap **Share** (□).

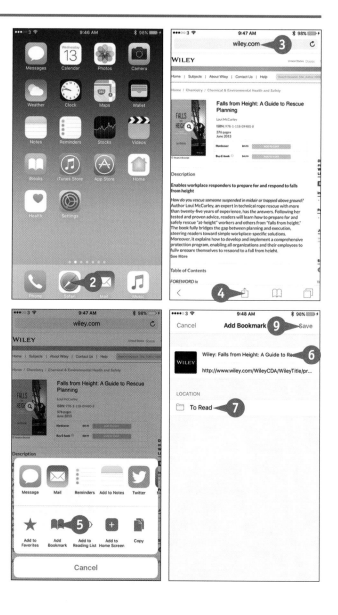

The Share sheet appears.

5 Tap **Add Bookmark** (□□).

The Add Bookmark screen appears.

6 Edit the suggested name, or type a new name.

7 Tap the current folder under the Location heading.

The Choose a Folder screen appears.

8 Tap the folder in which to store the bookmark.

The Add Bookmark screen appears.

9 Tap **Save**.

Create a New Folder for Bookmarks

1 In Safari, tap **Bookmarks** (📖).

The Bookmarks screen appears.

2 Tap **Edit**.

The editing controls appear.

A You can drag a handle (═) to change the order of the bookmark folders.

B You can tap **Delete** (⊖) and then tap the textual **Delete** button to delete a bookmark folder and its contents.

3 Tap **New Folder**.

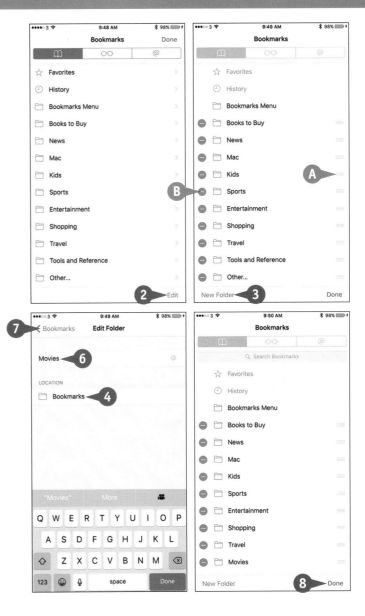

The Edit Folder screen appears.

4 Tap the folder under the Location heading.

The Choose a Folder screen appears.

5 Tap the folder in which to store the bookmark.

The Edit Folder screen appears again.

6 Type the name for the folder.

7 Tap **Bookmarks** (ᐸ).

The Bookmarks screen appears, still with editing controls displayed.

8 Tap **Done**.

TIP

Can I change a bookmark I have created?
Yes. Tap **Bookmarks** (📖) to display the Bookmarks screen, and then navigate to the bookmark you want to change. Tap **Edit** to switch to Editing Mode. You can then tap a bookmark to open it on the Edit Bookmark screen, where you can change its name, address, or location. In Editing Mode, you can also delete a bookmark by tapping **Delete** (⊖) and then tapping **Delete**, or rearrange your bookmarks by dragging the handle (═) up or down the list.

Keep a Reading List of Web Pages

Safari's Reading List feature enables you to save a web page for later without creating a bookmark. You can quickly add the current web page to Reading List by using the Share sheet. Once you have added pages, you access Reading List through the Bookmarks feature. When viewing Reading List, you can display either all the pages it contains or only those you have not read.

Keep a Reading List of Web Pages

Add a Web Page to Reading List

 Press **Home**.

The Home screen appears.

2 Tap **Safari** (⊘).

Safari opens and displays the last web page you were viewing.

3 Navigate to the web page you want to add to Reading List.

4 Tap **Share** (⬆).

The Share sheet appears.

5 Tap **Add to Reading List** (∞).

Safari adds the web page to Reading List.

Open Reading List and Display a Page

1 In Safari, tap **Bookmarks** (▢).

The Bookmarks screen appears.

2 Tap **Reading List** (∞).

Note: You can quickly display the Reading List screen from the Home screen by 3D-touching **Safari** (🧭) and then tapping **Show Reading List** on the Peek panel.

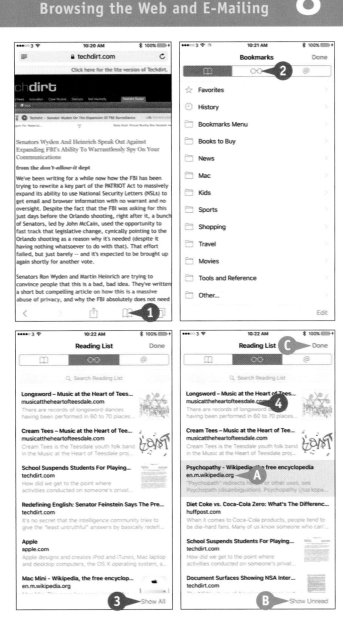

The Reading List screen appears.

3 Tap **Show All**.

Reading List displays all the pages it contains, including those you have read.

Ⓐ Pages you have read appear with gray shading.

Ⓑ You can tap **Show Unread** to display only unread pages.

4 Tap the page you want to open.

Ⓒ If you decide not to open a page from Reading List, tap **Done** to hide the Reading List screen.

TIP

How do I remove an item from Reading List?

To remove an item from Reading List, swipe it left and then tap the textual **Delete** button that appears.

When you swipe left, the Mark Read button also appears if you have not read the item; the Mark Unread button appears if you have read it. You can tap **Mark Read** or **Mark Unread** to switch the item's read status.

Share Web Pages with Others

When browsing the web, you will likely come across pages you want to share with other people. Safari makes it easy to share web page addresses via e-mail, instant messaging, Twitter, Facebook, and other apps. This section shows an example using the Mail app.

When others share web pages with you via Twitter and similar apps, Safari adds them to the Shared Links list. You can open this list, browse the pages, and quickly display any pages you want to view.

Share Web Pages with Others

Share a Web Page with Others

① Press **Home**.

The Home screen appears.

② Tap **Safari** (⊘).

Safari opens and displays the last web page you were viewing.

③ Navigate to the web page you want to share.

④ Tap **Share** (⬆).

The Share sheet appears, showing apps you can use for sharing.

⑤ Tap **Mail** (✉).

Your iPhone starts a new message in the Mail app.

Ⓐ The URL appears in the body of the message.

⑥ Tap **Add Contact** (⊕) and select an address for the message.

⑦ Edit the suggested subject line as needed.

⑧ Type any explanatory text needed.

⑨ Tap **Send**.

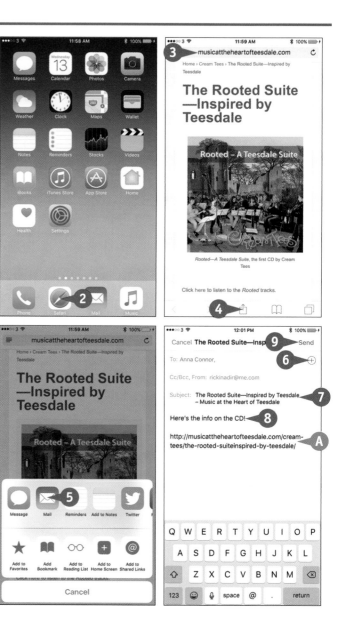

Open a Page Someone Has Shared with You

1 In Safari, tap **Bookmarks** ().

The Bookmarks screen appears.

2 Tap **Shared Links** (@).

The Shared Links list appears.

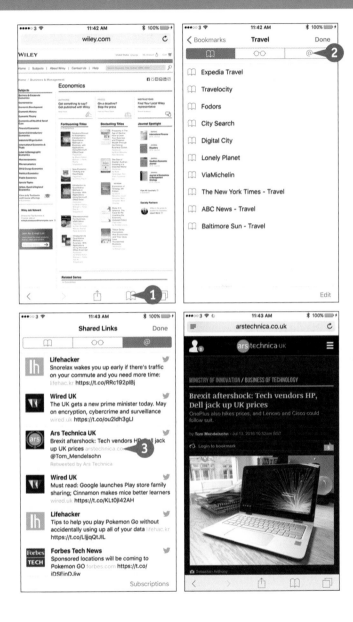

3 Tap the link.

Safari displays the linked page.

TIP

What other ways can I use to share a web page?
You can also share a web page address by including it in an instant message, by tweeting it to Twitter, or by posting it to Facebook. Another option is to use AirDrop to share the address with a local device. See Chapter 6 for instructions on using AirDrop.

Navigate Among Open Web Pages Using Tabs

If you browse the web a lot, you will probably need to open many web pages in Safari at the same time. Safari presents your open pages as a list of scrollable tabs, making it easy to navigate from one page to another.

You can change the order of the tabs to suit your needs, and you can quickly close a tab by either tapping its **Close** button or simply swiping it off the list.

Navigate Among Open Web Pages Using Tabs

Open Safari and Display the List of Tabs

 Press **Home**.

The Home screen appears.

 Tap **Safari** ().

Safari opens or becomes active.

Note: If Safari has hidden the on-screen controls, tap the screen and pull down a short way to display them.

3 Tap **Pages** (⬚).

The list of pages appears.

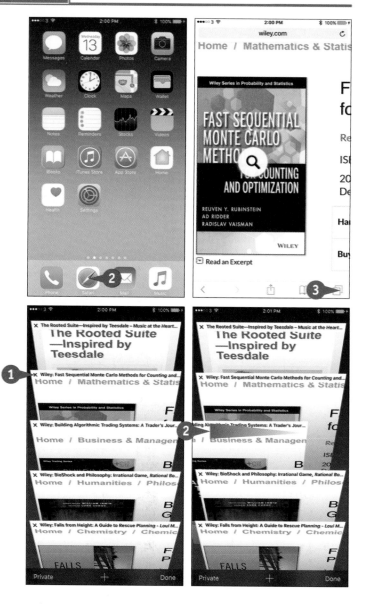

Close Pages You Do Not Need to Keep Open

1 Tap **Close** (✕) on the tab for a page you want to close.

The page closes, and the tab disappears from the list.

2 Alternatively, you can tap a tab and swipe it left off the screen.

The page closes, and the tab disappears from the list.

Note: You can turn a large-screen iPhone to landscape orientation and then tap **Close** (✕) to close the current tab.

Change the Order of the Pages

1 Tap and hold the tab for a page you want to move.

The tab moves to the foreground.

2 Drag the tab to where you want it to appear in the list, and then release it.

Find a Page and Display It

1 3D-touch the tab for the page you want to display.

The Peek panel for the page opens.

2 3D-touch further.

The page opens.

Note: You can also turn a large-screen iPhone to landscape orientation to display the tab bar at the top of the screen. You can then tap the tab you want to view.

How do I return from the list of tabs to the page I was viewing before?
To return to the page you were viewing before, either tap the page's tab in the list of tabs, or tap **Done** in the lower-right corner of the screen.

Tighten Up Safari's Security

To protect yourself against websites that infect computers with malware or try to gain your sensitive personal or financial information, turn on Safari's Fraudulent Website Warning feature. You can also turn off the JavaScript programming language, which can be used to attack your iPhone. Additionally, you can block pop-up windows, which some websites use to display unwanted information; choose which cookies to accept; and turn on the Do Not Track feature to request that sites not track your visits.

Tighten Up Safari's Security

① Press **Home**.

The Home screen appears.

② Tap **Settings** (⚙).

The Settings screen appears.

③ Tap **Safari** (🧭).

The Safari screen appears.

Ⓐ The AutoFill feature enables you to save information — such as your name, address, and credit card details — for filling out web forms quickly.

④ Set the **Block Pop-ups** switch to On (🔵) to block unwanted pop-up windows.

⑤ Set the **Do Not Track** switch to On (🔵) or Off ( ), as needed.

⑥ Tap **Block Cookies**.

The Block Cookies screen appears.

⑦ Tap **Always Block**, **Allow from Current Website Only**, **Allow from Websites I Visit**, or **Always Allow**, as needed. See the tip for advice.

⑧ Tap **Safari** (<).

The Safari screen appears again.

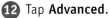 Set the **Fraudulent Website Warning** switch to On (○).

 Tap **Clear History and Website Data**.

A dialog opens.

Tap **Clear History and Data**.

The dialog closes.

Safari clears your browsing history and data.

Tap **Advanced**.

The Advanced screen appears.

Set the **JavaScript** switch to On (○) or Off ( ), as needed.

Note: Turning off JavaScript may remove some or most functionality of harmless sites.

Tap **Website Data**.

The Website Data screen appears.

Ⓑ You can tap **Remove All Website Data** to remove all website data.

Tap **Edit**.

A Delete icon (⊖) appears to the left of each website.

To delete a website's data, tap **Delete** (⊖), and then tap the textual **Delete** button that appears.

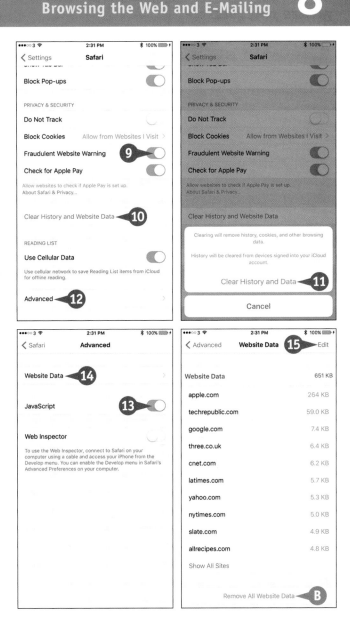

TIP

What are cookies, and what threat do they pose?

A *cookie* is a small text file that a website places on a computer to identify that computer in the future. This is helpful for many sites, such as shopping sites in which you add items to a shopping cart, but when used by malevolent sites, cookies can pose a threat to your privacy. You can set Safari to never accept cookies, but this prevents many legitimate websites from working properly. So accepting cookies only from sites you visit is usually the best compromise.

Read E-Mail

After you have set up Mail by synchronizing accounts via your computer, as described in Chapter 1, or by setting up accounts manually on the iPhone, as explained in Chapter 4, you are ready to send and receive e-mail messages using your iPhone.

This section shows you how to read your incoming e-mail messages. You learn to reply to messages and write messages from scratch later in this chapter.

Read E-Mail

Read a Message and View an Attached File

1 Press **Home**.

The Home screen appears.

A The badge shows the number of unread messages.

2 Tap **Mail** (icon).

The Mailboxes screen appears.

Note: If Mail does not show the Mailboxes screen, tap **Back** (<) until the Mailboxes screen appears.

3 Tap the inbox you want to open.

B To see all your incoming messages together, tap **All Inboxes**. Depending on how you use e-mail, you may find seeing all your messages together helpful.

C A blue dot indicates an unread message.

D A gray star indicates the message's sender is one of your VIPs. See the second tip for information about VIPs.

E A paperclip icon (icon) indicates one or more attachments.

4 Tap a message.

The message opens.

F You can tap **Previous** (∧) or **Next** (∨) to display another message.

G You can tap **Filter** (icon) to filter the messages by Unread status, displaying only unread messages. You can then tap **Unread** to apply a different filter.

5 If the message has an attachment, tap it.

The attachment opens in the viewer.

Note: Mail's viewer can display many types of attached files, but not all files.

Note: If Mail has hidden the controls at the top of the screen, tap the screen to display the controls.

⑥ If you want to send the file to an app or share it with others, tap **Share** (⬆).

The Share sheet opens.

⑦ Tap the means of sharing, such as **Copy to Pages** (◨) for a Word document.

⑧ Tap **Done**.

The message appears again.

Access New Messages Quickly from the Home Screen

① Press **Home**.

The Home screen appears.

② 3D-touch **Mail** (✉).

The Peek panel opens.

Ⓗ You can also tap another button, such as **VIP**.

Ⓘ You can tap a contact whose icon bears a badge to display a new message from that contact.

③ Tap **All Inboxes**.

The All Inboxes screen appears.

TIPS

How do I view the contents of another mailbox?

From an open message, tap **Inbox** (<) or **All Inboxes** (<) to return to the inbox or the screen for all the inboxes. Tap **Back** (<) to go back to the Mailboxes screen. You can then tap the mailbox you want to view.

What is the VIP inbox on the Mailboxes screen?

The VIP inbox is a tool for identifying important messages, no matter which e-mail account they come to. You mark particular contacts as being very important people to you, and Mail then adds messages from these VIPs to the VIP inbox. To add a VIP, tap the sender's name in an open message, and then tap **Add to VIP** on the Sender screen.

Reply To or Forward an E-Mail Message

Mail makes it easy to reply to an e-mail message or forward it to others. If the message had multiple recipients, you can choose between replying only to the sender of the message and replying to the sender and all the other recipients in the To field and the Cc field, if there are any. Recipients in the message's Bcc field, whose names you cannot see, do not receive your reply.

Reply To or Forward an E-Mail Message

Open the Message You Will Reply To or Forward

1 Press **Home**.

The Home screen appears.

2 Tap **Mail** (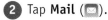).

The Mailboxes screen appears.

Note: When you launch Mail, the app checks for new messages. This is why the number of new messages you see on the Mailboxes screen may differ from the number on the Mail badge on the Home screen.

3 Tap the inbox you want to see.

The inbox opens.

4 Tap the message you want to open.

The message opens.

5 Tap **Action** ().

The Action dialog opens.

Note: You can also reply to or forward a message by using Siri. For example, say "Reply to this message" or "Forward this message to Alice Smith," and then tell Siri what you want the message to say.

Reply To the Message

1 In the Action dialog, tap **Reply**.

A To reply to all recipients, tap **Reply All**. Reply to all recipients only when you are sure that they need to receive your reply. Often, it is better to reply only to the sender.

A screen containing the reply appears.

2 Type your reply to the message.

3 Tap **Send**.

Mail sends the message.

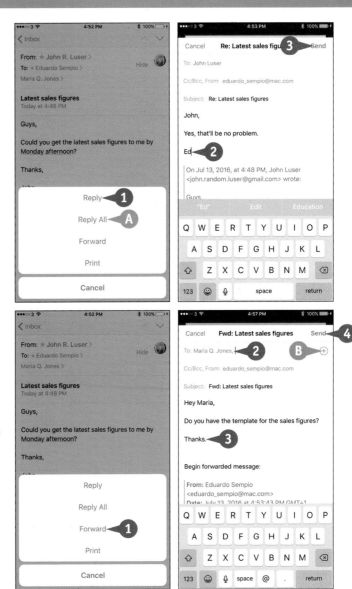

Forward the Message

1 In the Action dialog, tap **Forward**.

A screen containing the forwarded message appears.

2 Type the recipient's address.

B Alternatively, you can tap **Add Contact** (⊕) and choose the recipient in your Contacts list.

3 Type a message if needed.

4 Tap **Send**.

Mail sends the message.

TIPS

Can I reply to or forward only part of a message?
Yes. The quick way to do this is to select the part of the message you want to include before tapping **Action** (⤺). Mail then includes only your selection. Alternatively, you can start the reply or forwarded message, and then delete the parts you do not want to include.

How do I check for new messages?
In a mailbox, tap and drag your finger down the screen, pulling down the messages. When a progress circle appears at the top, lift your finger. Mail checks for new messages.

Organize Your Messages in Mailbox Folders

To keep your inbox or inboxes under control, you should organize your messages into mailbox folders.

You can quickly move a single message to a folder after reading it or after previewing it in the message list. Alternatively, you can select multiple messages in your inbox and move them all to a folder in a single action. You can also delete any message you no longer need.

Organize Your Messages in Mailbox Folders

Open Mail and Move a Single Message to a Folder

1 Press **Home**.

The Home screen appears.

2 Tap **Mail** (📧).

The Mailboxes screen appears.

3 Tap the mailbox you want to open.

The mailbox opens.

A The Replied arrow (↩) indicates you have replied to the message.

B The Forwarded arrow (➡) indicates you have forwarded the message.

4 Tap the message you want to open.

The message opens.

C You can delete the message by tapping **Delete** (🗑).

5 Tap **Move** (🗁).

The Move This Message to a New Mailbox screen appears.

6 Tap the mailbox to which you want to move the message.

Mail moves the message.

The next message in the mailbox appears, so that you can read it and file it if necessary.

Move Multiple Messages to a Folder

① In the mailbox, tap **Edit**.

② Tap the selection button (⃝ changes to ✓) next to each message you want to move.

③ Tap **Move**.

④ Tap the destination mailbox.

Note: To move the messages to a mailbox in another account, tap **Accounts** on the Move This Message to a New Mailbox screen, tap the account, and then tap the mailbox.

Move a Message from a Mailbox

① In the mailbox list, tap the message and swipe to the left.

Ⓓ Tap **Trash** (🗑) to delete the message.

② Tap **More**.

The More dialog opens.

③ Tap **Move Message**.

The Mailboxes screen appears.

④ Tap the mailbox to which you want to move the message.

TIP

What does the Mark command in the Action dialog do?

Tap **Mark** to display the Mark dialog. You can then tap **Flag** to set a flag on the message — for example, to indicate that you need to pay extra attention to it. The flag appears as an orange dot (●). In the Mark dialog, you can also tap **Mark as Unread** to mark the message as not having been read, even though you have opened it; if the message is marked as unread, you can tap **Mark as Read** instead. You can also mark a message as unread or by tapping it in the message list, swiping right, and then tapping **Unread** (✉) or **Read** (✅), as appropriate.

Write and Send E-Mail Messages

Your iPhone is great for reading and replying to e-mail messages you receive, but you will likely also need to write new messages. When you do, you can use the data in the Contacts app to address your outgoing messages quickly and accurately. If the recipient's address is not one of your contacts, you can type the address manually.

You can attach one or more files to an e-mail message to send those files to the recipient. This works well for small files, but many mail servers reject files larger than several megabytes in size.

Write and Send E-Mail Messages

① Press **Home**.

The Home screen appears.

② 3D-touch **Mail** ().

The Peek panel appears.

③ Tap **New Message** (📝).

Note: You can also tap **Mail** (✉) and then tap **New Message** (📝) to start a new message.

The New Message screen appears.

④ Tap **Add Contact** (⊕).

The Contacts list appears.

Note: If necessary, change the Contacts list displayed by tapping **Groups**, making your choice on the Groups screen, and then tapping **Done**.

Ⓐ If the person you are e-mailing is not a contact, type the address in the To area. You can also start typing here and then select a matching contact from the list that the Mail app displays.

Note: Contacts that appear in gray have no e-mail address.

⑤ Tap the contact you want to send the message to.

B The contact's name appears in the To area.

Note: You can add other contacts to the To area by repeating steps **4** and **5**.

6 If you need to add a Cc or Bcc recipient, tap **Cc/Bcc, From**.

The Cc, Bcc, and From fields expand.

7 Tap the Cc area or Bcc area, and then follow steps **4** and **5** to add a recipient.

C To change the e-mail account you are sending the message from, tap **From**, and then tap the account to use.

8 Tap **Subject**, and then type the message's subject.

D You can tap **Notifications** (🔔 changes to 🔔) to receive notifications when someone responds to the e-mail conversation.

9 Tap below the Subject line, and then type the body of the message.

Note: If you need to stop working on a message temporarily, tap its title bar and drag it down to the bottom of the screen. You can then work with other messages. To resume work on the parked message, tap its title bar.

10 Tap **Send**.

Mail sends the message.

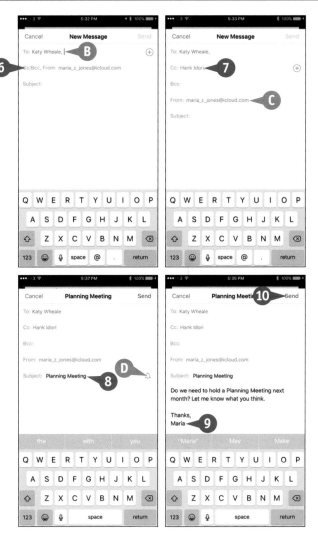

TIP

How do I attach a file to a message?

To attach a photo or video, tap and hold the message body area to display the contextual menu, and then tap **Insert Photo or Video**. On some iPhone models, you may need to tap **More** (▶) before tapping **Insert Photo or Video**.

To attach a file from iCloud Drive, tap and hold the message body area to display the contextual menu, and then tap **Add Attachment**. On some iPhone models, you may need to tap **More** (▶) before tapping **Add Attachment**.

To attach other types of files, start the message from the app that contains the file. Select the file, tap **Share** (⬆), and then tap **Mail** (✉). Mail starts a message with the file attached. You then address the message and send it.

CHAPTER 9

Keeping Your Life Organized

Your iPhone includes many apps for staying organized, such as Contacts, the Calendars, the Reminders, and Wallet. Other apps help you find your way, stay on time, and track stock prices, weather forecasts, and your own health.

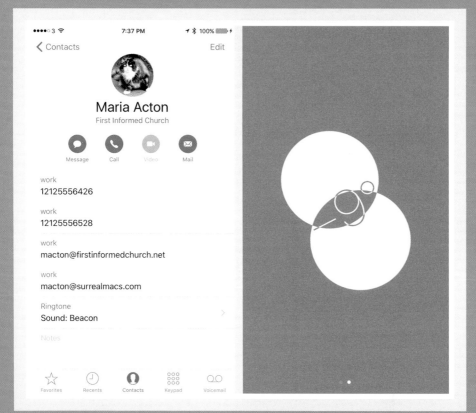

Browse or Search for Contacts

Your iPhone's Contacts app enables you to store contact data that you sync from your computer or online accounts or that you enter directly on your iPhone. You can access the contacts either via the Contacts app itself or through the Contacts tab in the Phone app.

To locate a particular contact, you can browse through the list of contacts or through selected groups, such as your friends, or use the Search feature.

Browse or Search for Contacts

Browse Your Contacts

 Press **Home**.

The Home screen appears.

 Tap **Extras** (⬚).

The Extras folder opens.

 Tap **Contacts** (👤).

The Contacts screen appears, showing either All Contacts or your currently selected groups.

Note: You can also access your contacts by pressing **Home**, tapping **Phone** (📞), and then tapping **Contacts** (👤 changes to 👤).

A To navigate the screen of contacts quickly, tap the letter on the right that you want to jump to. To navigate more slowly, scroll up or down.

 Tap the contact whose information you want to view.

The contact's screen appears.

Note: From the contact's screen, you can quickly phone the contact by tapping the phone number you want to use.

 If necessary, tap and drag up to scroll down the screen to display more information.

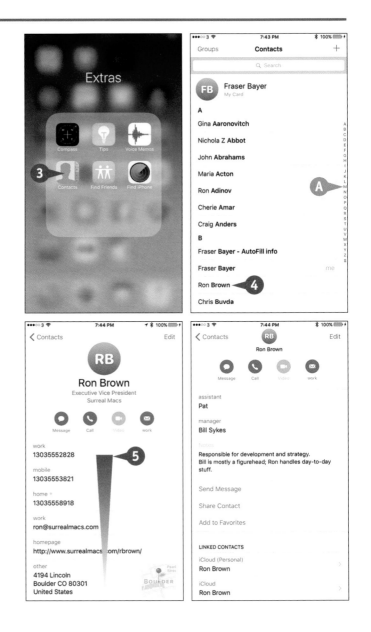

Choose Which Groups of Contacts to Display

1 From the Contacts screen, tap **Groups**.

The Groups screen appears.

2 Tap **Show All Contacts**.

Contacts displays a check mark next to each group.

Note: When you tap **Show All Contacts**, the Hide All Contacts button appears in place of the Show All Contacts button. You can tap **Hide All Contacts** to remove all the check marks.

3 Tap a group to apply a check mark to it or to remove the existing check mark.

4 Tap **Done**.

The Contacts screen appears, showing the contacts in the groups you selected.

Search for Contacts

1 From the Contacts screen, tap **Search** (🔍).

The Search screen appears.

2 Start typing the name you want to search for.

3 From the list of matches, tap the contact you want to view.

The contact's information appears.

TIP

How do I make my iPhone sort my contacts by last names instead of first names?
Press **Home**. Tap **Settings** (⚙) to display the Settings screen, and then tap **Contacts** (👤) to display the Contacts screen. Tap **Sort Order** to display the Sort Order screen, and then tap **Last, First**.

Create a New Contact

As well as syncing your existing contacts via cloud services such as iCloud or Yahoo!, your iPhone enables you to create new contact records directly on the device. For example, if you meet someone you want to remember, you can create a contact record for her — and take a photo using the iPhone's camera. You can then sync that contact record online, adding it to your other contacts.

Create a New Contact

1 Press **Home**.

The Home screen appears.

2 Tap **Phone** ().

The Phone app opens.

3 Tap **Contacts** ( changes to ).

The Contacts screen appears.

Note: You can also access the Contacts app by tapping **Extras** ( ) on the Home screen, and then tapping **Contacts** ( ) in the Extras folder.

4 Tap **Add** (+).

The New Contact screen appears.

5 Tap **First name**.

The on-screen keyboard appears.

6 Type the first name.

7 Tap **Last name**.

8 Type the last name.

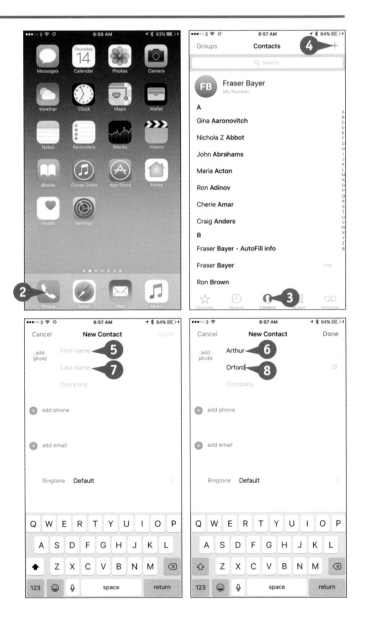

9 Add other information as needed by tapping each field and then typing the information.

10 To add a photo of the contact, tap **add photo**.

The Photo dialog opens.

11 Tap **Take Photo**.

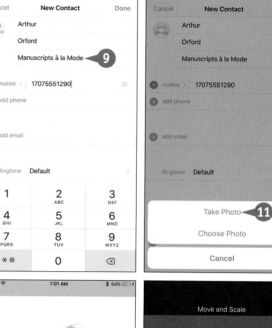

The Take Photo screen appears.

12 Compose the photo, and then tap **Take Photo** (◯).

The Move and Scale screen appears.

13 Position the part of the photo you want to use in the middle.

Note: Pinch in with two fingers to zoom the photo out. Pinch out with two fingers to zoom the photo in.

A You can tap **Retake** to take another photo.

14 Tap **Use Photo**.

The photo appears in the contact record.

15 Tap **Done**.

TIP

How do I assign my new contact an existing photo?

1 In the Photo dialog, tap **Choose Photo**.

2 On the Photos screen, tap the photo album.

3 Tap the photo.

4 On the Move and Scale screen, position the photo, and then tap **Choose**.

Browse Existing Events in Your Calendars

Your iPhone's Calendar app gives you a great way of managing your schedule and making sure you never miss an appointment.

After setting up your calendars to sync using iCloud or other calendar services, as described in Chapter 1, you can take your calendars with you everywhere and consult them whenever you need to. You can view either all your calendars or only those you choose.

Browse Existing Events in Your Calendars

Browse Existing Events in Your Calendars

1 Press **Home**.

2 Tap **Calendar** ( ).

A The black circle indicates the day shown. When the current date is selected, the circle is red.

B Your events appear on a scrollable timeline.

C An event's background color indicates the calendar it belongs to.

D You can tap **Today** to display the current day.

3 Tap the day you want to see.

The events for the day appear.

4 Tap the month.

The calendar for the month appears.

E You can tap the year to display the calendar for the full year, in which you can navigate quickly to other months.

5 Scroll up or down as needed, and then tap the date you want.

The date's appointments appear.

6 Tap **List** (☰ changes to ▤).

The appointments appear as a list, enabling you to see more.

7 Tap an event to see its details.

The Event Details screen appears.

8 To edit the event, tap **Edit**.

The Edit screen appears, and you can make changes to the event. When you finish, tap **Done**.

Choose Which Calendars to Display

1 Tap **Calendars**.

2 Tap to place or remove a check mark next to a calendar you want to display or hide.

F Tap **Show All Calendars** to place a check mark next to each calendar. Tap **Hide All Calendars** to remove all check marks.

G The Birthdays calendar automatically displays birthdays of contacts whose contact data includes the birthday.

H You can set the **Show Declined Events** switch to On (◯) to include invitations you have declined.

3 Tap **Done**.

The calendars you chose appear.

How can I quickly find an event?

In the Calendar app, tap **Search** (🔍). Calendar displays a list of your events. Type your search term. When Calendar displays a list of matches, tap the event you want to view.

Create New Events in Your Calendars

Y ou can create calendar events on your computer, or online using a web interface such as that of iCloud, and then sync the events to your iPhone. But you can also create new events directly on your iPhone. You can create either a straightforward, one-shot appointment or an appointment that repeats on a schedule. You can also choose the calendar in which to store the appointment.

Create New Events in Your Calendars

 Press **Home**.

The Home screen appears.

 Tap **Calendar** (22).

The Calendar screen appears.

3 Tap the day on which you want to create the new event.

Note: From the Home screen, 3D-touch **Calendar** (22) to display the Peek panel and then tap **Add Event** to start creating a new event. You will need to select the date.

Note: You can also leave the current date selected, and then change the date when creating the event.

 Tap **New** (+).

The New Event screen appears.

5 Tap **Title** and type the title of the event.

6 Tap **Location**.

Note: If the Allow "Calendar" to Access Your Location While You Use the App? dialog opens when you tap **Location**, tap **Allow** to use locations.

The Location screen appears.

A You can tap **Current Location** to use the current location.

7 Start typing the location.

8 Tap the appropriate match.

9 Tap **Starts**.

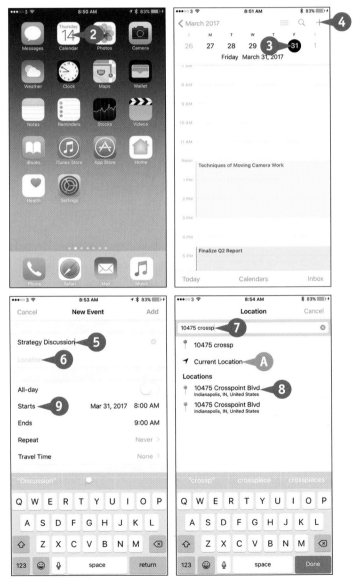

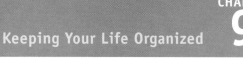

The time and date controls appear.

10 Tap the date and time controls to set the start time.

11 Tap **Ends**.

12 Tap the date and time controls to set the end time.

Ⓑ If this is an all-day appointment, set the **All-day** switch to On (⬤).

Ⓒ If you need to change the time zone, tap **Time Zone**, type the city name, and then tap the time zone.

13 Tap **Alert**.

The Alert screen appears.

14 Tap the timing for the alert, such as **30 minutes before**.

The New Event screen appears.

15 Tap **Calendar**.

The Calendar screen appears.

16 Tap the calendar for the event.

The New Event screen appears again.

17 Tap **Add**.

The event appears on your calendar.

TIPS

How do I set up an event that repeats every week?
On the New Event screen, tap **Repeat**. On the Repeat screen, tap **Every Week**, placing a check mark next to it, and then tap **Done**.

How do I set a time to the exact minute instead of to the nearest 5 minutes?
On the New Event screen, tap **Starts** to display the time and date controls. Double-tap the time readout — either the hours or the minutes — to switch the minutes between 5-minute intervals and single minutes.

Work with Calendar Invitations

As well as events you create yourself, you may receive invitations to events that others create. When you receive an event invitation attached to an e-mail message, you can choose whether to accept the invitation or decline it. If you accept the invitation, you can add the event automatically to your calendar.

Work with Calendar Invitations

Respond to an Invitation from an Alert

1 When an invitation alert appears, 3D-touch it.

The Peek panel displays the event's details, together with buttons for responding to the event.

2 Tap **Accept**, **Maybe**, or **Decline**, as needed.

Ⓐ You can tap **Close** (✕) to close the Peek panel without tapping one of the response buttons.

Respond to an Invitation from the Inbox Screen

1 Press **Home**.

The Home screen appears.

2 Tap **Calendar** ( ).

The Calendar screen appears.

Ⓑ The Inbox button shows the number of invitations.

3 Tap **Inbox**.

The Inbox screen appears.

Ⓒ You can tap **Accept**, **Maybe**, or **Decline** to deal with the invitation without viewing the details.

4 Tap the invitation whose details you want to see.

The Event Details screen appears.

⑤ Tap **Calendar** if you decide to accept the invitation.

The Calendar screen appears.

⑥ Tap the calendar to which you want to assign the event.

The Event Details screen appears again.

⑦ Tap **Alert**.

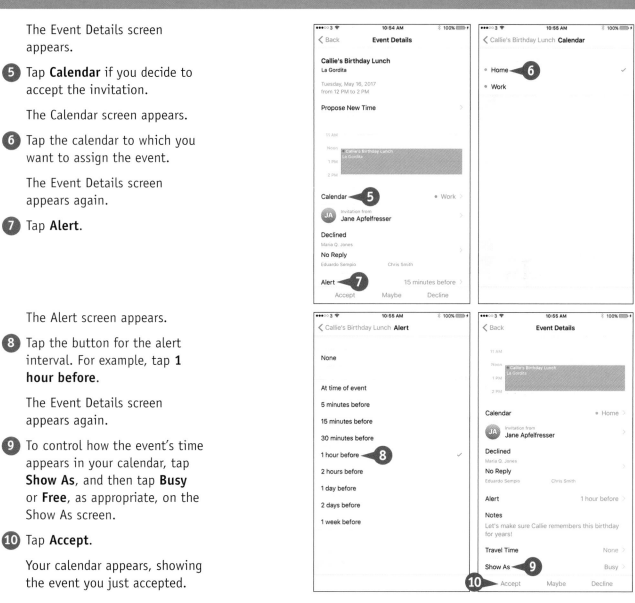

The Alert screen appears.

⑧ Tap the button for the alert interval. For example, tap **1 hour before**.

The Event Details screen appears again.

⑨ To control how the event's time appears in your calendar, tap **Show As**, and then tap **Busy** or **Free**, as appropriate, on the Show As screen.

⑩ Tap **Accept**.

Your calendar appears, showing the event you just accepted.

Track Your Commitments with Reminders

Your iPhone's Reminders app gives you an easy way to note your commitments and keep track of them. The Reminders app comes with a built-in list called Reminders, but you can create as many other lists as you need, giving each a distinctive color.

You can create a reminder with no due time or location or tie a reminder to a due time, arriving at or leaving a location, or both. Your iPhone can remind you of time- or location-based commitments at the appropriate time or place.

Track Your Commitments with Reminders

Open the Reminders App and Create Your Reminder Lists

 Press **Home**.

The Home screen appears.

2 Tap **Reminders** (⁝).

The Reminders app opens, displaying the Lists screen.

3 Tap **New** (➕).

The Create New dialog opens.

4 Tap **List**.

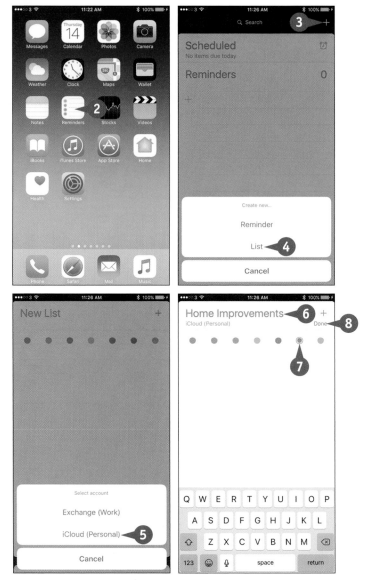

The Select Account dialog opens.

Note: If you have only one Reminders account, Reminders does not prompt you to choose which account to use.

 Tap the account in which you want to store the list.

The screen for creating the list appears.

6 Type the name for the list.

 Tap the color to use for the list.

8 Tap **Done**.

The list appears.

Create a New Reminder

1 To create a new reminder in this list, tap the first line.

A To return to the Lists screen so you can switch to another list, tap the tabbed pages at the bottom of the screen.

The keyboard appears.

2 Type the text for the reminder.

3 Tap **Information** (ⓘ).

The Details screen appears.

4 To create a time-based reminder, set the **Remind me on a day** switch to On (changes to ⬤).

The Alarm and Repeat controls appear.

5 Tap **Alarm**.

The date and time controls appear.

6 Set the date and time for the reminder.

7 If you need to repeat the reminder, tap **Repeat**, choose the repeat interval on the Repeat screen, and then tap **Details** to return to the Details screen.

TIP

How do I sync my iPhone's reminders with my Mac's reminders?

You can sync your iPhone's reminders with your Mac's reminders via your iCloud account, via one or more Exchange accounts, or via both types of accounts.

On your iPhone, press **Home** to display the Home screen, and then tap **Settings** (⚙) to display the Settings screen. Tap **iCloud** (☁) to display the iCloud screen, and then set the **Reminders** switch to On (⬤).

On your Mac, click **Apple** () and **System Preferences** to open System Preferences. Click **iCloud** (☁) to display the iCloud pane, and then click **Reminders** (changes to ☑).

continued ▶

You can assign different priorities to your reminders to give yourself a quick visual reference of their urgency. You can also add notes to a reminder to keep relevant information at hand. When you have completed a reminder, you can mark it as completed. You can view your list of scheduled reminders for quick reference, and you can choose whether to include your completed reminders in the list. If you no longer need a reminder, you can delete it from the list.

Track Your Commitments with Reminders (continued)

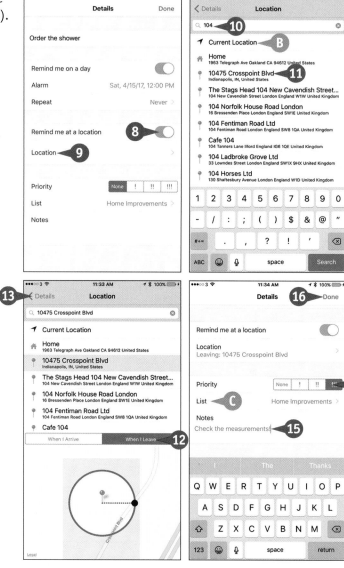

8 To create a location-based reminder, set the **Remind me at a location** switch to On (●).

Note: If Reminders prompts you to allow it to use your current location, tap **Allow**.

9 Tap **Location**.

The Location screen appears.

10 Start typing the location in the search box.

Ⓑ You can tap **Current Location** to use your current location.

11 Tap the location in the list of results.

The Location screen displays a map of the location.

12 Tap **When I Arrive** or **When I Leave**, as needed.

13 Tap **Details** (<).

The Details screen appears again.

14 To assign a priority to the reminder, tap **None**, **!**, **!!**, or **!!!**.

Ⓒ To assign the reminder to a different list than the current list, tap **List**. On the Change List screen, tap the list you want to use.

15 To add a note to the reminder, tap **Notes** and then type the text.

16 Tap **Done**.

The new reminder appears on your list of reminders.

17 Tap **New** (⊞) or anywhere on the next line to start creating a new reminder.

D When you finish a task, tap its button (○ changes to ◉) to mark the reminder as complete.

Note: To delete a reminder, tap **Edit** on the screen that contains it. Tap **Delete** (⊖) to the left of the reminder, and then tap **Delete**.

18 Tap the tabbed pages at the bottom of the screen to switch to another reminder list.

View a List of Your Scheduled Reminders

1 Tap **Scheduled** (⏰).

The Scheduled list appears.

2 Tap the reminder you want to see.

Note: You can turn a large-screen iPhone to landscape orientation to view both your reminder lists and the current list's reminders at the same time.

How do I change the default list that Reminders puts my reminders in?
Press **Home** to display the Home screen, and then tap **Settings** (⚙) to display the Settings screen. Tap **Reminders** (⋮) to display the Reminders screen, tap **Default List** to display the Default List screen, and then tap the list you want to make the default. On the Reminders screen, you can also tap **Sync** and choose how many reminders to sync — **Reminders 2 Weeks Back**, **Reminders 1 Month Back**, **Reminders 3 Months Back**, **Reminders 6 Months Back**, or **All Reminders**.

Keep Essential Documents at Hand with Wallet

allet is an app for storing payment cards and electronic versions of essential documents such as boarding passes, movie tickets, and hotel reservations. As explained in Chapter 1, the iPhone's setup routine walks you through adding a payment card for Apple Pay to Wallet; you can add other cards later, as needed.

You can add documents to Wallet from built-in apps such as Mail and Safari, as shown in this section, or by using custom apps for shopping, booking hotels, and booking flights.

Keep Essential Documents at Hand with Wallet

Add a Document to Wallet

1 In Mail, tap the message with the document attached.

The message opens.

2 Tap the document's button.

The document appears.

3 Tap **Add**.

Mail adds the document to Wallet.

The message appears again.

Note: In Safari, open the web page containing the document, and then tap **Add** to add the document to Wallet.

Open Wallet and Find the Documents You Need

1 Press **Home**.

The Home screen appears.

2 Tap **Wallet** ().

The Wallet app opens.

The documents you have added appear.

Note: Until you add one or more documents to Wallet, the app displays an information screen highlighting its uses.

3 Tap the document you want to view.

 The document appears above the other documents. You can then hold its barcode in front of a scanner to use the document.

4 To see another document, tap the current top document and swipe down.

Wallet reshuffles the documents so you can see them all.

Choose Settings for a Document or Delete It

1 Tap **Information** (ⓘ).

The document rotates so you can see its back.

2 Set the **Automatic Updates** switch to On (◯) if you want to receive updates to this document.

3 Set the **Suggest on Lock Screen** switch to On (◯) if you want notifications about the document to appear on the lock screen.

B If you have no further need for the document, tap **Remove Pass** to remove it.

4 When you finish reviewing the document, tap **Done**.

The document rotates to display its front.

TIP

What other actions can I take with documents in Wallet?
You can share a document with other people via e-mail, instant messaging, or AirDrop. To access these features, tap **Share** (⬆), and then tap **AirDrop**, **Mail**, or **Message** on the Share sheet that appears.

Get Your Bearings with Compass

When you need to get your bearings, use the Compass app that comes installed on your iPhone. With Compass, you can establish your relationship to the points of the compass, learn your precise GPS location, and measure an angle between two points.

Compass includes the Level feature that you can use to level an object or surface precisely or to measure its current slant.

Get Your Bearings with Compass

Open Compass and Get Your Bearings

 Press **Home**.

The Home screen appears.

 Tap **Extras** (📷).

The Extras folder opens.

③ Tap **Compass** (🧭).

Note: If Compass displays a message prompting you to complete the circle to calibrate it, turn your iPhone this way and that until the circle is filled in. The compass then appears.

④ Point your iPhone in the direction whose bearing you want to take.

Ⓐ The readout shows the bearing.

Ⓑ You can tap the GPS location to switch to the Maps app and display the map for that location.

Ⓒ The readout shows the approximate elevation above sea level.

Measure an Angle

① On the Compass screen, tap anywhere on the compass to fix the current bearing.

Ⓓ The bearing appears at the top of the compass.

② Turn the iPhone toward the target point.

Ⓔ The red arc measures the difference between the two bearings.

③ Tap anywhere to release the compass.

Use the Level Feature

1 From the Compass screen, tap and drag left or swipe left.

F You can also tap the gray dot to switch to the Level screen.

The Level screen appears.

G The figure shows the angle of the object or surface.

2 Tilt your iPhone toward a level position to move the circles on top of each other.

3 If the black-and-white color scheme is hard to see, tap anywhere on the screen.

The background color changes to red.

Note: You can tap again to switch the background color from red back to black.

H When you align the circles, the screen goes green.

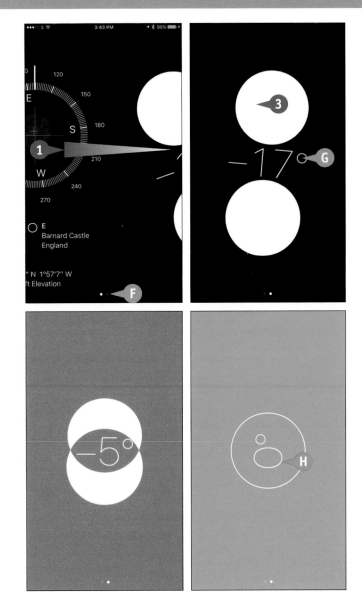

TIP

Does the Compass app use True North or Magnetic North?
The Compass app can show either True North or Magnetic North. To switch, press **Home**, and then tap **Settings** (⚙). In the Settings app, tap **Compass** (🧭), and then set the **Use True North** switch to On (⬤) or Off ( ), as needed.

Find Your Location with Maps

Your iPhone's Maps app can pinpoint your location by using the Global Positioning System, known as GPS, or wireless networks. You can view your location on a road map, display a satellite picture with or without place labels, or view transit information. You can easily switch among map types to find the most useful one. To help you get your bearings, the Tracking feature in the Maps app can show you which direction you are facing.

Find Your Location with Maps

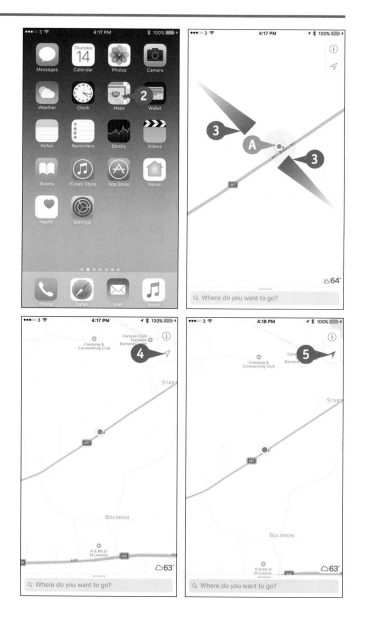

1 Press **Home**.

The Home screen appears.

2 Tap **Maps** ( ).

The Maps screen appears.

A A blue dot shows your current location. The expanding circle around the blue dot shows that Maps is determining your location.

Note: It may take a minute for Maps to work out your location accurately. While Maps determines the location, the blue dot moves, even though the iPhone remains stationary.

3 Place your thumb and finger apart on the screen and pinch inward.

Note: You can place your thumb and finger on the screen and pinch apart to zoom in.

The map zooms out, showing a larger area.

4 Tap **Location** (⊲ changes to ◀), turning on the Location service.

5 Tap **Location** (◀ changes to ⋀).

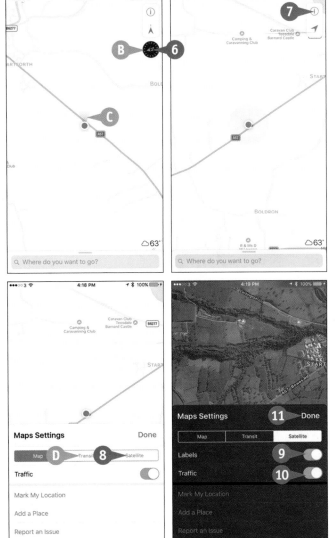

B The Compass icon appears (⬤). The red arrow indicates north.

C The map turns to show the direction the iPhone is facing, so that you can orient yourself.

6 When you need to restore the map orientation, tap **Compass** (⬤).

The map turns so that north is upward.

The Compass icon disappears.

7 Tap **Information** (ⓘ).

The Maps Settings dialog opens.

D You can tap **Transit** to display transit information for the area.

8 Tap **Satellite**.

The satellite map appears, showing photos with street and place names overlaid on them.

9 Set the **Labels** switch to On (⬤) to display labels.

10 Set the **Traffic** switch to On (⬤) or Off ( ), as needed.

11 Tap **Done**.

The Maps Settings dialog closes.

Note: The satellite photos may be several years old and no longer accurate.

TIPS

How can I tell the scale of the map?

Place two fingers on the screen as if about to pinch outward or inward. Maps displays a scale in the upper-left corner of the screen.

How can I share my location?

Tap and hold the location you want to share. A Marked Location pin appears, and the Marked Location panel opens. Tap **Share** (⬆) to display the Share sheet. You can then tap the means of sharing — such as AirDrop, Message, Mail, or Twitter — and follow the prompts to send or post your location.

Find Directions with Maps

Your iPhone's Maps app can give you directions to where you want to go. Maps can also show you current traffic congestion in some locales to help you identify the most viable route for a journey.

Maps displays driving directions by default, but you can make it display public transit directions and walking directions.

Find Directions with Maps

1 Press **Home**.

The Home screen appears.

2 Tap **Maps** ().

The Maps screen appears.

3 Tap **Where do you want to go?**.

Note: If you want the directions to start from your current location, leave Current Location in the Start field. Go to step **7**.

The Directions screen appears.

4 Start typing your destination.

A list of suggested matches appears.

5 Tap the correct match.

A map of the destination appears.

6 Tap **Directions**.

Note: If you want the directions to start from your current location, leave Current Location in the Start field. Go to step **10**.

7 Tap **Current Location**.

The Change Route dialog opens.

 Tap **From** and start typing the start location for the directions.

 Tap the correct match.

Ⓐ You can tap **Switch Places** (⇅) to switch the start location and end location.

⑩ Tap **Route**.

A screen showing the driving directions appears.

Ⓑ If multiple routes are available, tap a time button to view a different route. The time button changes to blue to indicate it is active.

Ⓒ You can tap **Walk** (🚶) to see walking directions.

Ⓓ You can tap **Transit** (🚃) to see transit directions.

Ⓔ You can tap **Ride** (🚶) to see ride-sharing apps that are available.

⑪ Tap **Go**.

The first screen of directions appears.

⑫ Swipe left to display the next direction.

Note: When you start navigating the route, the directions change automatically to reflect your progress.

⑬ To finish using the directions, tap **End**.

The map appears again.

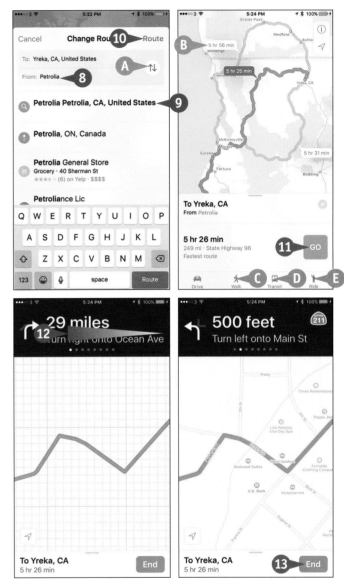

TIP

What else should I know about the directions for walking or public transit?

You should be aware that walking directions may be incomplete or inaccurate. Before walking the route, check that it does not send you across pedestrian-free bridges or through rail tunnels.

The Maps app provides transit information for only some routes. Even for these, it is advisable to double-check the information via online schedules, such as on the website of the transit company involved.

Explore with 3D Flyover

Maps is not only great for finding out where you are and for getting directions to places, but it can also show you 3D flyovers of the places on the map. Flyovers can be a useful way to explore a place virtually so that you can find your way around later in real life.

After switching on the 3D feature, you can zoom in and out, pan around, and move backward and forward.

Explore with 3D Flyover

1 Press **Home**.

The Home screen appears.

2 Tap **Maps** ( ).

The Maps screen appears.

3 Display the area of interest in the middle of the screen. For example, tap and drag the map, or search for the location you want.

4 Tap **Information** ( ).

The Maps Settings dialog opens.

5 Tap **Satellite**.

The map switches to Satellite view.

6 Tap **Done**.

The Maps Settings dialog closes.

7 Swipe up the screen with two fingers.

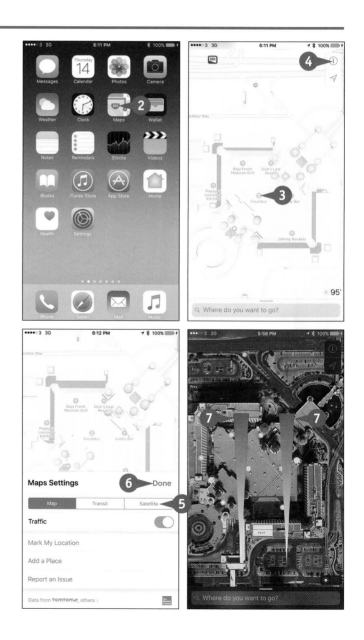

The map switches to 3D view.

8 Place your thumb and finger on the screen and pinch outward.

The map zooms in.

Note: You can place your thumb and finger on the screen and pinch inward to zoom out.

Note: Tap and drag to scroll the map as needed.

9 Place two fingers on the screen and twist clockwise or counterclockwise to rotate the view.

The rotated view appears.

A The Compass arrow () appears. You can tap it to restore the direction to north.

Note: Pan and zoom as needed to explore the area.

10 Tap and drag up with two fingers.

The viewing angle becomes shallower.

11 Tap **2D**.

The two-dimensional map reappears.

TIP

What does 3D do with the standard map?
When you swipe up the screen with two fingers to switch on Flyover with the standard map displayed, Maps tilts the map at an angle, as you might do with a paper map. In cities, building shapes appear when you zoom in on the map, enabling you to see the layout without using the full detail of the satellite photos.

Using Maps' Favorites and Contacts

When you want to return to a location easily in the Maps app, you can create a favorite for the location.

Similarly, you can add a location to your contacts, so that you can access it either from the Contacts app or from the Maps app. You can either create a new contact or add the location to an existing contact. You can also return quickly to locations you have visited recently but for which you have not created a favorite or contact.

Using Maps' Favorites and Contacts

Create a Favorite in Maps

1 Press **Home**.

The Home screen appears.

2 Tap **Maps** (🗺️).

The Maps screen appears.

3 Find the place for which you want to create a favorite. For example, tap and drag the map, or search for the location you want.

4 Tap and hold the place for which you want to create a favorite.

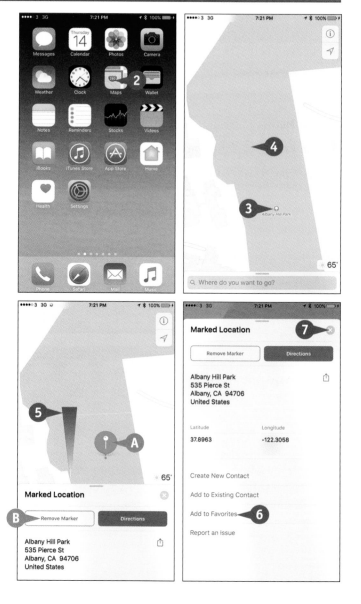

A The Maps app drops a pin on the place.

The Marked Location panel opens.

B You can tap **Remove Marker** to remove a marker you have placed accidentally.

5 Swipe up.

The Marked Location panel opens further.

6 Tap **Add to Favorites**.

The Maps app creates a favorite for the location.

7 Tap **Close** (❌).

The Marked Location panel closes.

Create a Contact in Maps

1 Find the place for which you want to create a contact. For example, tap and drag the map, or search for the location you want.

2 Tap and hold the appropriate place.

The Maps app drops a pin on the place.

The Marked Location panel opens.

3 Swipe up.

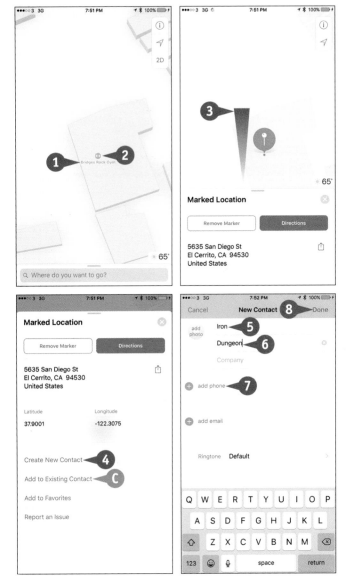

The Marked Location panel opens further.

4 Tap **Create New Contact**.

Ⓒ You can tap **Add to Existing Contact** and then tap the contact to which you want to add the location instead.

The New Contact screen appears.

5 Type the first name for the contact record.

6 Type the last name for the contact record.

7 Add any other information the contact record requires.

8 Tap **Done**.

The Maps app creates the contact record for the location.

TIP

How do I go to a location for which I have created a favorite or a contact?

In the Maps app, tap **Where do you want to go?** to display the Search screen. Start typing the name of the favorite or contact, and then tap the appropriate search result.

Take Notes

Your iPhone is a great device for taking notes no matter where you happen to be. The Notes app enables you to create notes stored in an e-mail account — such as your iCloud account — or on your iPhone.

You can create straightforward notes in plain text for any account you add to Notes. For notes stored on Exchange, IMAP, or Google accounts, you can also add formatting. For notes stored in iCloud, you can add check boxes, photos, and sketches.

Take Notes

1 Press **Home**.

The Home screen appears.

2 Tap **Notes** (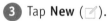).

The Notes app opens.

Note: To change the account or folder in which you are working, tap **Back** (<), and then tap the account or folder you want to use.

3 Tap **New** (✎).

A new note opens.

4 Type the title or first paragraph of the note.

5 Tap **More** (⊕).

The More bar appears.

6 Tap **Formatting** (Aa).

Ⓐ You can tap **Photo** (📷) to add a photo to the note.

Ⓑ You can tap **Sketch** (✍) to add a sketch to the note.

Ⓒ You can tap **Close** (✕) when you no longer need the More bar displayed.

The Formatting pane appears.

7 Tap the style you want to apply to the paragraph.

The paragraph takes on the style.

8 Tap **Done**.

The Formatting pane closes.

9 Tap **return**.

The insertion point moves to a new paragraph.

10 Tap **Check box** (⊘).

D The Notes app inserts a check box on the current line.

11 Type the text to accompany the check box.

12 Tap **return** twice.

The Notes app creates a new paragraph and discontinues the check boxes.

13 When you finish working on the note, tap **Done**.

The Notes app hides the keyboard.

14 Tap **Notes** (‹).

The Notes screen appears again, and you can work with other notes.

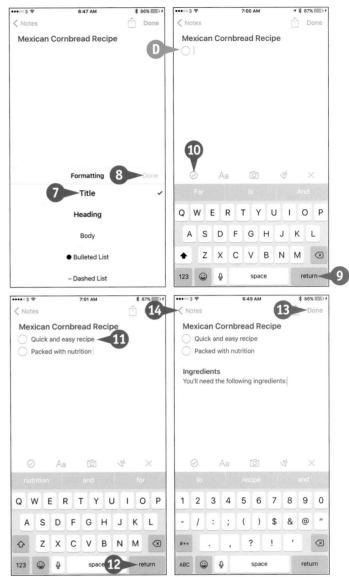

TIPS

How do I tell Siri into which account to put new notes?

Press **Home** to display the Home screen, tap **Settings** (⚙) to display the Settings screen, and then tap **Notes** ( ). On the Notes screen, tap **Default Account for Siri** to display the Default Account for Siri screen, and then tap the appropriate account; or tap **On My iPhone** to store the notes only on your iPhone.

What other settings can I configure for Notes?

You can choose the default style for the first line in each new note. Open the Notes screen in the Settings app as explained in the previous tip, tap **New Notes Start With**, and then tap the appropriate style — **Title**, **Heading**, or **Body** — on the New Notes Start With screen.

Using Stocks, Weather, and Clock

The iPhone includes several built-in apps that enable you to keep track of important information throughout the day. You can use the Stocks app to track stock prices so that you can take immediate action when it becomes necessary. You can use the Weather app to learn the current weather conditions and forecast for your current location and as many cities as you need. And you can use the Clock app's World Clock, Alarm, Bedtime, Stopwatch, and Timer features to track and measure time.

Using the Stocks App

The Stocks app enables you to track a customized selection of stock prices.

Tap **Stocks** (⬛) on the Home screen to launch the Stocks app. The Stocks screen appears, showing the default selection of stocks.

To change the stocks displayed, tap **Info** (▤). On the Stocks configuration screen that appears, tap **Add** (+) to display the Search screen. Type the name or stock symbol of the stock you want to add, and then tap the matching entry in the list. You can tap stock handles (▤) and drag the stocks into your preferred order. Tap **percentage**, **price**, or **market cap** to control which statistic the Stocks app displays first, and then tap **Done** to return to the Stocks screen.

Using the Weather App

The Weather app lets you stay in touch with current weather conditions and forecasts for multiple locations.

Tap **Weather** (⬤) on the Home screen to launch the Weather app. You can then swipe left or right at the top of the screen, or tap the dots at the bottom of the screen, to display the city you want to see. Swipe the timeline left to see later hours. Swipe up to display further details, such as sunrise and sunset times, humidity, and wind.

To customize the locations, tap **Cities** (▤). You can then tap **Add** (⊕) to add a location, swipe a location left and tap **Delete** to delete it, or tap and hold and then drag to move a city up or down the list. When you finish customizing the list, tap the city whose weather you want to display.

Using the Clock App

The Clock app, which you can launch by tapping **Clock** () on the Home screen, has five main features: World Clock, Alarm, Bedtime, Stopwatch, and Timer. You tap the buttons at the bottom of the screen to select the feature you want to use.

The World Clock feature enables you to easily keep track of the time in different cities. From the list, you can remove a city by swiping its button left and then tapping **Delete**. To add cities, tap **Add** (▦) and select the city on the Choose a City screen. To change the order of the list, tap **Edit** and drag cities up or down by their handles (≡); tap **Done** when you finish.

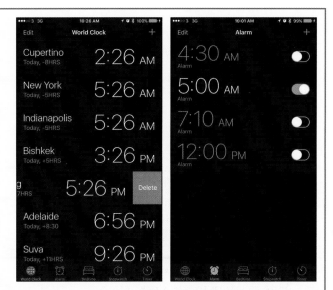

The Alarm feature lets you set as many alarms as you need, each with a different schedule and your choice of sound. Tap **Add** (▦) to display the Add Alarm screen, set the details for a new alarm, and then tap **Save**. On the Alarm screen, you can set each alarm's switch to On (◯) or Off (◯), as needed.

The Bedtime feature encourages you to follow consistent times for going to bed and waking. It also provides sleep analysis.

The Stopwatch feature allows you to time events to the hundredth of a second. You can switch between the analog-look stopwatch and the digital-look stopwatch by swiping left or right. Tap **Start** to start the stopwatch, tap **Lap** to mark a lap time, and tap **Stop** to stop the stopwatch.

The Timer feature enables you to count down a set amount of time and play a sound when the timer ends. You can also use the Timer to play music or other media for a set amount of time. To do this, tap **When Timer Ends**, tap **Stop Playing** on the When Timer Ends screen, and then tap **Set**.

Using the Health App

The Health app integrates with third-party hardware and software to enable you to keep tabs on many different aspects of your health, ranging from your weight and blood pressure to your nutrition, activity levels, and body mass index. Press **Home** to display the Home screen, and then tap **Health** (♥) to launch the Health app.

Track Your Health with Health Data

The Health Data screen provides quick access to the health information you want to track closely.

Tap **Health Data** (⊞ changes to ⊞) to display the Health Data screen. You can then tap one of the main four areas — Activity, Mindfulness, Nutrition, or Sleep — at the top of the screen to explore the data available. Further down the screen, you can tap **Body Measurements**, **Health Records**, **Reproductive Health**, **Results**, or **Vitals** to access those categories. For example, Body Measurements enables you to track your height, weight, body mass index, body fat percentage, and lean body mass.

Examine Today's Statistics

The Today screen provides an easy way to look at a day's activity and vital statistics.

Tap **Today** (▦ changes to ▦) to display the Today screen, which displays the Favorites list, showing items you have designated as favorites; the Activity list, which shows items such as Resting Energy, Active Energy, and Steps; and the Vitals list, which shows any vital signs measured by your iPhone, Apple Watch, or other hardware sources you have connected to Health.

Tap a button on the Today screen to display more detail. For example, tap **Walking + Running Distance** to display the Walking + Running Distance screen, where you can view graphs for day, week, month, and year; set the **Add to Favorites** switch to On (🔵) to make the item a favorite; or tap **Data Sources & Access** to examine or change the data sources used.

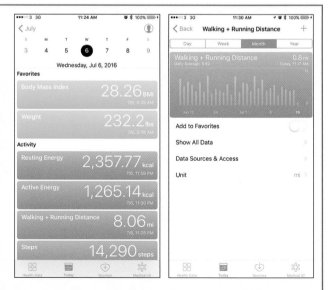

Add Data Points

The Health app can automatically accept data points from sources you approve, as explained next, but you can also add data points manually. For example, if you weigh yourself on a manual scale or have your blood pressure taken, you can add your latest readings to the Health app so that you can track your weight and blood pressure over time.

Tap **Vitals** on the Health Data screen to display the Vitals screen. You can then tap the appropriate button to reach its screen. For example, tap **Blood Pressure** to display the Blood Pressure screen. You can then tap **Add** (+) to display the Add Data screen. Enter the date, time, and systolic and diastolic pressures, and then tap the **Add** button.

Add Sources

Tap **Sources** (⏱ changes to ♥) to display the Sources screen. Here you can review the list of apps that have requested permission to update the data in the Health app; you can remove any apps that you no longer want to permit to update the data. You can also review the list of hardware devices that have gotten permission to update the data — for example, your Apple Watch — and revoke permissions as needed.

Add Your Medical ID

Tap **Medical ID** (❄ changes to ✳) to display the Medical ID screen. You can then tap **Edit** to open the data for editing so that you can enter details of your medical conditions, medications, emergency contact, and blood type. Set the **Show When Locked** switch to On (⬤) if you want to display your medical ID on the lock screen, enabling others to access your essential information to help if you become unwell.

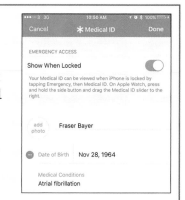

CHAPTER 10

Enjoying Music, Videos, and Books

As well as being a phone and a powerful handheld computer, your iPhone is also a full-scale music and video player. To play music and listen to radio, you use the Music app; to play videos, you use the Videos app. You can read digital books and PDF files using the iBooks app.

The Music app enables you to enjoy music you have loaded on your iPhone, music you have stored on Apple's iTunes Match service, and music on the Apple Music Radio service.

The Music app packs a wide range of functionality into its interface. The For You feature enables you to set — and reset — your musical preferences. The Radio feature allows you to listen to Apple Music Radio. And the Connect feature lets you connect to artists online.

Navigate the Music App and Set Preferences

1 Press **Home**.

The Home screen appears.

2 Tap **Music** (♫).

The Music app opens.

3 If Library is not selected, tap **Library** (♫ changes to ♫).

The Library screen appears, showing your music library.

Ⓐ You can tap an item, such as Playlists or Artists, to browse the library.

Ⓑ The Recently Added section shows items added recently.

4 Tap **Edit**.

The Library screen opens for editing.

5 Tap an empty selection circle to select it (○ changes to ✓), adding that item to the Library list.

6 Tap a selected selection circle to deselect it (✓ changes to ○), removing that item from the Library list.

7 Drag a selection handle up or down to move an item in the list.

8 Tap **Done**.

The Library screen displays the customized list.

9 Tap **For You** (♥ changes to ♥).

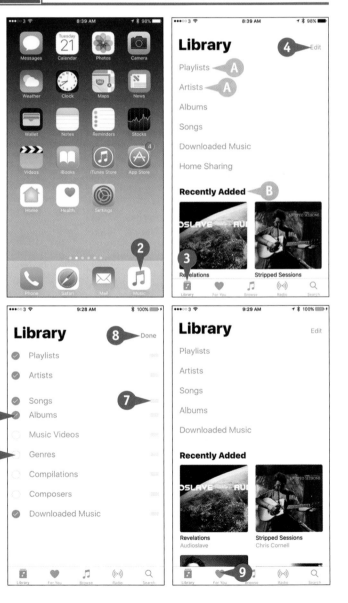

The For You screen appears, showing music suggestions for you.

Note: On the For You screen, you can scroll down to see different categories of items, such as Artist Playlists and New Releases for you. Scroll a category left to see more items in it.

 You can tap your initials to display the Account screen. From here, tap **Choose Artists For You** to launch a feature for specifying the genres and artists you like.

⑩ Tap **Browse** (♫ changes to ♪).

The Browse screen appears, providing ways to browse music.

⑪ Tap **Radio** ((••)) changes to ((•))).

The Radio screen appears.

Ⓓ You can tap a station to start it playing.

Note: See the section "Listen to Apple Music Radio," later in this chapter, for more information on the Radio feature.

⑫ Tap **Search** (Q changes to Q).

The Search screen appears.

Ⓔ You can tap the Search box and type a search term.

Ⓕ You can tap a recent search to repeat it.

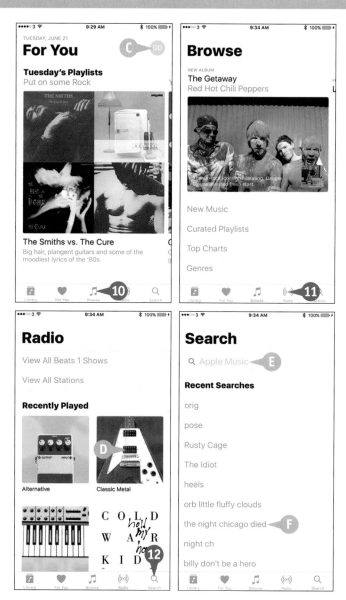

How does the Search function work?

The Search function enables you to search both your own music and the Apple Music service. Tap **Search** (Q changes to Q) to display the Search screen, and then type your search terms in the box at the top of the screen. Tap the **Apple Music** tab button to see matching searches you can perform on Apple Music; you can then tap a search to perform it. Tap the **In Library** tab button to see matching items in your music, broken down into categories such as Artists, Albums, or Songs. When you locate the item you want, tap the item to go to it.

Play Music Using the Music App

After loading music on your iPhone, as described in the section "Choose Which Items to Sync from Your Computer" in Chapter 1, you can play it back using the Music app. You can play music by song or by album, as described in this section. You can play songs in exactly the order you want by creating a custom playlist, as described in the later section, "Create a Music Playlist and Add Songs." You can also play by artist, genre, or composer.

Play Music Using the Music App

① Press **Home**.

The Home screen appears.

② Tap **Music** (🎵).

The Music app opens.

③ Tap **Library** (🎵 changes to 🎵).

The Library screen appears.

Ⓐ The Recently Added section shows items added recently. You can scroll up to see more.

④ Tap the button for the means by which you want to browse your library. This example uses **Songs**.

The Songs screen appears.

⑤ Tap the letter that starts the name of the item you want to play.

That section of the list appears.

Note: You can also swipe or drag your finger up the screen to scroll down.

Note: Tap above the letter A in the navigation letters to go back to the top of the screen.

⑥ Tap the song you want to play.

The song starts playing.

B The song appears on the Now Playing button.

C You can tap **Pause** (❚❚) to pause the song.

D You can tap **Next** (▶▶) to skip to the next song.

7 Tap **Now Playing** — either the song name or the album art.

The Now Playing screen appears.

8 Tap and drag the playhead to move through the song.

9 Tap and drag the volume control to change the volume.

10 Tap **More** (•••).

The More pop-up panel appears.

E You can tap **Add to a Playlist** (⊕≣) to add the song to a new or existing playlist.

F You can tap **Create Station** ((•)) to create a station based on the song.

G You can tap **Love** (♥) or **Dislike** (🖐) to indicate your feeling toward the song.

H You can tap **Remove** (🗑) to remove the song.

11 Tap the song name.

The Now Playing screen appears again.

12 Tap **Back** (⌐).

The list of songs appears again.

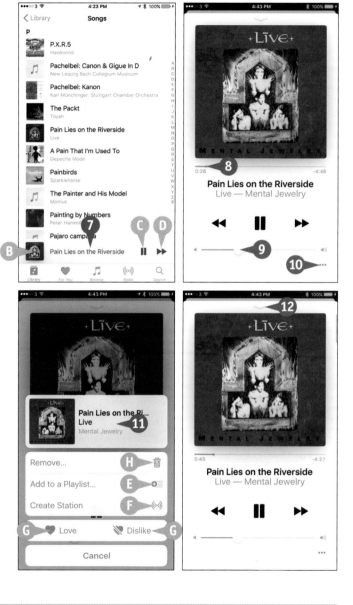

TIPS

How else can I control playback?
Swipe up from the bottom of the screen to display Control Center; if the Music panel does not appear at first, swipe left to display it. You can then use the playhead to move through the song, control playback using the playback buttons, and tap and drag the volume slider to adjust the volume.

Where are the Shuffle button and the Repeat button?
Scroll the Now Playing screen up to display the Shuffle button, the Repeat button, and the Up Next list, which shows you the list of songs that will play next.

Play Videos Using the Videos App

To play videos — such as movies, TV shows, or music videos — you use the iPhone's Videos app. You can play a video on the iPhone's screen, which is handy when you are traveling; on a TV to which you connect the iPhone; or on a TV connected to an Apple TV box. Using a TV is great when you need to share a movie or other video with family, friends, or colleagues.

Play Videos Using the Videos App

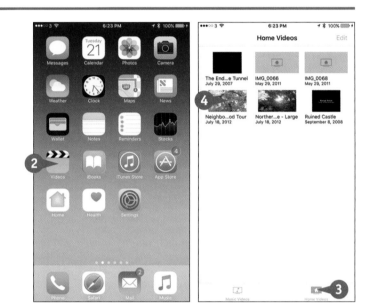

1 Press **Home**.

The Home screen appears.

Note: You can also play videos included on web pages. To do so, press **Home**, tap **Safari**, navigate to the page, and then tap the video.

2 Tap **Videos** ().

The Videos screen appears.

3 Tap the video category you want to browse, such as **Music Videos** (☑ changes to ▣) or **Home Videos** (☐ changes to ▣).

The screen for that video category appears.

4 Tap the video you want to play.

The video starts playing.

Note: If the video is in landscape format, turn your iPhone sideways to view the video in landscape orientation.

5 When you need to control playback, tap the screen.

The playback controls appear.

Ⓐ You can drag the playhead to move through the video.

Ⓑ You can drag the volume control to change the volume.

Ⓒ You can tap **Pause** (❚❚) to pause playback. Tap **Play** (▶) to resume playback.

Ⓓ Tap and hold **Rewind** (◀◀) to rewind the video a few seconds at a time.

Ⓔ Tap and hold **Fast-Forward** (▶▶) to fast-forward the video a few seconds at a time.

6 Tap **Done** when you want to stop playing the video.

The details screen for the video appears.

Ⓕ You can tap a video category to display it.

Ⓖ You can tap **Play** (▶) to play the video again.

7 Tap **Back** (‹).

The screen for the video category appears.

Neighborhood Tour
July 18, 2012

Length	Size
12 sec	6.1 MB

Dimensions	Codec
960 × 540	H.264

TIPS

How do I play videos on my television from my iPhone?

If you have an Apple TV or AirPlay-compatible device, use AirPlay, as explained in the next section, "Play Music and Videos Using AirPlay." Otherwise, use the Apple Lightning Digital AV Adapter and an HDMI cable to connect your iPhone to a TV.

What other video content can I watch on my iPhone?

You can also use your iPhone to watch or listen to *podcasts*, which are video or audio programs released via the Internet. The Podcasts app enables you to access podcasts covering many different topics, and the iTunes U app is your gateway to podcasts containing educational content, some free and some paid.

Play Music and Videos Using AirPlay

Using the AirPlay feature, you can play music from your iPhone on remote speakers connected to an AirPlay-compatible device such as an AirPort Express or Apple TV. Similarly, you can play video from your iPhone on a TV or monitor connected to an Apple TV. Even better, you can use the iOS feature called *AirPlay Mirroring* to display an iPhone app on a TV or monitor. For example, you can display a web page in Safari on your TV screen.

Play Music and Videos Using AirPlay

Play Music on External Speakers or an Apple TV

 Press **Home**.

The Home screen appears.

 Tap **Music** (♫).

The Music app opens.

 Navigate to the song you want to play. For example, tap **Library** (🎵 changes to 🎵), tap **Songs**, and then tap the song.

The song appears on the Now Playing button.

4 Swipe up from the bottom of the screen.

Control Center opens.

Note: If the Music panel of Control Center does not appear, swipe left to display it.

5 Tap **Now Playing on iPhone**.

The AirPlay pop-up panel appears.

6 Tap the speakers or Apple TV you want to use.

7 Tap **Now Playing On**. The button shows the name of the device you tapped.

The AirPlay pop-up panel closes.

The music starts playing through the AirPlay device.

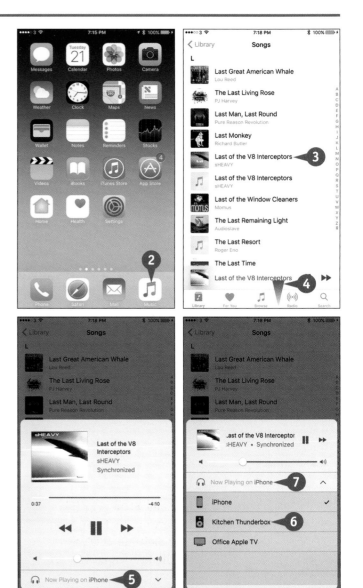

Play Video or an App on an Apple TV

1 Open the app you want to use. This example uses **Notes** ( ).

2 Swipe up from the bottom of the screen.

Note: In landscape view, swipe up once to display an arrow button in the center of the bottom of the screen. Tap this button or swipe up again to open Control Center.

> Control Center opens.

3 Tap **AirPlay Screen** ( ).

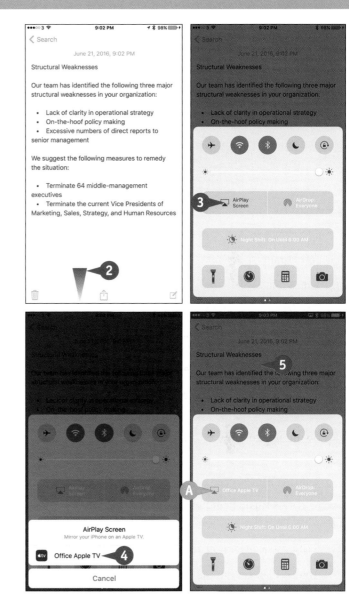

> The AirPlay Screen pop-up panel opens.

4 Tap the Apple TV you want to use.

> The AirPlay Screen pop-up panel closes.

Ⓐ The AirPlay button shows the Apple TV you selected.

> The app or video appears on the screen connected to the Apple TV.

5 Tap in the app above Control Center.

> Control Center closes, and the app appears full-screen.

Why does the AirPlay button not appear in Control Center?

The AirPlay button appears only when your iPhone is connected to a wireless network that has AirPlay devices attached. If you use multiple wireless networks, make sure your iPhone is connected to the right network.

Can AirPlay play music through multiple sets of speakers at the same time?

AirPlay on the Mac or PC can play music through two or more sets of speakers at the same time, enabling you to play music throughout your home. However, as of this writing, AirPlay on the iPhone can play only to a single device at a time.

Create a Music Playlist and Add Songs

Instead of playing individual songs or playing a CD's songs from start to finish, you can create a playlist that contains only the songs you want in your preferred order. Playlists are a great way to enjoy music on your iPhone.

To help identify a playlist, you can add a new photo or an existing photo. Alternatively, you can let the Music app create a thumbnail from the covers of the songs you add to the playlist.

Create a Music Playlist and Add Songs

Create a Music Playlist

1. Press **Home**.

   The Home screen appears.

2. Tap **Music** (♫).

   The Music screen appears.

3. Tap **Library** (♫ changes to ♫).

   The Library screen appears.

4. Tap **Playlists**.

   The Playlists screen appears.

5. Tap **New Playlist**.

   The New Playlist screen opens.

6. Tap **Playlist Name** and type the name for the playlist.

7. Optionally, tap **Description** and type a description for the playlist.

8. Optionally, tap **Photo** (📷), tap **Take Photo** or **Choose Photo**, and follow the prompts to add a photo.

   Ⓐ You can tap **Add Music** to display the Add Music screen, navigate to the songs you want, and then tap them. Alternatively, follow the steps in the next subsection.

9. Tap **Done**.

238

Add Songs to a Playlist

1 In the Music app, tap **Library** (changes to 🎵).

The Library screen appears.

Note: This example uses the Songs list to add songs to a playlist, but you can also add songs by other means, such as browsing or searching.

2 Tap **Songs**.

The Songs screen appears.

3 3D-touch the first song you want to add.

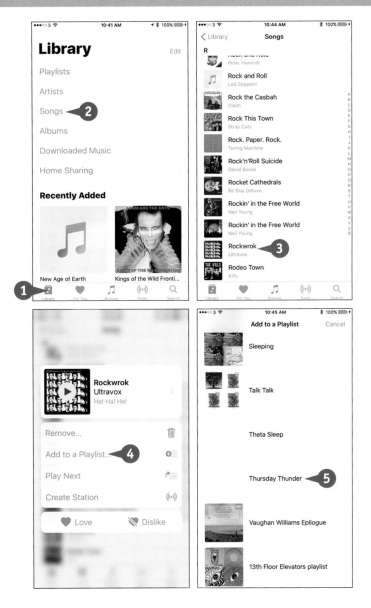

The Peek panel appears.

4 Tap **Add to a Playlist** (⊕≡).

The Add to a Playlist screen appears.

5 Tap the appropriate playlist.

The Music app adds the song to the playlist.

You can now add other songs to the playlist, as needed.

TIP

How do I change the order of the songs I have added to a playlist?
Press **Home**. Tap **Music** (🎵), tap **Library** (🎵 changes to 🎵), and then tap **Playlists**. On the Playlists screen, tap the playlist you want to edit, and then tap **Edit** to open the playlist for editing. Tap a song's selection handle (≡) and drag the song up or down to change the playlist order. When you finish editing the playlist, tap **Done**.

Listen to Apple Music Radio

The Radio feature in the Music app enables you to listen to the Apple Music Radio service. Apple Music Radio has two main parts, one free and one paid. The free part comprises the Beats 1 global radio station and other live radio stations. The paid part is curated, on-demand radio stations and custom radio stations, which require a subscription to the Apple Music service. An individual subscription costs $9.99 per month; a family subscription, which covers up to six people, costs $14.99 per month.

Listen to Apple Music Radio

1 Press **Home**.

The Home screen appears.

2 Tap **Music** (♫).

The Music app opens.

3 Tap **Radio** ((•) changes to (•)).

The Radio screen appears.

A You can tap **View All Beats 1 Shows** to display a screen that lists Beats 1 shows.

B The Recently Played list shows stations you have played recently. Scroll up to see more of the list.

4 Tap **View All Stations**.

The Stations screen appears.

C The top of the Stations list shows some featured stations such as Charting Now, Pop Hits, Dance, and Classical. Scroll left to browse the stations.

D The Featured Stations list shows a fuller list of featured stations. You can tap **See All** to see all the featured stations.

5 Swipe up to scroll down.

The All Genres list appears.

6 Tap the genre you want to browse.

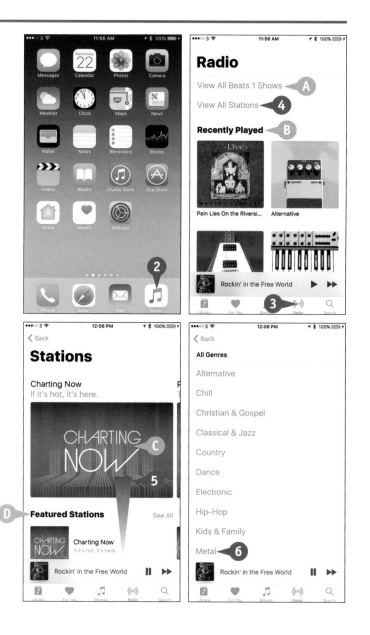

The list of stations in that genre appears.

Note: To share a station, 3D-touch the station and then tap **Share Station** (⬆️).

7 Tap the station you want to play.

Ⓔ The current song on that station starts playing. The song appears on the Now Playing button.

Ⓕ You can tap **Pause** (❚❚) to pause playback.

Ⓖ You can tap **Skip** (▶▶) to skip to the next song.

8 Tap **Now Playing**.

The Now Playing screen appears.

Ⓗ You can tap **Back** (‹) to return to the Radio screen.

Ⓘ You can drag the playhead to move through the song.

Ⓙ You can drag the volume control to change the volume.

Ⓚ You can tap **Add** (+) to add the song to your library.

9 Tap **More** (•••).

The More panel appears.

Ⓛ You can tap **Love** (♥) or **Dislike** (🚫) to express your feelings about the song.

Ⓜ You can tap **Add to a Playlist** (⊕≡) to add the song to a playlist.

Ⓝ You can tap **Create Station** ((•)) to create a station based on the song.

Ⓞ You can tap **Share Song** (⬆️) to share the song with others.

TIP

What do the Share Station and Share Song commands do?

The Share Station command enables you to share a link to a station on Apple Music Radio. Similarly, the Share Song command lets you share a link to a song on the iTunes Store. You can use various means of sharing, such as sending the link via Mail or Messages, posting it to Facebook or Twitter, or simply setting yourself a reminder to listen to — or avoid — the music.

Read Digital Books with iBooks

The iBooks app enables you to read e-books or PDF files that you load on the iPhone from your computer or sync via iCloud. You can also read e-books and PDFs you download from online stores, download from web pages, or save from e-mail messages.

If you have already loaded some e-books, you can read them as described in this section. If iBooks contains no books, tap the **Store** button and browse the iBooks Store or sync books from your computer using iTunes.

Read Digital Books with iBooks

1 Press **Home**.

The Home screen appears.

2 Tap **iBooks** (📖).

iBooks opens, and a screen such as the All Books screen or the Books screen appears.

Ⓐ If the Audiobooks screen or the PDFs screen appears, tap **Audiobooks** or **PDFs**. On the Collections screen that appears, tap **All Books** or **Books** to display the All Books screen or the Books screen.

3 To view the books as a list, tap **List** (☰ changes to ▦) at the top of the screen.

Ⓑ You can tap **Search** (🔍) and search to locate the book you want.

The list of books appears.

Ⓒ You can tap **Recent**, **Titles**, **Authors**, or **Categories** to sort the books differently.

4 Tap the book you want to open.

The book opens.

Note: When you open a book, iBooks displays your current page. When you open a book for the first time, iBooks displays the book's cover, first page, or default page.

Ⓓ To change the font, tap **Font Settings** (ₐA) and work in the Font Settings dialog.

5 Tap anywhere on the screen to hide the reading controls.

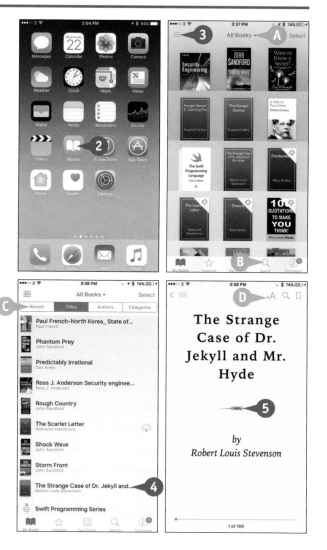

The reading controls disappear.

Note: To display the reading controls again, tap anywhere on the screen.

6 Tap the right side of the page to display the next page.

Note: To display the previous page, tap the left side of the page. Alternatively, tap the left side of the page and drag to the right.

7 To look at the next page without fully revealing it, tap the right side and drag to the left. You can then either drag further to turn the page or release the page and let it fall closed.

8 To jump to another part of the book, tap **Table of Contents** (≡).

Note: Alternatively, you can drag the slider at the bottom of the screen.

The table of contents appears.

9 Tap the part of the book you want to display.

10 To search in the book, tap **Search** (🔍).

The Search screen appears.

11 Type the search term.

The list of search results appears.

12 Tap the result you want to display.

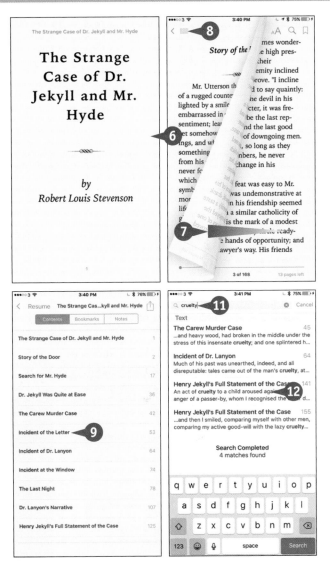

TIPS

How do I get my books from iBooks on my Mac onto my iPhone?

Use iTunes to sync your books. Connect your iPhone to your Mac, and then click **iPhone** (📱) on the navigation bar. Click **Books** in the Settings list in the sidebar, and then click **Sync Books** (☐ changes ☑). To sync all your books, click **All books** (◯ changes to ◉); to sync books you choose, click **Selected books** (◯ changes to ◉) and then click each book (☐ changes to ☑).

Where can I find free e-books to read in iBooks?

On the iBooks Store, tap **Featured** and then tap **Free Books** in the Browse area. Other sources of free e-books include ManyBooks.net (www.manybooks.net), Project Gutenberg (www.gutenberg.org), and the Baen Free Library (www.baen.com/library).

CHAPTER 11

Working with Photos and Video

Your iPhone's Camera app enables you to take high-quality still photos and videos. You can edit photos or apply filters to them, trim video clips down to length, and easily share both photos and videos.

Take Photos with the Camera App

Your iPhone includes a high-resolution rear camera and a lower-resolution screen-side camera. Both cameras can take photos and videos, and the screen-side camera works for video calls, too. To take photos using the camera, you use the Camera app. This app includes a digital zoom feature for zooming in and out; a flash that you can set to On, Off, or Auto; and a High Dynamic Range (HDR) feature that combines several photos into a single photo with adjusted color balance and intensity.

Take Photos with the Camera App

Open the Camera App

1 Press **Home**.

The Home screen appears.

Note: From the lock screen, you can open the Camera app by swiping left.

2 Tap **Camera** ( ).

The Camera app opens and displays whatever is in front of the lens.

Compose the Photo and Zoom if Necessary

1 Aim the iPhone so that your subject appears in the middle of the photo area. To focus on an item not in the center of the frame, tap that item to move the focus rectangle to it.

Note: If you need to take tightly composed photos, get a tripod mount for the iPhone. You can find various models on eBay and photography sites.

2 If you need to zoom in, place two fingers together on the screen and pinch outward.

The zoom slider appears.

3 Tap **Zoom In** ( ) to zoom in or **Zoom Out** ( ) to zoom out. Tap as many times as needed.

Ⓐ You can also zoom by tapping and dragging the zoom slider ( ).

Note: On the iPhone 7 Plus, tap **2X** to zoom in quickly using optical zoom.

Choose Flash and HDR Settings

1 Tap **Flash** (⚡, ⚡, or ⚡).

The Flash settings appear.

2 Tap **On** to use the flash, **Auto** to use the flash if there is not enough light without it, or **Off** to turn the flash off.

3 Tap **HDR**.

The HDR settings appear.

4 Tap **Auto**, **On**, or **Off**, as needed.

Note: You cannot use the flash with HDR. Turning HDR on turns the flash off, and vice versa.

Take the Photo and View It

Ⓑ HDR appears if HDR is on.

1 Tap **Take Photo** (○).

Note: You can tap and hold **Take Photo** (○) to take a burst of photos.

The Camera app takes the photo and displays a thumbnail.

2 Tap the thumbnail.

The photo appears.

Ⓒ From the photo screen, swipe or tap a thumbnail to display another photo. Tap **Delete** (🗑) to delete the current photo.

3 Tap **Camera** (<) when you want to go back to the Camera app.

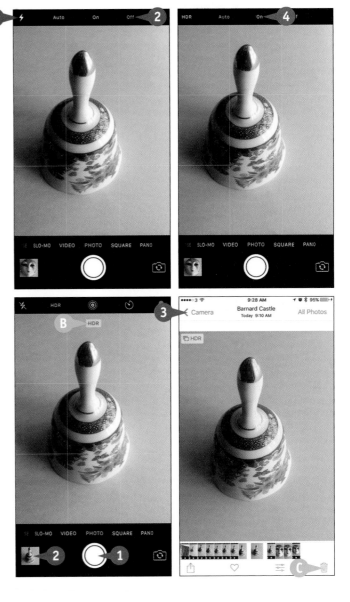

TIP

How do I switch to the front-facing camera?
Tap **Switch Cameras** (📷) to switch from the rear-facing camera to the front-facing camera. The image that the front-facing camera is seeing appears on-screen, and you can take pictures as described in this section. HDR is available for the front-facing camera; flash is available only on some iPhone models. Tap **Switch Cameras** (📷) again when you want to switch back to the rear-facing camera.

Take Live, Timed, Square, and Panorama Photos

The Camera app's Live Photo feature enables you to capture several seconds of video around a still photo. Live Photo is great for photographing moving subjects or setting the scene.

The self-timer feature lets you set the app to take a burst of 11 photos after a delay of 3 seconds or 10 seconds, which is good for group shots and for avoiding camera shake. You can also capture square photos, panoramas, and time-lapse movies.

Take Live, Timed, Square, and Panorama Photos

Open the Camera App, Take a Live Photo, and View It

1 Press **Home**.

   The Home screen appears.

2 Tap **Camera** (📷).

   The Camera app opens.

3 Tap **Live** (◉ changes to ◉).

Note: Live Photo starts recording video as soon as you enable the feature. Live Photo discards the video except for the segments before and after photos you shoot.

Ⓐ The Live badge appears briefly.

4 Take **Take Photo** (◯).

   The Camera app captures the Live Photo.

5 Tap the photo's thumbnail.

   The photo opens.

   The Live Photo segment plays.

6 Tap and hold the photo to play the Live Photo segment again.

7 Tap **Back** (〈).

   The Camera app appears again.

Take a Timed Photo

1 Tap **Timer** ().

The Timer settings appear.

2 Tap **3s** or **10s** to set the delay.

The delay appears next to the Timer icon.

3 Tap **Take Photo** (○).

Note: The Camera app displays an on-screen countdown, and the rear flash flashes to indicate the countdown to the subject.

When the countdown ends, the Camera app takes a burst of 11 photos.

Note: The timer remains set until you change it.

Take a Square Photo

1 Tap **Square**.

Note: Square photos are useful for adding to contact records and similar needs.

Camera reduces the frame to a square.

2 Tap **Take Photo** (○).

Camera takes a photo.

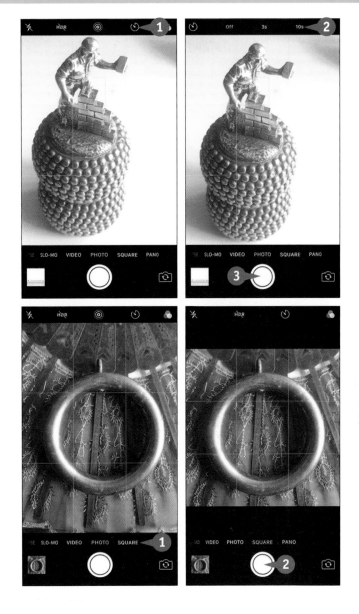

TIPS

How do I take panorama photos?
Tap **Pano**. Holding the iPhone in portrait orientation, aim at the left end of the panorama. Tap **Take Photo** (○); gradually move the iPhone to the right, keeping the white arrow on the horizontal line; and then tap **Stop** (○).

How do I take time-lapse movies?
Tap **Time-Lapse**; if you cannot see Time-Lapse, drag the current setting to the right first. Set the iPhone up on a tripod or other steady holder, aim it at the subject, and then tap **Start** (○). When you have captured enough, tap **Stop** (○) to stop shooting.

Apply Filters to Your Photos

Y ou can use the Filter feature in the Camera app to change the look of a photo by applying a filter such as Mono, Tonal, Chrome, Transfer, or Instant.

You can apply a filter either before taking the photo or after taking it. If you apply the filter before taking the photo, you can remove the filter afterward; the filter is an effect applied to the photo, not an integral part of the photo.

Apply Filters to Your Photos

1 Press **Home**.

The Home screen appears.

2 Tap **Camera** (📷).

The Camera app opens.

3 Tap **Filters** (⬤).

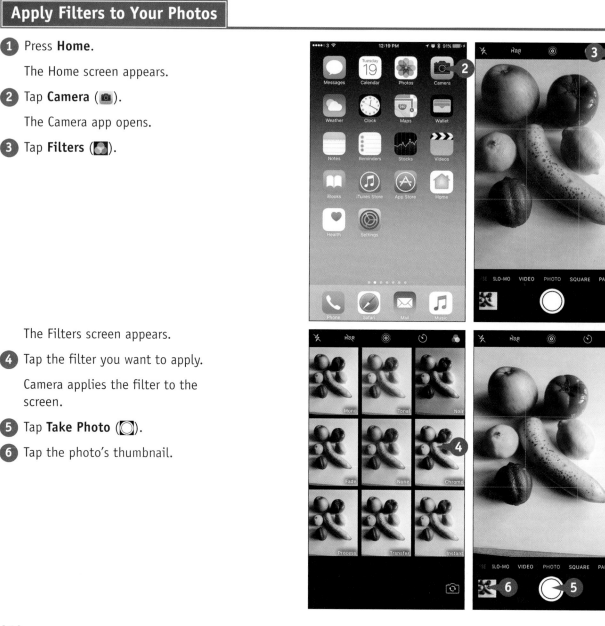

The Filters screen appears.

4 Tap the filter you want to apply.

Camera applies the filter to the screen.

5 Tap **Take Photo** (◯).

6 Tap the photo's thumbnail.

The photo appears.

7 Tap **Edit** ().

The Edit Photo screen appears, showing the editing tools.

8 Tap **Filters** ().

The Choose Filter screen appears.

9 Tap the filter you want to apply. Scroll left or right to display other filters.

Note: Tap **None** if you want to remove filtering.

10 Tap **Done**.

iOS saves the change to the photo.

11 Tap **Camera** (<) to return to the Camera app.

TIP

Is it better to apply a filter before taking a photo or after taking it?
This is up to you. Sometimes it is helpful to have the filter effect in place when composing a photo so that you can arrange the composition and lighting to complement the filtering. Other times, especially when you do not have time to experiment with filters, it is more practical to take the photos and then try applying filters afterward.

251

Edit Your Photos

To improve your photos, you can use the powerful but easy-to-use editing tools your iPhone includes. These tools include rotating a photo to a different orientation, straightening it by rotating it a little, and cropping off the parts you do not need.

You can access the editing tools either through the Recently Added album in the Photos app or through the Photos app. To start editing a photo, you open the photo by tapping it, and then tap **Edit**.

Edit Your Photos

Open a Photo for Editing

1 Press **Home**.

The Home screen appears.

2 Tap **Photos** (✳).

The Photos app opens.

3 Navigate to the photo you want to edit.

Ⓐ If the photo is part of a burst, the Burst readout appears. You can tap **Select** to select another photo from the burst instead of the default photo.

4 Tap **Edit** (⚊).

The Editing controls appear.

Crop, Rotate, and Straighten a Photo

1 Tap **Crop** (▣).

The tools for cropping, straightening, and rotating appear.

Ⓑ You can tap **Rotate** (◤) to rotate the photo 90 degrees counterclockwise.

2 Tap and hold the degree dial.

Ⓒ The grid appears.

3 Drag the degree dial left or right to straighten the photo.

Ⓓ You can tap **Reset** to reset the photo.

④ Tap and hold an edge or corner of the crop box.

ⓔ The nine-square grid appears. This is to help you compose the cropped photo.

⑤ Drag the edge or corner of the crop box to select only the area you want to keep.

Enhance the Colors in a Photo

① Tap **Auto-Enhance** (🪄 changes to 🪄).

iOS enhances the colors.

Note: Tap **Auto-Enhance** again (🪄 changes to 🪄) if you want to remove the color change.

Note: You can tap and hold the photo to display the original photo for as long as you hold. Displaying the original helps you see the effects of your changes.

TIP

What does the three-squares button on the cropping screen do?
The button with three squares (▤) is the Aspect button. Tap **Aspect** (▤) when you need to crop to a specific aspect ratio, such as a square or the 16:9 widescreen aspect ratio. In the Aspect dialog that opens, tap the constraint you want to use. iOS adjusts the current cropping to match the aspect ratio. You may then need to move the portion of the photo shown to get the composition you want. If you adjust the cropping, tap **Aspect** (▤) again and reapply the aspect ratio.

continued ▶

The Red-Eye Reduction feature enables you to restore feral eyes to normality. The Enhance feature enables you to adjust a photo's color balance and lighting quickly using default algorithms that analyze the photo and try to improve it. The Enhance feature often works well, but for greater control, you can use the Light settings and the Color settings to tweak the exposure, highlights, shadows, brightness, black point, contrast, vibrancy, and other settings manually.

Edit Your Photos (continued)

Remove Red Eye from a Photo

Note: You may need to zoom in on the photo in order to touch the red-eye patches accurately.

 Tap **Red-Eye Reduction** (◯).

iOS prompts you to tap each eye.

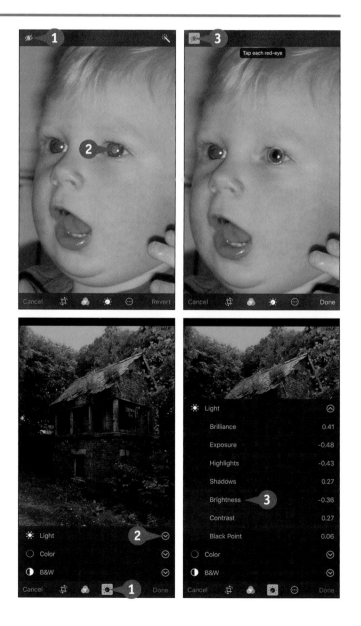 Tap each red eye.

iOS removes the red eye.

 Tap **Red-Eye Reduction** (◯).

iOS turns off the Red-Eye Reduction tool.

Adjust the Colors in a Photo

 Tap **Adjust** (◯).

The Adjust controls appear.

 Tap **Expand** (◯) on the Light bar.

Note: To adjust all the light settings at once, using Photos' automated adjustments, tap **Light**.

The Light settings appear.

 Tap the setting you want to adjust. This example uses **Brightness**.

4 Drag the scale to adjust the setting.

Following this example, the photo becomes brighter.

5 Tap **List** (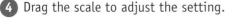).

The list of Light settings appears.

6 Tap **Expand** (⌄) on the Color line.

Note: To adjust all the color settings at once, using Photos' automated adjustments, tap **Color**. Similarly, you can tap **B&W** to adjust all the black-and-white settings at once.

The list of Color settings appears.

7 Tap the setting you want to adjust. This example uses **Saturation**.

8 Drag the scale to adjust the setting.

9 Tap **List** (▤).

The list of settings appears, and you can adjust further settings as needed.

TIPS

How do I save the changes I have made to a photo?
When you finish making changes to a photo, tap **Done** to save the changes.

How do I get rid of changes I have made to a photo?
Tap **Cancel**, and then tap **Discard Changes** in the confirmation dialog that opens.

Capture Video

As well as capturing still photos, your iPhone's camera can capture high-quality, full-motion video in either portrait orientation or landscape orientation. To capture video, you use the Camera app. You launch the Camera app as usual, and then switch it to Video Mode for regular-speed shooting or to Slo-Mo Mode to shoot slow-motion footage. You can use flash, but it is effective only at close range for video. After taking the video, you can view it on the iPhone's screen.

Capture Video

1 Press **Home**.

The Home screen appears.

2 Tap **Camera** ().

The Camera screen appears, showing the image the lens is seeing.

Ⓐ Tap **Slo-Mo** if you want to shoot slow-motion footage.

3 Tap **Video**.

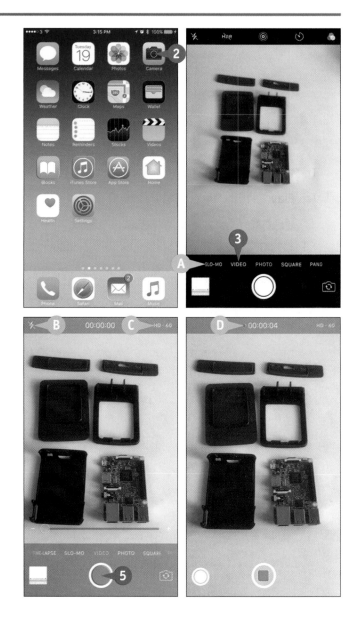

The video image and video controls appear.

4 Aim the camera at your subject.

Ⓑ If you need to use the flash for the video, tap **Flash** (⚡, ⚡, or ✕), and then tap **Auto** or **On**.

Ⓒ This readout shows the definition, such as HD, and the frame rate in frames per second, such as 60.

Note: To focus on a particular area of the screen, tap that area.

5 Tap **Record** (◉).

Ⓓ The camera starts recording, and the time readout shows the time that has elapsed.

6 To zoom in, place two fingers on the screen and pinch outward. You can then tap ➕ to zoom in, tap ➖ to zoom out, or drag the zoom slider (●).

E To take a still photo while shooting video, tap **Take Photo** (○).

7 To finish recording, tap **Stop** (●).

The Camera app stops recording and displays a thumbnail of the video's first frame.

8 Tap the thumbnail.

The video appears.

9 Tap **Play** (▶).

The video starts playing.

10 Tap anywhere on the screen to display the video controls. These disappear automatically after a few seconds of not being used.

11 When you finish viewing the video, tap **Camera** (<).

Note: If you want to trim the video, follow the procedure described in the next section, "Edit Video with the Trim Feature," before tapping **Camera** (<).

The Camera app appears again.

TIPS

How can I pause shooting a video?

As of this writing, you cannot pause while shooting. Either shoot separate video clips or trim out unwanted footage afterward.

What does the bar of miniature pictures at the bottom of the video playback screen do?

The navigation bar gives you a quick way of moving forward and backward through the video. Tap the thumbnails and drag them left or right until the part of the video you want to view is at the vertical blue playhead bar. You can use the navigation bar either when the video is playing or when it is paused.

Edit Video with the Trim Feature

When you capture video, you normally shoot more footage than you want to keep. You then edit the video to keep only the footage you need.

The Camera app includes a straightforward Trim feature that you can use to trim the beginning and end of a video clip to where you want them. For greater precision in editing, or to make a movie out of multiple clips, you can use the iMovie app, which is available from the App Store.

Edit Video with the Trim Feature

1 Press **Home**.

The Home screen appears.

2 Tap **Photos** (⚘).

The Photos app opens.

3 Tap **Albums**.

The Albums screen appears.

4 Tap **Videos**.

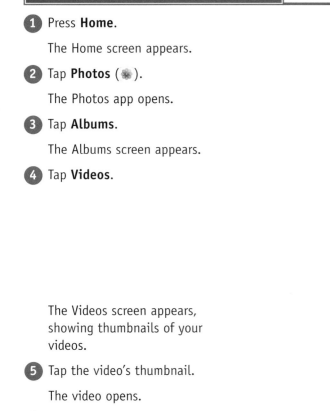

The Videos screen appears, showing thumbnails of your videos.

5 Tap the video's thumbnail.

The video opens.

6 Tap **Edit** (⟛).

The controls for editing the video appear.

7 Tap the left trim handle and drag it to the right until the frame appears where you want the trimmed clip to start.

8 Tap the right handle and drag it to the left until the frame appears where you want the trimmed clip to end.

9 Tap **Done**.

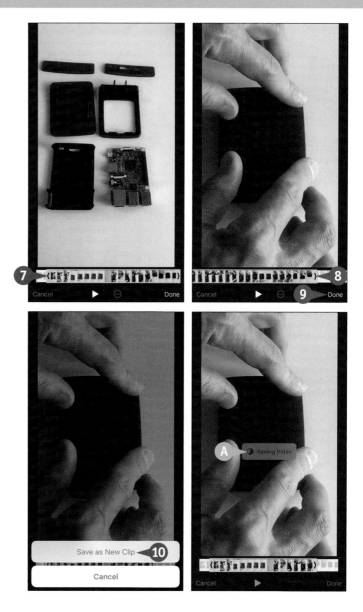

The Trim dialog appears.

10 Tap **Save as New Clip**.

A The Saving Video progress indicator appears while the Camera app trims and saves the video.

Note: Tap **Play** (▶) if you want to play back the trimmed video.

11 Tap **Back** (‹).

The Videos screen appears.

TIP

Is there an easier way of trimming my videos?

If you need to trim your videos on your iPhone, try turning the iPhone to landscape orientation. This makes the navigation bar longer and the trimming handles easier to use.

You can also trim your videos, edit them, and create movies from them by using Apple's iMovie app, which is available from the App Store. If you have a Mac, you can trim your videos more precisely and make many other changes by importing the clips into iMovie on the Mac, and then working with them there.

You can use the Photos app to browse the photos you have taken with your iPhone's camera, photos you have synced using iTunes or via iCloud's Shared Streams feature, and images you save from e-mail messages, instant messages, or web pages.

You can browse your photos by dates and locations using the smart groupings that Photos creates. Each Year grouping contains Collections, which contain Moments, which contain your photos. Alternatively, you can browse by albums, as explained in the section "Browse Photos Using Albums," later in this chapter.

Browse Photos Using Years, Collections, and Moments

1 Press **Home**.

The Home screen appears.

2 Tap **Photos** (❁).

The Photos app opens.

3 Tap **Photos** (◻ changes to ▦).

The Photos screen appears, showing the Years list.

4 Tap the year you want to open.

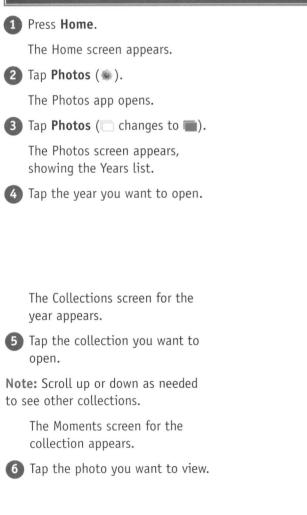

The Collections screen for the year appears.

5 Tap the collection you want to open.

Note: Scroll up or down as needed to see other collections.

The Moments screen for the collection appears.

6 Tap the photo you want to view.

The photo opens.

A You can tap **Edit** (⊜) to edit the photo, as explained earlier in this chapter.

B You can tap **Share** (⬆) to share the photo, as explained later in this chapter.

C You can tap **Favorite** (♡ changes to ♥) to make the photo a favorite.

D You can tap **Trash** (🗑) to delete the photo.

Note: The Trash icon does not appear for photos you cannot delete, such as photos in a shared photo stream.

⑦ In the thumbnail bar, tap the photo you want to view.

Note: You can also swipe left or right to display other photos.

The photo appears.

⑧ Tap **Back** (<).

The Moments screen appears.

Note: You can scroll up or down to display other moments.

⑨ Tap **Collections** (<).

The Collections screen appears.

Note: You can scroll up or down to display other collections.

⑩ Tap **Years** (<).

The Years screen appears, and you can navigate to another year.

How can I move a photo to a different year?

To move a photo to a different year, you need to change the date set in the photo's metadata. You cannot do this with the Photos app, but you can change the date with a third-party app such as Pixelgarde, which is free from the App Store at this writing. Alternatively, if you sync the photos from your computer, you can change the date in the photo on your computer. For example, in Photos on the Mac, click **Image** on the menu bar and then click **Adjust Date and Time**.

Browse Photos Using Memories

The Memories feature in the Photos app presents a movie of photos from a particular period of time, such as a given year or a trip to a certain geographical location.

You can customize the settings for a memory. You can either customize them quickly by choosing roughly how long a memory should be and what atmosphere it should have, or you can take complete control and specify exactly which items to include and which music to play.

Browse Photos Using Memories

1. Press **Home**.

   The Home screen appears.

2. Tap **Photos** (✳).

   The Photos app opens.

3. Tap **Memories** (◉ changes to ◈).

   The Memories screen appears.

4. Tap the memory you want to view.

   The screen for the memory opens.

   Ⓐ You can tap **Show All** to show all the photos.

   Ⓑ You can tap **Select** to select the photos you want to include.

5. Tap **Play** (▶).

   The memory starts playing.

6. Tap the screen.

   The customization controls appear.

7. Tap the desired mood, such as **Happy** or **Gentle**.

8. Tap **Short**, **Medium**, or **Long**, as needed.

9. For greater control, tap **Edit** (⚏).

   The Edit screen appears.

10. Choose settings for Title, Music, Duration, and Photos & Videos.

11. Tap **Done**.

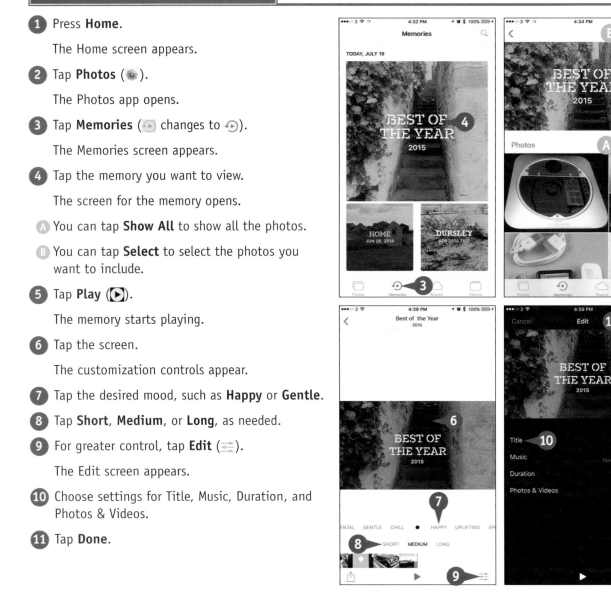

Browse Photos Using the Map

The Camera app automatically stores the GPS location in each photo and video you take, enabling the Photos app to sort your photos and videos by their locations. Starting from any photo, you can display other nearby photos, identifying them by their locations on the map. You can then browse the photos taken in a particular location.

Browse Photos Using the Map

1 In the Photos app, navigate to the photo from which you want to start browsing.

2 Tap **Details**.

The Details screen for the photo appears.

Note: You can also swipe up to display the Details screen.

Ⓐ The map shows the location at which the photo was taken.

3 Tap **Show Nearby Photos**.

The Map screen appears.

Ⓑ You can tap **Grid** to display the places as a list.

4 Tap the place you want to view.

The photos in the place appear.

Ⓒ You can tap **Show All** to display all the photos in a group.

5 Tap the photo you want to view.

The photo opens.

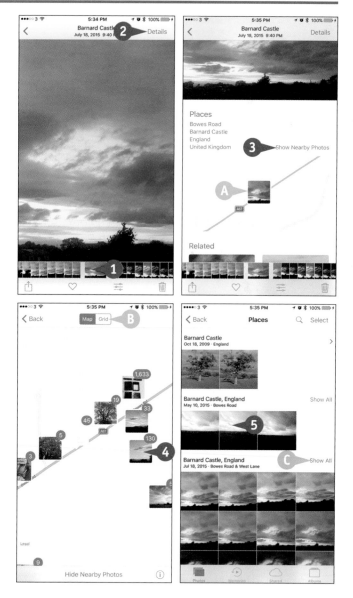

Your iPhone's Photos app includes a feature called iCloud Photo Sharing that enables you to share photos easily with others via iCloud and enjoy the photos they are sharing. You can add other people's shared albums to the Photos app on your iPhone by accepting invitations. You can then browse the photos those people are sharing.

The section "Share Photo Streams with Other People," later in this chapter, shows you how to share your own photos via iCloud Photo Sharing.

Browse Photos Using iCloud Photo Sharing

Accept an Invitation to a Shared Album

1 When you receive an invitation to subscribe to shared photos, open the e-mail message in Mail.

2 Tap **Subscribe**.

The Photos app becomes active, and the album opens.

3 Tap the thumbnail for the photo you want to view.

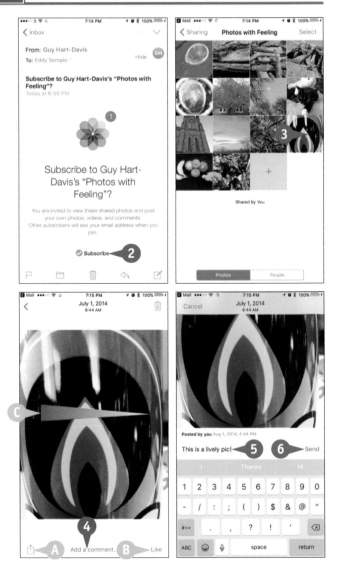

The photo opens.

Ⓐ You can tap **Share** (⬆) to share the photo with others.

Ⓑ You can tap **Like** to like the photo.

Ⓒ You can swipe left or right to display other photos.

4 Tap **Add a comment** if you want to add a comment on the photo.

The comment field opens.

The keyboard appears.

5 Type the comment.

6 Tap **Send**.

Photos sends the comment.

Browse the Latest Activity on iCloud Photo Sharing

1 In the Photos app, tap **Shared** (○ changes to ●).

The iCloud Photo Sharing screen appears.

2 Tap **Activity**.

Note: The Activity item shows new activity on your shared albums. When you add a shared album, the Activity thumbnail shows the new album's thumbnail.

The Activity screen appears.

3 Swipe up to scroll down.

Other items appear.

4 Tap a photo.

The photo opens.

5 Tap **Activity** (〈).

The Activity screen appears.

6 When you finish browsing the latest activity, tap **Sharing** (〈).

The iCloud Photo Sharing screen appears.

How do I remove a shared album?

In the Photos app, tap **Shared** (○ changes to ●) to display the iCloud Photo Sharing screen. Tap **Edit** to turn on Editing Mode, and then tap **Delete** (⊖) to the left of the stream you want to remove. In the Unsubscribe From dialog that opens, tap **Unsubscribe**. Tap **Done** to turn off Editing Mode.

Browse Photos Using Albums

Along with browsing by collections and browsing shared albums, you can browse your photos by albums. The Camera app automatically stores each conventional photo you take in the All Photos album, each burst photo in an album called Bursts, and each video in an album called Videos. You can also create other albums manually from your photos or sync existing albums from your computer.

Browse Photos Using Albums

Open the Photos App and Browse an Album

 Press **Home**.

The Home screen appears.

 Tap **Photos** (✽).

The Photos app opens.

 Tap **Albums** (☐ changes to ▣).

The Albums screen appears.

 Tap the album you want to browse. This example uses the Favorites album.

Note: The All Photos album contains all the photos you take; photos you save from web pages, e-mail messages, instant messages, and social media apps; and photos you edit from other people's streams.

The album appears.

Note: The People album contains faces identified in photos. You can browse the photos in which a particular person appears.

 Tap the photo you want to view.

The photo opens.

Note: Swipe left to display the next photo or right to display the previous photo.

 Tap **Back** (‹).

The album appears.

 Tap **Albums** (‹).

The Albums screen appears.

Create an Album

1 In the Photos app, tap **Albums**
(🔲 changes to 📁).

The Albums screen appears.

2 Tap **New** (+).

The New Album dialog opens.

3 Type the name to give the album.

4 Tap **Save**.

The screen for adding photos
appears.

5 Tap the source of the photos. For
example, tap **Albums**, and then
tap the album.

6 Tap each photo to add to the
collection, placing ✓ on each.

7 Tap **Done**.

A The album appears on the Albums
screen.

TIPS

How can I move through a long list of photos more quickly?

You can move through the photos more quickly by using momentum scrolling. Tap and flick up with your finger to set the photos scrolling. As the momentum drops, you can tap and flick up again to scroll further. Tap and drag your finger in the opposite direction to stop the scrolling.

How can I recover photos I deleted by mistake?

Tap **Albums**, and then tap **Recently Deleted**. In the Recently Deleted album, tap **Select**, tap the photos, and then tap **Recover**. Alternatively, tap **Recover All** to recover all the photos without selecting any.

Share Photos Using My Photo Stream

If you have an iCloud account, you can use the My Photo Stream feature to upload your photos to iCloud, making them available to all your iOS devices and your computer.

After you turn on My Photo Stream on your iPhone, other iOS devices, and your Macs or PCs, Photo Stream automatically syncs your 1,000 most recent photos among your devices and your computers.

Share Photos Using My Photo Stream

Turn On My Photo Stream on Your iPhone

1 Press **Home**.

The Home screen appears.

2 Tap **Settings** (⊚).

The Settings screen appears.

3 Tap **iCloud** (☁).

The iCloud screen appears.

4 Tap **Photos** (✿).

The Photos screen appears.

A You can set the **iCloud Photo Library** switch to On (⬤) to store your photo library in iCloud.

5 Set the **Upload to My Photo Stream** switch to On (⬤).

B You can set the **Upload Burst Photos** switch to On (⬤) to upload all bursts of photos instead of only favorite bursts.

6 If you also want to share your iCloud photo streams with others, set the **iCloud Photo Sharing** switch to On (⬤). See the next section, "Share Photo Streams with Other People," for more information.

7 Tap **iCloud** (く).

The iCloud screen appears.

Turn On Photo Stream on Your Mac

1 Click **Apple** ( ) and then click **System Preferences**.

The System Preferences window opens.

2 Click **iCloud** ( ).

The iCloud pane appears.

3 Click **Photos** (changes to ☑).

4 Click **Options**.

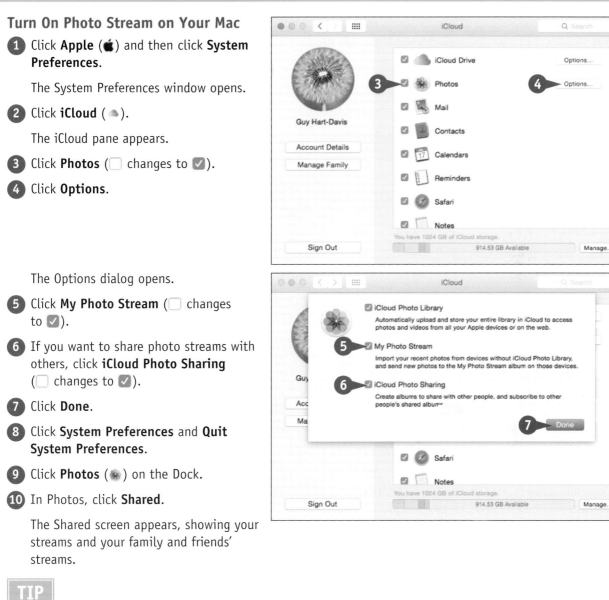

The Options dialog opens.

5 Click **My Photo Stream** (changes to ☑).

6 If you want to share photo streams with others, click **iCloud Photo Sharing** (changes to ☑).

7 Click **Done**.

8 Click **System Preferences** and **Quit System Preferences**.

9 Click **Photos** ( ) on the Dock.

10 In Photos, click **Shared**.

The Shared screen appears, showing your streams and your family and friends' streams.

TIP

How do I use Photo Stream in Windows?

On Windows, you must install Apple's iCloud for Windows software, which you can download from www.apple.com/icloud/setup/pc.html. Then click **Start**, click **All Apps**, and then click **iCloud Photos**.

In the iCloud Photos window, click **Open iCloud**. Type your Apple ID and password and then click **Sign in**. Click **Photos** (☐ changes to ☑). Click **Options** to display the Photos Options dialog. Click **My Photo Stream** (☐ changes to ☑) and **iCloud Photo Sharing** (☐ changes to ☑). Click **Change** and select the folder for photos if necessary. Click **OK** and then click **Apply**.

Share Photo Streams with Other People

After turning on iCloud Photo Sharing as described in the previous section, you can create shared photo albums, invite people to subscribe to them, and add photos.

You can also control whether subscribers can post photos and videos to your shared photo album, decide whether to make the album publicly available, and choose whether to receive notifications when subscribers comment on your photos or post their own.

Share Photo Streams with Other People

1 Press **Home**.

The Home screen appears.

2 Tap **Photos** (⚘).

The Photos app opens.

3 Tap **Shared** (☁ changes to ☁).

The iCloud Photo Sharing screen appears.

4 Tap **New** (+).

The iCloud dialog opens.

5 Type the name for the album.

6 Tap **Next**.

Another iCloud dialog opens.

7 Tap **Add Contact** (⊕) to display the Contacts screen, and then tap the contact to add.

8 Repeat step **7** to add other contacts as needed. You can also type contact names or tap names that the list automatically suggests.

9 Tap **Create**.

The iCloud Photo Sharing screen appears.

10 Tap the new album.

The album's screen appears.

 Tap **Add** (+).

The Moments screen appears, with the selection controls displayed.

Note: You can navigate to other collections or albums as needed.

12 Tap each photo you want to add.

13 Tap **Done**.

Another iCloud dialog opens.

14 Type the text you want to post with the photos.

15 Tap **Post**.

The album's screen appears.

16 Tap **People**.

The People screen appears.

Ⓐ To invite others to the album, tap **Invite People**.

17 Set the **Subscribers Can Post** switch to On (⬤) or Off ( ), as needed.

18 Set the **Public Website** switch to On (⬤) or Off ( ) to control whether to make the album publicly accessible on the iCloud.com website.

19 Set the **Notifications** switch to On (⬤) or Off ( ), as needed.

20 Tap **Sharing** (‹).

The iCloud Photo Sharing screen appears.

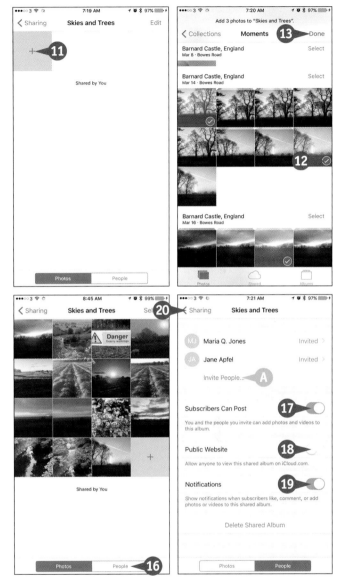

TIP

If I make a photo album public, how do people find the website?

When you set the **Public Website** switch on the People screen for a photo album to On (⬤), a Share Link button appears. Tap **Share Link** to display the Share sheet, and then tap the means of sharing you want to use — for example, Messages, Mail, Twitter, or Facebook.

Share and Use Your Photos and Videos

After taking photos and videos with your iPhone's camera, or after loading photos and videos on the iPhone using iTunes, you can share them with other people.

This section explains how to tweet photos to your Twitter account, assign photos to contacts, use photos as wallpaper, and print photos. Chapter 6 explains how to share items via the AirDrop feature.

Share and Use Your Photos and Videos

Select the Photo or Video to Share

1 Press **Home**.

The Home screen appears.

2 Tap **Photos** ().

3 On the Photos screen, tap the item that contains the photo or video you want to share. For example, tap an album such as **Camera Roll**.

4 Tap the photo or video you want to share.

5 Tap **Share** (⬆) to display the Share sheet.

Share a Photo on Twitter

A You can tap the selection button (⃝ changes to ✅) to include another item in the sharing.

1 On the Share sheet, tap **Twitter** (🐦).

The Twitter dialog opens.

2 Type the text of the tweet.

3 Tap **Post**.

Your iPhone posts the tweet to Twitter.

Assign a Photo to a Contact

1 On the Share sheet, tap **Assign to Contact** ().

The list of contacts appears.

2 Tap the contact to which you want to assign the photo.

The Move and Scale screen appears.

3 If necessary, move the photo so that the relevant part appears centrally.

4 If necessary, pinch in to shrink the photo or pinch out to enlarge it.

5 Tap **Choose**.

Set a Photo as Wallpaper

1 On the Share sheet, tap **Use as Wallpaper** (□).

The Move and Scale screen appears.

2 Move the photo to display the part you want.

3 If necessary, pinch in to shrink the photo or pinch out to enlarge it.

4 Tap **Still** if you want the photo to be still, or tap **Perspective** to use perspective movement.

5 Tap **Set**.

The Set Wallpaper dialog appears.

6 Tap **Set Lock Screen**, **Set Home Screen**, or **Set Both**, as needed.

TIP

How do I print a photo?

Display the photo you want to print, and then tap **Share** (⬆) to display the Share sheet. Tap **Print** (🖨) to display the Printer Options screen. If the Printer readout does not show the correct printer, tap **Select Printer** and then tap the printer. Back on the Printer Options screen, tap **Print** to print the photo.

Play Slide Shows of Photos

Your iPhone can not only display your photos, but also play a sequence of photos as a slide show. You can choose which theme to use, which music to play, and whether to repeat the slide show when it reaches the end. You can adjust the running speed of the slide show as a whole, but you cannot adjust individual slides.

Play Slide Shows of Photos

 Press Home.

The Home screen appears.

Note: To play your photos on a bigger screen, either use AirPlay to play a TV connected to an Apple TV or use the Apple Lightning Digital AV Adapter and an HDMI cable to connect your iPhone to a TV or monitor with an HDMI input.

 Tap **Photos** (✹).

The Photos app opens.

③ Navigate to the photo with which you want to start the slide show. For example, tap **Photos** (▢ changes to ▦), tap the appropriate year, tap the appropriate collection, and then tap the moment that contains the photo.

The moment or other photo collection opens.

④ Tap the photo you want to use at the beginning of the slide show.

The photo opens.

⑤ Tap **Share** (⬆).

The Share sheet appears.

⑥ Tap **Slideshow** (▶).

274

The slide show starts playing, using the default theme and music.

7 Tap the screen.

The controls appear.

 You can tap **AirPlay** () to play the slide show to an Apple TV.

8 Tap **Options**.

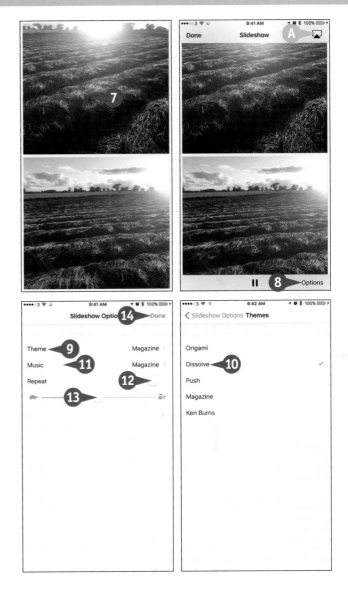

The Slideshow Options screen appears.

9 Tap **Theme**.

The Themes screen appears.

10 Tap the theme you want.

The Slideshow Options screen appears.

11 Tap **Music** and choose the music to play.

12 Set the **Repeat** switch to On () if you want the slide show to repeat.

13 Drag the **Speed** slider as needed to change the speed.

14 Tap **Done**.

The slide show resumes, using the settings you chose.

TIP

How do I choose music for a slide show?

First, choose the theme for the slide show, as explained in the main text. When you choose the theme, Photos automatically selects the theme's default music as the music for the slide show.

Next, tap **Music** on the Slideshow Options screen to display the Music screen. Here, you can either tap a different theme's music in the Theme Music list or tap **iTunes Music** to select music from your iTunes Music library.

CHAPTER 12

Advanced Features and Troubleshooting

You can connect your iPhone to VPNs and Exchange Server, troubleshoot problems, and locate it when it goes missing.

Connect to a Network via VPN

Virtual private networking, or VPN, enables you to connect your iPhone securely to a network across the Internet. For example, you can connect to a network at your workplace — or to your home network, if you set up a VPN server on it.

To set up a VPN connection, you enter the settings, username, and password in the Settings app. You normally get this information from the network's administrator.

Connect to a Network via VPN

Set Up the VPN Connection on the iPhone

1 Press **Home**.

The Home screen appears.

2 Tap **Settings** ().

The Settings screen appears.

Note: After you have set up a VPN configuration, the VPN switch appears in the top section of the Settings screen. You can connect to the currently selected virtual private network by setting the switch to On (changes to).

3 Tap **General** ().

The General screen appears.

4 Toward the bottom of the screen, tap **VPN**.

The VPN screen appears.

5 Tap **Add VPN Configuration**.

Note: If your iPhone already has a VPN configuration you want to use, tap it, and then go to step **1** of the next set of steps, "Connect to the Virtual Private Network."

The Add Configuration screen appears.

6 Tap **Type**.

The Type screen appears.

7 Tap the VPN type: **IKEv2**, **IPSec**, or **L2TP**.

8 Tap **Add Configuration** (<).

The Add Configuration screen appears again.

9 Fill in the details of the virtual private network.

Note: Set the **Send All Traffic** switch to On (○) if you want your iPhone to send all Internet traffic across the virtual private network after you connect.

10 Tap **Done**.

The VPN configuration appears on the VPN screen.

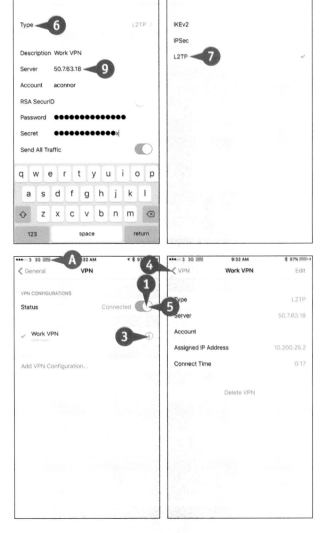

Connect to the Virtual Private Network

1 On the VPN screen, set the **Status** switch to On (changes to ○).

The iPhone connects to the virtual private network.

A The VPN indicator appears in the status bar.

2 Work across the network connection as if you were connected directly to the network.

3 To see how long your iPhone has been connected, or to learn its IP address, tap **Information** (ⓘ).

4 Tap **VPN** (<) to return to the VPN screen.

5 When you are ready to disconnect from the virtual private network, set the **Status** switch to Off (○ changes to).

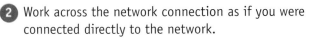

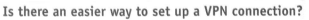

TIPS

Is there an easier way to set up a VPN connection?
Yes. An administrator can provide the VPN details in a configuration profile. This is a settings file that the administrator either installs directly on your iPhone or shares via e-mail or a website so that you can install it. Installing the profile adds its settings, such as the VPN details or the settings needed to connect to an Exchange Server system, to your iPhone. You can then connect to the virtual private network.

What can I do if my iPhone cannot connect to my company's VPN type?
Look in the App Store for an app for that VPN type.

Connect Your iPhone to Exchange Server

You can set up your iPhone to connect to Exchange Server or Office 365 for e-mail, contacts, calendaring, reminders, and notes.

Before setting up your Exchange account, ask an administrator for the connection details you need: your e-mail address, your password, the server name if required, and the domain name if required. You may be able to set up the account using only the e-mail address and password, but often you need the server name and domain as well.

Connect Your iPhone to Exchange Server

1 Press **Home**.

The Home screen appears.

2 Tap **Settings** (⚙).

The Settings screen appears.

Note: If you have not yet set up an e-mail account on the iPhone, you can also open the Add Account screen by tapping **Mail** (✉) on the iPhone's Home screen.

3 Tap **Mail** (✉).

The Mail screen appears.

4 Tap **Accounts**.

The Accounts screen appears.

5 Tap **Add Account**.

The Add Account screen appears.

6 Tap **Exchange**.

Note: You can also set up an Exchange account using a configuration profile file that an administrator provides.

The Exchange screen appears.

7 Type your e-mail address.

8 Type your password.

9 Type a descriptive name for the account field.

10 Tap **Next**.

Note: If Mail needs more information, another screen appears. Type the server's address; type the domain, if it is needed; and type your username. Then tap **Next**.

The Exchange screen appears.

11 Set the **Mail** switch to On (⬤) or Off (◯).

12 Set the **Contacts** switch to On (⬤) or Off (◯).

13 Set the **Calendars** switch to On (⬤) or Off (◯).

14 Set the **Reminders** switch to On (⬤) or Off (◯).

15 Set the **Notes** switch to On (⬤) or Off (◯).

16 Tap **Save**.

A The new account appears on the Mail screen.

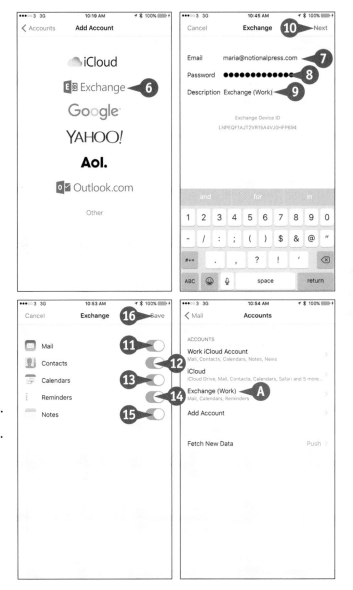

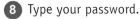
TIPS

How do I know whether to enter a domain name when setting up my Exchange account?
You need to ask an administrator, because some Exchange implementations require you to enter a domain, whereas others do not.

How do I set up an Office 365 e-mail account?
Use the method explained in this section, but use outlook.office365.com as the server's address. Your username is typically your full e-mail address; if in doubt, ask an administrator.

Update Your iPhone's Software

Apple periodically releases new versions of the iPhone's software to fix problems, improve performance, and add new features. To keep your iPhone running quickly and smoothly, and to add any new features, update its software when a new version becomes available.

You can update your iPhone's software either directly on the iPhone or by using iTunes on your computer. Both the iPhone and iTunes notify you automatically when an update is available. You can also check for updates manually.

Update Your iPhone's Software

Update Your iPhone's Software on the iPhone

1 Press **Home**.

The Home screen appears.

A The badge on the Settings icon indicates that an update is available.

2 Tap **Settings** (⚙).

The Settings screen appears.

3 Tap **General** (⚙).

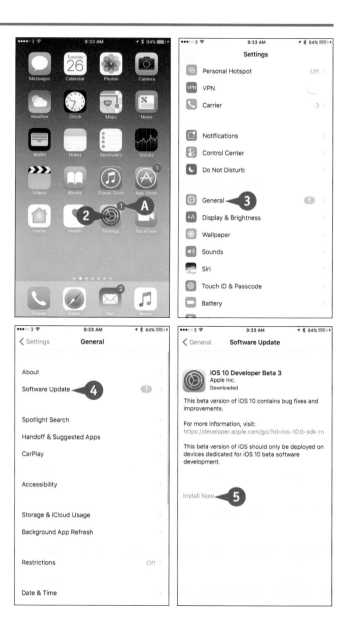

The General screen appears.

4 Tap **Software Update**.

The Software Update screen appears.

5 Tap **Install Now**.

The installation procedure begins.

6 Follow the prompts to complete the installation.

Update Your iPhone's Software Using iTunes on Your Computer

① Connect your iPhone to your computer via the USB cable.

The iPhone appears on the navigation bar in iTunes.

A dialog appears, telling you that a new software version is available.

② Click **Update**.

iTunes downloads the new software, extracts it, and begins to install it.

When the installation is complete, iTunes displays a dialog telling you that the iPhone will restart in 15 seconds.

③ Click **OK**, or wait for the countdown to complete.

The iPhone restarts, and its button then appears on the navigation bar in iTunes.

④ Disconnect your iPhone from the USB cable. You can now start using the iPhone as usual.

A new iPhone software version (10.0.1) is available for the iPhone "iPhone". Would you like to update your iPhone now?

iTunes will verify the software update with Apple.

Later   Update ②

Your iPhone has been updated, and is restarting. Please leave your iPhone connected. It will appear in the iTunes window after it restarts.

This message will be dismissed in 8 seconds.

OK ③

TIP

How do I make iTunes check for a new version of my iPhone's software?

Connect your iPhone to your computer via the USB cable so that the iPhone appears on the navigation bar in iTunes. Click **iPhone** to display the Summary screen, and then click **Check for Update** in the upper area.

Extend Your iPhone's Runtime on the Battery

To extend your iPhone's runtime on the battery, you can reduce the power usage by dimming the screen, turning off Wi-Fi and Bluetooth when you do not need them, and setting your iPhone to go to sleep quickly.

When the battery reaches 20 percent power, your iPhone prompts you to turn on Low Power Mode, which disables background app refreshing, slows down the processor, and turns off some demanding graphical features. You can also enable Low Power Mode manually anytime you want.

Extend Your iPhone's Runtime on the Battery

Dim the Screen

1 Press **Home**.

The Home screen appears.

2 Swipe up from the bottom of the screen.

Control Center opens.

3 Drag the **Brightness** slider to the left.

4 Tap above Control Center.

Control Center closes.

Turn Off Wi-Fi and Bluetooth

1 Press **Home**.

The Home screen appears.

2 Swipe up from the bottom of the screen.

Control Center opens.

A You can turn off all communications by tapping **Airplane Mode** (changes to).

3 To turn off Wi-Fi, tap **Wi-Fi** (changes to).

4 To turn off Bluetooth, tap **Bluetooth** (changes to).

5 Tap above Control Center.

Control Center closes.

Turn On Low Power Mode Manually

1 Press **Home**.

The Home screen appears.

2 Tap **Settings** (⚙).

The Settings screen appears.

3 Tap **Battery** (▭).

The Battery screen appears.

Ⓑ You can set the **Battery Percentage** switch to On (⬤) to display the battery percentage in the status bar.

Ⓒ You can tap a button in the Battery Life Suggestions list to see any recommendations for increasing battery life.

4 Set the **Low Power Mode** switch to On (⬤ changes to ⬤).

The first time you set the Low Power Mode switch to On, the Low Power Mode dialog opens.

5 Tap **Continue**.

Your iPhone enables Low Power Mode.

TIP

What else can I do to save power?

If you do not need your iPhone to track your location, you can turn off the GPS feature. Press **Home**, tap **Settings** (⚙), and then tap **Privacy** (✋) to display the Privacy screen. Tap **Location Services** (➤) to display the Location Services screen, and then set the **Location Services** switch to Off ( ).

You can also set a short time for Auto-Lock. Press **Home**, tap **Settings** (⚙), tap **Display & Brightness** (AA), and then tap **Auto-Lock**. Tap a short interval — for example, **1 Minute**.

Back Up and Restore Using Your Computer

When you sync your iPhone with your computer, iTunes automatically backs up the iPhone's data and settings, unless you have chosen to back up your iPhone to iCloud instead.

If your iPhone suffers a software or hardware failure, you can use iTunes to restore the data and settings to your iPhone or to a new iPhone, an iPad, or an iPod touch. You must turn off the Find My iPhone feature before restoring your iPhone.

Back Up and Restore Using Your Computer

Turn Off the Find My iPhone Feature on Your iPhone

1 Press **Home**.

The Home screen appears.

2 Tap **Settings** (⚙).

The Settings screen appears.

3 Tap **iCloud** (☁).

The iCloud screen appears.

4 Tap **Find My iPhone** (⊙).

The Find My iPhone screen appears.

5 Set the **Find My iPhone** switch to Off (⚪ changes to ⚪).

The Apple ID Password dialog opens.

6 Type the password for your Apple ID.

7 Tap **Turn Off**.

The iPhone turns off the Find My iPhone feature.

Back Up and Restore Your iPhone

1️⃣ Connect your iPhone to your computer via the USB cable or via Wi-Fi.

The iPhone appears on the navigation bar in iTunes.

2️⃣ Click **iPhone** (📱) on the navigation bar.

The iPhone's management screens appear.

3️⃣ Click **Summary** if the Summary screen is not yet shown.

4️⃣ Click **Back Up Now**.

iTunes backs up your iPhone.

5️⃣ Click **Restore iPhone**.

iTunes asks you to confirm that you want to restore the iPhone to its factory settings.

6️⃣ Click **Restore**.

iTunes backs up the iPhone's data, restores the software on the iPhone, and returns the iPhone to its factory settings.

Note: Do not disconnect the iPhone during the restore process. Doing so can leave the iPhone in an unusable state.

iTunes displays the Welcome to Your New iPhone screen.

7️⃣ Click **Restore from this backup** (⭕ changes to ◉).

8️⃣ Click 🔽 and choose your iPhone by name.

9️⃣ Click **Continue**.

iTunes restores the data and settings to your iPhone.

Your iPhone restarts, appears on the navigation bar in iTunes, and then syncs.

🔟 Disconnect the iPhone.

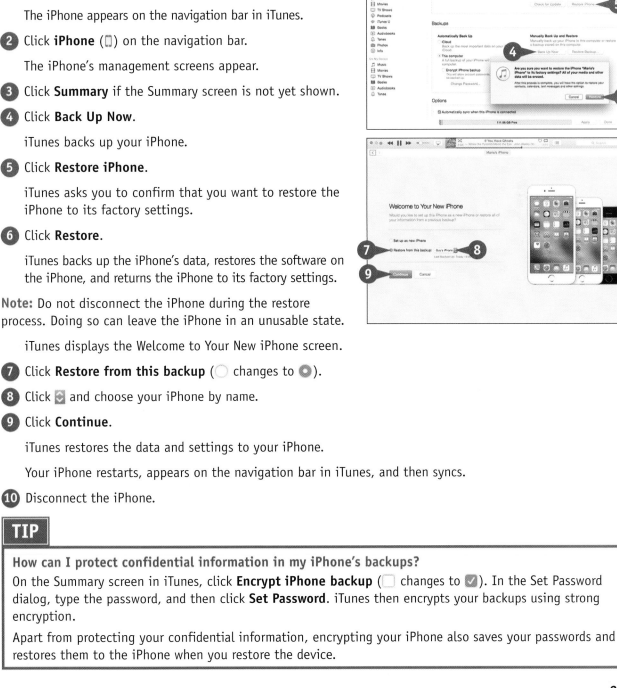

TIP

How can I protect confidential information in my iPhone's backups?

On the Summary screen in iTunes, click **Encrypt iPhone backup** (☐ changes to ✅). In the Set Password dialog, type the password, and then click **Set Password**. iTunes then encrypts your backups using strong encryption.

Apart from protecting your confidential information, encrypting your iPhone also saves your passwords and restores them to the iPhone when you restore the device.

Back Up and Restore Using iCloud

Instead of backing up your iPhone to your computer, you can back it up to iCloud, preferably via Wi-Fi, but optionally — if you have a generous data plan — via the cellular network. If your iPhone suffers a software or hardware failure, you can restore its data and settings from backup.

You can choose which items to back up to iCloud. You do not need to back up apps, media files, or games you have bought from the iTunes Store, because you can download them again.

Back Up and Restore Using iCloud

1 Press **Home**.

The Home screen appears.

2 Tap **Settings** ().

The Settings screen appears.

3 Tap **iCloud** ( ) to display the iCloud screen.

Note: The 5GB of storage in a standard free iCloud account is enough space to store your iPhone's settings and your most important data and files.

A If you need more storage space, tap **Storage** to display the Account screen, and then tap **Buy More Storage**.

4 Choose the data you want to synchronize with iCloud by setting the **Mail, Contacts, Calendars, Reminders, Safari, Notes, News**, and **Wallet** switches to On ( ) or Off ( ), as needed.

5 Tap **iCloud Drive**.

6 Set the **iCloud Drive** switch to On ( ).

7 In the apps list, set each app's switch to On ( ) or Off ( ), as needed.

8 Set the **Use Cellular Data** switch to On ( ) or Off ( ), as needed.

9 Tap **iCloud** ( ).

The iCloud screen appears again.

10 Tap **Photos**.

The Photos screen appears.

11 Set the **iCloud Photo Library** switch to On (⬤) if you want to store all your photos in iCloud.

12 If you enable iCloud Photo Library, tap **Optimize iPhone Storage** or **Download and Keep Originals**, as needed.

13 Set the **Upload to My Photo Stream** switch to On (⬤) if you want to upload all your new photos.

14 Set the **iCloud Photo Sharing** switch to On (⬤) if you want to share albums with others via iCloud.

15 Tap **iCloud** (‹).

The iCloud screen appears again.

16 Tap **Backup** (◎).

The Backup screen appears.

17 Set the **iCloud Backup** switch to On (⬤).

18 If you want to back up your iPhone now, tap **Back Up Now**.

Your iPhone begins backing up its contents to iCloud.

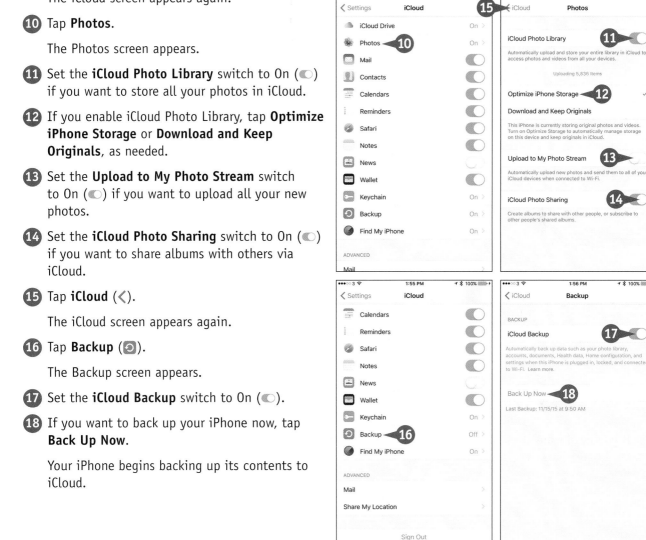

How do I restore my iPhone from its iCloud backup?
First, reset the iPhone to factory settings. Press **Home**, tap **Settings** (⚙), tap **General** (⚙), tap **Reset**, and tap **Erase All Content and Settings**. Tap **Erase iPhone** in the confirmation dialog. When the iPhone restarts and displays its setup screens, choose your language and country. On the Set Up iPhone screen, tap **Restore from iCloud Backup**, and then tap **Next**. On the Apple ID screen, enter your Apple ID, and then tap **Next**. On the Choose Backup screen, tap the backup you want to use — normally, the most recent backup — and then tap **Restore**.

Reset Your iPhone's Settings

If your iPhone malfunctions, you can reset its network settings, reset the Home screen's icons, reset your keyboard dictionary, reset your location and privacy settings, or reset all settings to eliminate tricky configuration issues. If your iPhone has intractable problems, you can back it up, erase all content and settings, and then set it up from scratch. You can also erase your iPhone before selling or giving it to someone else; you must turn off Find My iPhone first.

Reset Your iPhone's Settings

Display the Reset Screen

1 Press **Home**.

The Home screen appears.

2 Tap **Settings** (⚙).

The Settings screen appears.

Note: If your iPhone is not responding to the Home button or your taps, press and hold the Sleep/Wake button and **Home** for about 15 seconds to reset the iPhone.

3 Tap **General** (⚙).

The General screen appears.

4 Tap **Reset**.

The Reset screen appears.

You can then tap the appropriate button: **Reset All Settings**, **Erase All Content and Settings**, **Reset Network Settings**, **Reset Keyboard Dictionary**, **Reset Home Screen Layout**, or **Reset Location & Privacy**.

Reset Your Network Settings

 On the Reset screen, tap **Reset Network Settings**.

Note: If your iPhone prompts you to enter your passcode at this point, do so.

A dialog opens, warning you that this action will delete all network settings and return them to their factory defaults.

2 Tap **Reset Network Settings**.

iOS resets your iPhone's network settings.

Restore Your iPhone to Factory Settings

Note: If you intend to sell or give away your iPhone, turn off Find My iPhone before restoring your iPhone to factory settings. See the second tip.

1 On the Reset screen, tap **Erase All Content and Settings**.

Note: Enter your passcode if prompted to do so.

A dialog opens to confirm that you want to delete all your media and data and reset all settings.

2 Tap **Erase iPhone**.

A second dialog opens.

3 Tap **Erase iPhone**.

iOS wipes your media and data and restores your iPhone to factory settings.

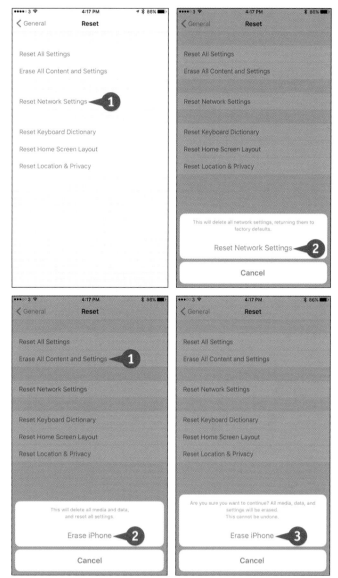

TIPS

Does the Reset All Settings command delete my data and my music files?

No. When you reset all the iPhone's settings, the settings go back to their defaults, but your data remains in place. But you need to set the iPhone's settings again, either by restoring them using iTunes or by setting them manually, in order to get your iPhone working the way you prefer.

How do I turn off the Find My iPhone feature?

Press **Home**, tap **Settings** (⚙️), and then tap **iCloud** (☁️). Tap **Find My iPhone** (🔵), and then set the **Find My iPhone** switch to Off (⬤ changes to ◯).

Troubleshoot Wi-Fi Connections

To avoid exceeding your data plan, use Wi-Fi networks whenever they are available instead of using your cellular connection.

Normally, the iPhone automatically reconnects to Wi-Fi networks to which you have previously connected it and maintains those connections without problems. But you may sometimes need to request your iPhone's network address again, a process called *renewing the lease* on the IP address. You may also need to tell your iPhone to forget a network, and then rejoin the network manually, providing the password again.

Troubleshoot Wi-Fi Connections

Renew the Lease on Your iPhone's IP Address

1 Press **Home**.

The Home screen appears.

Note: You can sometimes resolve a Wi-Fi problem by turning Wi-Fi off and back on. Swipe up from the bottom of the screen to open Control Center, tap **Wi-Fi** (changes to), and then tap **Wi-Fi** again (changes to).

2 Tap **Settings** ( ).

The Settings screen appears.

3 Tap **Wi-Fi** ( ).

The Wi-Fi screen appears.

4 Tap **Information** (ⓘ) to the right of the network for which you want to renew the lease.

The network's screen appears.

5 Tap **Renew Lease**.

The Renew Lease dialog opens.

6 Tap **Renew Lease**.

7 Tap **Wi-Fi** (‹).

The Wi-Fi screen appears.

Forget a Network and Then Rejoin It

1 On the Wi-Fi screen, tap **Information** (ⓘ) to the right of the network.

The network's screen appears.

2 Tap **Forget This Network**.

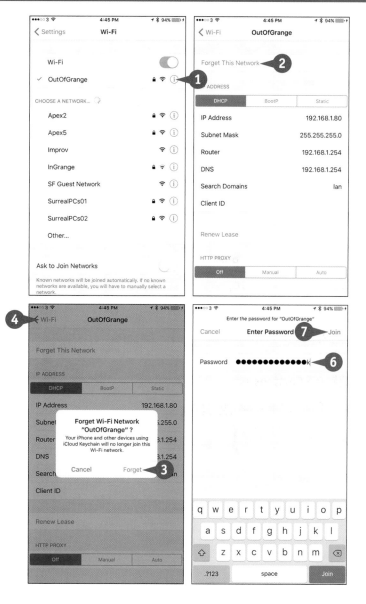

The Forget Wi-Fi Network dialog opens.

3 Tap **Forget**.

The iPhone removes the network's details.

4 Tap **Wi-Fi** (〈).

The Wi-Fi screen appears.

5 Tap the network's name.

The Enter Password screen appears.

6 Type the password for the network.

7 Tap **Join**.

The iPhone joins the network.

TIP

What else can I do to reestablish my Wi-Fi network connections?

If you are unable to fix your Wi-Fi network connections by renewing the IP address lease or by forgetting and rejoining the network, as described in this section, try restarting your iPhone. If that does not work, reset your network settings, as described earlier in this chapter, and then set up each connection again manually.

Locate Your iPhone with Find My iPhone

If you have an iCloud account, you can use the Find My iPhone feature to locate your iPhone if it has been lost or stolen. You can also display a message on the iPhone — for example, to tell the finder how to contact you — or remotely wipe the data on the iPhone.

To use Find My iPhone, you must first set up your iCloud account on your iPhone, and then enable the Find My iPhone feature.

Locate Your iPhone with Find My iPhone

Turn On the Find My iPhone Feature

1 Set up your iCloud account on your iPhone as discussed in "Set Up Your iPhone as New Using iCloud" in Chapter 1.

Note: You may have turned on the Find My iPhone feature when setting up your iCloud account.

2 Press **Home**.

The Home screen appears.

3 Tap **Settings** (⚙).

The Settings screen appears.

4 Tap **iCloud** (☁).

The iCloud screen appears.

5 Tap **Find My iPhone** (◉).

The Find My iPhone screen appears.

6 Set the **Find My iPhone** switch to On (changes to ⬤).

7 Set the **Send Last Location** switch to On (changes to ⬤) if you want your iPhone to send Apple its location when the battery runs critically low.

8 Tap **iCloud** (‹).

The iCloud screen appears.

9 Tap **Settings** (‹).

The Settings screen appears.

Locate Your iPhone Using Find My iPhone

1 Open a web browser, such as Microsoft Edge, Internet Explorer, Chrome, or Safari.

2 Click the Address box.

3 Type **www.icloud.com** and press `Enter` in Windows or `Return` on a Mac.

The Sign in to iCloud web page appears.

4 Type your username.

5 Type your password.

6 Click **Sign In** (→).

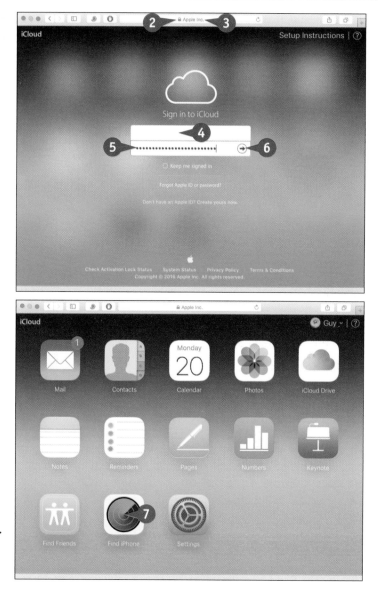

The iCloud site appears, displaying either the Home page or the page you last used.

Note: If you have set up two-step verification on your Apple ID, the Verify Your Identity screen may appear. Click the device to use for verification, and then enter the code sent to the device on the Enter Verification Code screen. In the Trust This Browser? dialog that opens, click **Trust** or **Don't Trust**, as appropriate.

Note: If iCloud displays a page other than the Home page, click **iCloud** and then click **Find iPhone** (●) on the pop-up panel. Go to step **8**.

7 Click **Find iPhone** (●).

TIP

Is it worth displaying a message on my iPhone, or should I simply wipe it?
Almost always, it is definitely worth displaying a message on your iPhone. If you have lost your iPhone and someone has found it, that person may be trying to return it to you. The chances are good that the finder is honest, even if he has not discovered that you have locked the iPhone with a passcode. That said, if you are certain someone has stolen your iPhone, you may prefer simply to wipe it, using the technique explained next.

continued ▶

Find My iPhone is a powerful feature you can use when your iPhone goes missing.

If Find My iPhone reveals someone has taken your iPhone, you can wipe its contents to prevent anyone from hacking into your data. However, know that wiping your iPhone prevents you from locating the iPhone again — ever — except by chance. Wipe your iPhone only when you have lost it, you have no hope of recovering it, and you must destroy the data on it.

Locate Your iPhone with Find My iPhone (continued)

The iCloud Find My iPhone screen appears.

8 Click the pop-up menu at the top. Normally, this shows All Devices at first.

The My Devices pop-up panel appears.

9 Click your iPhone.

A Your iPhone's location appears.

The Info dialog appears, showing when the iPhone was last located.

10 If you want to play a sound on the iPhone, click **Play Sound** (◀). This feature is primarily helpful for locating your iPhone if you have mislaid it somewhere nearby.

B A message indicates that the iPhone has played the sound.

Lock the iPhone with a Passcode

1 Click **Lost Mode** (◉) in the Info dialog.

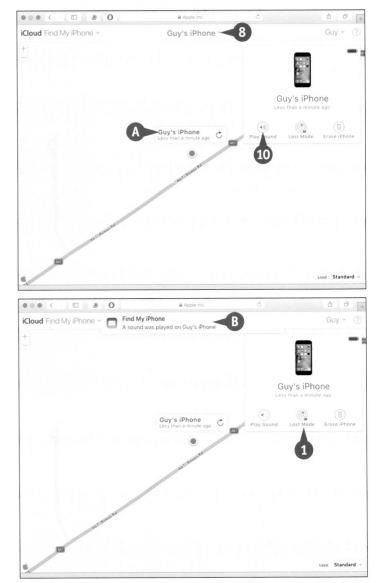

The Lost Mode dialog appears, prompting you to enter a phone number where you can be reached.

② Optionally, click **Number** and type the number.

③ Click **Next**.

The Lost Mode dialog prompts you to enter a message.

④ Type a message to whoever finds your iPhone.

⑤ Click **Done**.

iCloud sends the lock request to the iPhone, which locks itself.

Remotely Erase Your iPhone

① Click **Erase iPhone** (⌫) in the Info dialog.

The Erase This iPhone? dialog opens.

Note: If this iPhone is the last trusted device for your Apple ID, the Erase Last Trusted Device? dialog opens instead of the Erase This iPhone? dialog. Read the warning about having to use your Recovery Key to access your Apple ID. If you are sure you want to erase the iPhone, click **Erase**.

② Click **Erase**.

iCloud sends the erase request to the iPhone, which erases its data.

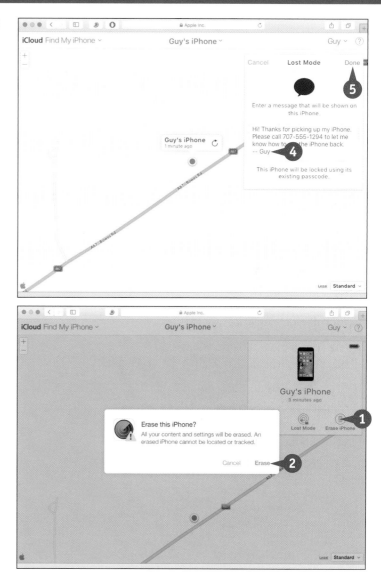

TIP

Can I remotely wipe the data on my iPhone if I do not have an iCloud account?
You can set a passcode for the iPhone, as discussed in the section "Secure Your iPhone with Touch ID or a Passcode" in Chapter 2, and then set the **Erase Data** switch on the Touch ID & Passcode screen to On (⬤). This setting makes the iPhone automatically erase its data after ten successive failed attempts to enter the passcode. After five failed attempts, the iPhone enforces a delay before the next attempt; further failures increase the delay.

Index

A